BLACK WRITERS, WHITE PUBLISHERS

BLACK WRITERS, WHITE PUBLISHERS

Marketplace Politics in Twentieth-Century African American Literature

John K. Young

University Press of Mississippi / *Jackson*

www.upress.state.ms.us

The University Press of Mississippi is a member of the
Association of American University Presses.

First edition 2006

Library of Congress Cataloging-in-Publication Data

Young, John K. (John Kevin), 1968–
    Black writers, white publishers : marketplace politics in twentieth-century
African American literature / John K. Young.— 1st ed.
        p. cm.
    Based on the author's thesis (Ph.D., Northwestern University, 1998).
    Includes bibliographical references and index.
    ISBN 1-57806-846-0 (alk. paper)
1. American literature—African American authors—History and criticism.
2. American literature—African American authors—Publishing—History—
20th century. 3. Literature publishing—Political aspects—United States—
History—20th century. 4. Politics and literature—United States—History—20th
century. 5. Authors and publishers—United States—History—20th century.
6. Literature publishing—United States—History—20th century. 7. American
literature—20th century—History and criticism. 8. African Americans—Intellectual
life—20th century. 9. African Americans in literature. 10. Race in literature. I. Title.
    PS153.N5Y625   2006
    810.9'896073—dc22   2005020010

British Library Cataloging-in-Publication Data available

CONTENTS

ACKNOWLEDGMENTS

Contemporary editorial theory holds authorship to be a fundamentally social process, and I have learned just how true that idea is in the course of producing this book. Beginning with my intellectual debts, I am grateful for the insightful comments on an early version of chapter 4 provided by my graduate colleagues at Northwestern University, especially Barbara Baumgartner, Joshua Charlson, Joe Kraus, and Celia Marshik. The two readers for my dissertation, Betsy Erkkila and Lawrence Lipking, offered numerous helpful suggestions about its future. My dissertation director, Christine Froula, has always been generous with her professional guidance and friendship, from my first days in graduate school to the present. During a two-year stay as an adjunct instructor at the University of Michigan, I learned a great deal from discussions about textual scholarship and modernism with George Bornstein and John Whittier-Ferguson and about Toni Morrison with my office mate, Vincent O'Keefe. While at Marshall University, I have benefited from grants of reassigned time and summer research funding, for which I am grateful to Dean Leonard Deutsch of the Graduate College and Dean Christina Murphy of the College of Liberal Arts, as well as the faculty committees who reviewed my applications. My department chair, David Hatfield, has been unfailingly supportive of both the teaching and scholarly aspects of my career, which have intersected in numerous ways during the course of this project. I am also thankful for five years of feedback and collegiality from the readers in our departmental first-draft group, whose former and present members include Richard Badenhausen, Janet Badia, Kellie Bean, Chris Green, Mary Moore, Donna Pasternak, Katharine Rodier, Sherri Smith, and Lachlan Whalen. Two other Marshall colleagues, Lee Erickson and Dolores Johnson, have offered useful ideas and advice about this project as well. My still developing ideas about material textuality and race in America have grown from the opportunity to teach frequently in both areas and to work with many engaging thinkers among my department's majors and MA students.

I have presented earlier versions of chapter 1 at the University of Tulsa's Comparative Literature Symposium, "The Sociomaterial Turn: Excavating Modernism," and at the 2002 convention of the Modern Language Association; chapter 2 at the 1998 Twentieth-Century Literature Conference at the University of Louisville and at the 2001 meeting of the Society for Textual Scholarship; and chapter 4 at that same STS session, all of which provided useful feedback. An earlier version of chapter 1 appeared as "Teaching Texts Materially: The Ends of Nella Larsen's *Passing*" in *College English* 66 (2004): 632–51, copyright 2004 by the National Council of Teachers of English, and reprinted with permission. An earlier version of chapter 4 appeared in *African American Review* 35 (2001): 181–203.

I thank Christopher C. De Santis for permission to reprint quotations from his interview with John Callahan, which was published in *African American Review* 34 (2000): 601–20. Figure 1 appears here courtesy of Northwestern University Library, Special Collections Department, and Random House, Inc. Figures 2, 4, 5, 6, 7, and 8 appear by permission of Random House, Inc., and figures 4 and 5 by permission of Plume as well. Figure 3 appears by permission of Nora Brooks Blakely. Unpublished material from the Ishmael Reed Papers at the University of Delaware is reproduced by permission of Ishmael Reed. For their assistance in locating documents and published sources, I am grateful to the librarians at the University of Texas's Harry Ransom Humanities Research Center, the University of Delaware's Special Collections Department, the University of Toledo's Ward M. Canady Center for Special Collections, and the ILL staff at Marshall University. Russell Maylone, director of the Northwestern University Library's Special Collections Department, has been of particular assistance over the life of this project.

At the University Press of Mississippi, I thank Seetha Srinivasan for her initial interest in and continued support of this project, as well as Walter Biggins, Karen Johnson, and Anne Stascavage for their work on its production. I am especially grateful for several insightful points, regarding both the details and broader strokes of my argument, contributed by the press's reviewer.

Finally, I owe the deepest debts to my family. Thanks to my mother, Judy Young, for teaching me to love reading and always beginning with the copyright page; to my father, Byron Young, for teaching me to love working; and to my brother, Alex Young, for explaining the legal definition of "misadventure." Alexandra Bradner has been a constant source of philosophical rigor and editorial advice. And our daughter, Vivian, has taught me of the other ways in which books are material objects.

BLACK WRITERS, WHITE PUBLISHERS

INTRODUCTION

Real Fictions of Race and Textuality

Boni and Liveright advertised *Cane* (1923) as "a book about Negroes by a Negro," despite Jean Toomer's express request not to promote the book along such racial lines (Larson 25; Toomer 157). Nella Larsen agreed to switch the title of her second novel from *Nig* to *Passing* (1929) because an editor at Knopf felt the original title "might be too inflammatory for a novel by an unproven writer, while 'Passing,' and the phenomenon's connection to miscegenation, would incite interest without giving offense" (T. Davis 306–7). Richard Wright revised and deleted several scenes in *Native Son* (1940) depicting Bigger Thomas masturbating, as well as those showing Mary Dalton's desire for Bigger, in order to publish his first novel as a Book-of-the-Month Club main selection. Zora Neale Hurston criticized American racial policy in her autobiography, *Dust Tracks on a Road* (1942), noting that "President Roosevelt could extend his four freedoms to people right here in America." But she cut this passage and others like it after an editor at Lippincott wrote, "Suggest eliminating *international* opinions as irrelevant to autobiography" (Hemenway 287, 288, emphasis added). Toni Morrison revised the last "racially charged but figuratively coherent" word of *Beloved* (1987) at her editor's request ("Home" 8), and changed the title of *Paradise* (1998) from *War* to allay Knopf's marketing concerns (see Mulrine 22).

These examples share a marked power imbalance between white editors and publishers and African American authors. To some extent this is, of course, a normal publisher-writer relationship: Theodore Dreiser muted several of his novels' passages deemed to be too sexually explicit; the British editions of *Moby Dick* were similarly softened, without Melville's consent; and literary history provides numerous other such cases. And there are certainly instances of productive interracial literary relationships; Ralph Ellison, for example, followed editor Albert Erskine to Random House in 1947. As Lawrence Jackson reports, Ellison "liked the atmosphere at [Random House], which had braved litigation to bring out James Joyce's *Ulysses*, as well as the fact that they were impressed enough with his work to offer to buy out his old contract and pay him an additional $500 advance" (360). Additionally, the "range of [Erskine's] travels and experiences, his familiarity with the South and broad ease with differing literary approaches, and ultimately his saturation in the New Criticism made him an apt match for Ellison's projects" (426). But generally what sets the white publisher–black author relationship apart is the underlying social structure that transforms the usual unequal relationship into an extension of a much deeper cultural dynamic. The predominantly white publishing industry reflects and often reinforces the racial divide that has always defined American society, representing "blackness" as a one-dimensional cultural experience. Minority texts are edited, produced, and advertised as representing the "particular" black experience to a "universal," implicitly white (although itself ethnically constructed) audience.[1] The American publishing industry, that is, has historically inscribed a mythologized version of the "black experience" onto all works marked by race, in much the same way that, for much of the twentieth century, American jurists ascribed an innate blackness to all bodies marked as such, even if at the invisible and seemingly unknowable level of a drop of blood.

The 1896 Supreme Court ruling instituting the "one-drop-of-blood rule," *Plessy v. Ferguson*, "was a landmark case," Eric Sundquist writes, "not because it drastically altered the direction of legislation and judicial thought but because it concluded the process of transfiguring dual *constitutional* citizenship into dual *racial* citizenship which had unfolded since the end of Reconstruction" (241, original emphasis). The cultural analogue of this legal shift is a similar duality for African American authors, who are marked in advertisements, prefaces, and other paratextual material as black, even when their texts themselves might belie such a strict classification. (I refer here to Gérard Genette's definition of paratexts as "verbal or other productions, such as an author's name, a title, a preface, illustrations," which "ensure the text's presence in the world, its 'reception' and consumption in the form (nowadays at least) of a book" [*Paratexts* 1].) It is this cultural anxiety about racial classification that motivates advertisements marking *Cane* as a "Negro" text, marking the book's ambiguous "inside" with a clear external indication of racial identity—even while Toomer's grandfather, ironically, was on the Louisiana train with Homer Plessy when he challenged the segregationist law (Sundquist 234). In addition to the advertisement cited above, the first-edition dust jacket calls the book a "black vaudeville," marking both its racial and cultural forms (Scruggs and Vandemarr 176).[2] Just as northern courts, in the wake of the *Plessy* decision, largely adopted a southern approach to containing the race "problem" (Sundquist 241), so too did New York and other publishers maintain systems of racial classification that perpetuated African American literature's identity as raced, even when that literature was produced in an increasingly hybrid environment.

This book examines twentieth-century literature produced as "black" in light of the circumstances of textual production: I argue that through a historicist attention to these social and cultural contexts we can best understand both the complex negotiations required to produce African American texts through a predominantly white publishing industry and the material marks of those negotiations. I should point out here that in referring to the mainstream publishing industry as "white," I intend this reference neither metonymically nor metaphorically. That is, I do not mean for the presence of individual white editors and publishers to stand in for publishing as an institution; neither do I mean to suggest an essential quality of whiteness to publishing which would be expressed by a reference to the institution as a whole as white. The "black" writers and "white" publishers of the book's title should thus refer more to racial cultural constructions than to static biological categories; my focus lies on the ways in which both groups work against and with each other in publishing blackness. Indeed, I have sought to investigate the production of "race" outside of reductive binaries, bearing in mind Anthony Appiah's admonition: "Even if the concept of race *is* a structure of oppositions—white opposed to black (but also to yellow), Jew opposed to Gentile (but also to Arab)—it is a structure whose realization is, at best, problematic and, at worst, impossible" ("Uncompleted" 134). Along those intersecting racial lines, it is worth remembering that, especially in the first half of the twentieth century, popular discourse routinely referred to a range of white ethnic identities with varying degrees of social and cultural associations. Jewishness functioned in such discourse largely as a racial category, as was the case in different ways and to lesser degrees for Irishness and other ethnic markers. As Sander L. Gilman observes, images of Jewishness have historically confronted "an absolute boundary of the difference of the Jew even as this boundary historically shifts and slides" (11). Abraham Cahan's *The Rise of David Levinsky*, for example, first appeared in four installments in *McClure's* in 1913, alongside such vitriolic articles as "The Jewish Invasion of America" and stereotypically anti-Semitic illustrations accompanying Cahan's stories (Chametzky xiv–xviii). The rhetorical ethnic markings produced by the variability of white ethnicity is also evident in such materials as a 1923 *Sporting News* editorial, which claimed that aside from major league baseball's "tacit understanding that a player of Ethiopian descent is ineligible" it remained true that "The Mick, The Sheeny, the Wop, the Dutch and the Chink, the Cuban, the Indian, the Jap or the so-called Anglo-Saxon—his 'nationality' is never a matter of moment if he can pitch, hit, or field" (quoted in White 245). Such rhetoric demonstrates the still inviolable boundary between all other races and blackness. As G. Edward White shows, the discourse surrounding baseball in the first half of the century reflected broader popular conceptions of racial and ethnic identity, with Jewish and Italian players constituting "the last two significant groups to be treated as 'remarkable' ethnics" (248–49) into the early 1940s, just before Jackie Robinson crossed the color line.

My focus throughout this book on cultural interactions among writers, editors, and publishers who are identified socially as black or white thus operates at the level of power, in the Foucauldian sense: I investigate the ways in which a concentration of money and cultural authority in mainstream publishers works to produce images of blackness that perpetuate an implicit black-white divide between authors and readers, with publishers acting as a gateway in this interaction. As Hurston once explained to an interviewer, "Rather than get across all of the things which you want to say, you must compromise and work within the limitations [of those people] who have the final authority in deciding whether or not a book shall be printed" (quoted in Hemenway 286–87).

In order to study such compromises through the material traces they leave—manuscripts, drafts, book covers, colophons, advertisements, and other vestiges of textual production—I apply editorial theory to a range of twentieth-century African American literary examples. This branch of literary scholarship is best suited to such an enterprise, I will argue, because its purview is precisely the interaction between the material and immaterial aspects of textuality, what Jerome McGann terms bibliographic and linguistic codes. At the same time, an emphasis on race enriches editorial theory, first, because this discipline has focused primarily on canonical, Anglo-Saxon, male authors and, second, because the notion of authorship as a socialized process—an idea which, in various forms, holds wide currency within the field presently—expands that network beyond its local participants (author, editor, printer, publisher) to the broader social dimension that informs the particular exchanges involved in textual production. In applying editorial theory to African American literature, I have necessarily understood "race" as a cultural concept that has been historically grounded in allegedly scientific descriptions of raced bodies. Even as African American thinkers since W. E. B. Du Bois and Alain Locke have insisted on the idea that a "viable concept of race must be grounded on cultural criteria" (Lott 152), the publishing "final authority" that Hurston cites has repeated the scientistic urge to mark and measure blackness by reifying cultural (mis)conceptions of race in material texts and paratexts. I pursue each of these points in greater depth in the remainder of this introduction, progressing from the historical factors motivating this study to the conceptual connections between theories of raced bodies and material texts.

"A BIT ON THE RAW SIDE": BETWEEN HYBRIDITY AND PARTICULARITY

In citing my opening examples, I recognize that a historical overview of twentieth-century African American literature that simply reduces the field to oppressive white editors and publishers and ultimately powerless black authors would be both simplistic and inaccurate. As George Hutchinson, George Bornstein, and several other scholars have demonstrated, many New Negro Renaissance texts express a cultural hybridity that undoes and exceeds basic racial dichotomies. Such hybrid interactions, however, do not in my view outweigh the continuing drive to publish and market black authors in racially marked terms; while these accounts of culturally hybrid textual production operate across horizontal lines of mutual influence, the publishing industry's underlying structure inheres across vertical lines of economic and cultural power. Most of the Jewish publishers interested in

New Negro works—such as Alfred and Blanche Knopf, Ben Heubsch, and Horace Liveright—were themselves marginalized by the mainstream Protestant New York firms and, therefore, turned to minority literature as a way to establish new and independent backlists. As Hutchinson demonstrates in his extensive study, the major publishers of African American literature during this period "were an entirely *new* group, with new attitudes in every phase of the business, from stylistic and ideological preferences, to cultural and geographical range, to marketing techniques, typography, and jacket design" (*Harlem* 349). These firms published New Negro books as part of a range of modernist titles; thus, Larsen and Langston Hughes at Knopf, Jessie Redmon Fauset and Toomer at Boni and Liveright, and Du Bois and Claude McKay at Harcourt saw their work feed into and draw influence from various avant-garde thinkers (Hutchinson, *Harlem* 350).

Claims of white publishers' repression of black literature can certainly be taken too far. As Hutchinson notes of George Doran's rejection of Walter White's novel *The Fire in the Flint* in 1922, Doran had championed such virulently racist authors as Irvin Cobb, making Doran "about as unlikely a choice as could be imagined for White's manuscript" (*Harlem* 348). But considering that Knopf accepted the book soon thereafter, it is difficult to accept this as a typical instance of interactions between white publishers and black authors. It is also worth noting here that James Weldon Johnson related to the Knopfs on the same plane as white writers; as Randolph Robert Lewis notes, "When a dust jacket blurb did not suit Johnson's taste, he ordered all 3,700 copies recalled in a tone reserved for peers" (69). (Lewis refers to a blurb for Johnson's 1930 history, *Black Manhattan*.)

Of Knopf, arguably the most important New Negro Renaissance publisher, Hutchinson concludes: "There is just not much evidence that Knopf was guilty of the sort of exploitative mentality that supposedly typified the white publishers' approach to black authors' works" (*Harlem* 365). Knopf published several volumes critical of dominant racial structures, such as James Weldon Johnson's *Autobiography*, White's *The Fire in the Flint*, and Hughes's *The Ways of White Folks*, for which Blanche Knopf suggested the title.[3] Similarly, Hutchinson concludes that Liveright's marketing of Toomer as a "Negro" in the ads for *Cane* should not "suggest . . . that Liveright wanted to pigeonhole African American authors" (*Harlem* 369–70), as evidenced by Liveright's interest in publishing Countee Cullen in 1923, "before the Negro was in vogue" (370). To me, however, the revealing element of the *Cane* ads is not the question of whether Liveright was interested in publishing black writers, but rather how the firm decided a book like *Cane* would best be marketed—with its author's race emphasized, thus circumscribing the book within the usual dynamic of representing the exotic black experience to curious, implicitly white readers. Such marketing appeals did not help the book commercially, however, as *Cane*'s initial sales covered only about half of Toomer's $150 advance in the first year (Larson 27). Boni and Liveright issued a small second edition of five hundred copies (one hundred of which were never bound) in 1927, but by 1938 *Cane* was out of print and would remain so until 1969 (Larson 34).

Publishers marketed white accounts of Harlem life in similar terms. For example, the dust jacket for Carl Van Vechten's *Nigger Heaven*, published by Knopf in 1926, reads, "In this, his fifth novel, Carl Van Vechten continues to act as a historian of contemporary New York life, drawing a curious picture of a fascinating group hitherto neglected by writers of fiction." The book adds to this "curious picture" with its closing "Glossary of Negro Words and Phrases." As Werner Sollors notes, however, the glossary is also "humorously turned against the reader's expectations," for instance defining "boody" and "hootchie-pap" only in terms of the other word. I would point out that such playfulness extends Van Vechten's image of the "real" Harlem for his white readers in terms of a language which is inscrutable (or at least autotelic). While such prominent New Negro writers as James Weldon Johnson, Hughes, Walter White, and Rudolph Fisher had collaborated with Van Vechten on his manuscript's "authenticity" (Gubar 155), the title alone prompted widespread denunciation in Harlem, with the author hung in effigy on 135th Street. Overall sales were strong, however, as the novel went through nine printings in its first four months (Flora 72, 74). And as Emily Bernard notes, several African American writers included positive references to Van Vechten, with characters modeled on him appearing in several later novels "as counterpoints to the unwanted white interlopers who had insinuated themselves into Harlem night life" ("What" 540); similarly, Fisher's 1928 novel, *The Walls of Jericho*, also included a glossary "for the black cultural neophyte" (539).

Bornstein examines the period's hybridity through the original edition of *The New Negro* and its illustrations by Bavarian artist Winold Reiss, including his drawing *The Brown Madonna* opposite the title page. Because the contemporary reprint erases these markers of Reiss's influence, it suppresses the anthology's status "as a biracial, collaborative project from the start" (Bornstein, *Material* 150). While I agree with Bornstein's analysis, I would point to countervailing marketing factors in this case as well. As Arnold Rampersad notes in his introduction to the reprint, "liberal whites were probably the major target of *The New Negro* and efforts like it. Through the display of black sensitivity, intelligence, and artistic versatility, it was believed, whites would come to a new understanding of the humanity of African-Americans and help to accelerate social change" (xvi). In his introduction to the reprint, Rampersad acknowledges that the "the role of the illustrations by Winold Reiss cannot be underestimated" (xviii). Reiss's prominent place on the original title page signals his intimate involvement with the project, but this indication that Reiss and Locke were "as though coequal" (Bornstein, *Material* 150) simultaneously reassures potential white readers that the anthology will be culturally "safe." To be sure, Weiss's illustrations themselves express what Cary Nelson calls "an explicitly contemporary rearticulation of African materials, not an essentialist claim of immediate and instinctual identity across cultural, historical, and geographical boundaries" (91). But I see this artistic effect as working both in concert and in competition with the anthology's marketing toward its double audiences, in much the same way that white artists and audiences occupy an inevitably conflicted position in relation to the "Harlem" of the Renaissance. Such appeals to white audiences do not negate the artistic hybridity that produced *The New Negro,* but they do reveal the intersection of the creative and marketing spheres of textual production. The turn in editorial theory toward a socialized model of authorship bears particularly important consequences for literature marked as racially or ethnically "other," for the writing and the selling of a book almost always work in concert and conflict, as reflections of broader social and cultural hybridities and hierarchies.

An interesting exception to the problems of the white market for black literature, however, is Nancy Cunard's massive anthology, *Negro,* published by the obscure London firm Wishart & Company in 1934, with Cunard herself providing £1,500 in production costs. Most of those funds came from the settlement of Cunard's libel suit against several British newspapers for their salacious coverage of her relationship with Henry Crowder, an African American pianist (Cunard xix). *Negro* was an enormous book, both in physical size, with 12-by-10-inch pages and weighing nearly eight pounds, and in scope, with its 855 pages and 385 illustrations covering poetry, history, law, politics, music, sculpture, and anthropology in the United States, Africa, West Indies, South America, and Europe (xxiii n18). Among the American contributors, who comprise more than half of the collection, such New Negro writers as Hurston, Locke, Du Bois, White, Sterling Brown, Cullen, Georgia Douglas Johnson, and Hughes appear alongside a broad spectrum of white modernists, including William Carlos Williams, Dreiser, Alfred Kreymborg, Carl Rakosi, Louis Zukofsky, Ezra Pound, and Cunard herself. (As a publisher through her Hours Press in Paris, Cunard also issued Pound's *A Draft of XXX Cantos*, two books by Laura Riding, one by Robert Graves, Samuel Beckett's *Whoroscope*, Bob Brown's *Words*, W. H. Auden's *Spain*, and several volumes by Richard Aldington and George Moore.) Although not produced in the biracial atmosphere of *The New Negro*, Cunard's collection is certainly more hybrid in its contents, as well as more international in its focus (a breadth suggested by the working title, *Color*). Despite all of these factors, *Negro* has been too large (even Continuum's 1996 abridged paperback reprint checks in at 457 12-by-9-inch pages), too European, and perhaps too tainted by Cunard herself to have made its way into standard histories of modernist literature on race.

In addition to these examples of white publishers issuing important black texts, the twentieth century has witnessed several books published by black-owned presses or other groups. These titles were largely self-published; for instance, Sutton Griggs's Orion Publishing in Nashville issued only his four novels, including one sponsored by the National Baptist Convention as a response to Thomas Dixon's *The Leopard's Spots: A Romance of the White Man's Burden*. The Colored Co-Operative Publishing Company produced just one book, Pauline Hopkins's novel *Contending Forces* in 1900, focusing primarily on *Colored American Magazine*, in which *Contending Forces* was serialized, along with two other Hopkins novels. Similarly, Du Bois and Dill, a firm launched by Du Bois and the *Crisis* business manager, produced the monthly *Brownies' Book* for two years, along with one book-length biographical collection, *Unsung Heroes*. J. A. Rogers Publications, based in Chicago and probably the most prolific black publisher before the 1960s, was a one-man company focusing largely on Rogers's own work.[4] These firms operated not so much alongside as outside the white publishing mainstream, at a double remove from the traditional houses that had already marginalized Knopf and other new publishers of his generation. Orion and its cousins clearly aimed at an African American audience first and foremost, with mixed results. Griggs called *The Hindered Hand*, his Baptist-sponsored novel, a "financial failure," and the company closed in 1913, when Griggs moved to Memphis to serve as a Baptist pastor (Joyce 176–77). It seems clear that, in the end, none of these firms possessed the necessary capital to sustain themselves beyond a narrow audience.

Those financial realities changed with such Black Arts publishers as Dudley Randall at Broadside Press and Haki Madhubuti at Third World Press. Melba Joyce Boyd reports that Broadside published more than five hundred thousand copies of its various titles over a thirty-five-year history, most with runs of five thousand to ten thousand volumes (3). While such circulation certainly does not rival a mainstream firm's, it demonstrates a distinct market for an independent press. I discuss Broadside and Third World further in chapter 3, in relation to Gwendolyn Brooks's later career, and so proceed to note here the gradual curricular effects of the civil rights movement, effects which have also meant the consequent canonization of several African American writers and texts. As I will point out, though, such canon formation has largely occurred at the level of the syllabus, not the scholarly edition, a distinction that reinforces the cultural distinctiveness of most minority literature, as opposed to those works that appear in editions designed for posterity.

Against this historical backdrop, then, I would argue that the basic dynamic through which most twentieth-century African American literature has been produced derives from an expectation that the individual text will represent the black experience (necessarily understood as exotic) for the white, and therefore implicitly universal, audience. (This dynamic is doubly in effect for a minority woman writer, who is expected to "speak for her gender *and* her race and culture" [Burr 113].) Consider the example of Johnson's *The Autobiography of an Ex-Coloured Man*, which the Knopfs issued in 1927 as part of their Blue Jade Library, a series launched two years earlier to feature " 'semi-classic, semi-curious books . . . which for one reason or another have enjoyed great celebrity but little actual distribution' " (quoted in Madison 325). Johnson's autobiographical novel had first appeared anonymously in 1912 from Sherman, French, a small press that lasted only a few years and saw most of its titles, including Johnson's, fall out of print. As Eugene Levy notes, other than Booker T. Washington and Paul Laurence Dunbar, "no black author could sustain success in this period, and, moreover, the white public was not interested in a novel critical of national racial practices. Nor were there enough black readers to produce large sales" (128). The literary publics—both white and black—had changed by 1927, when Knopf reissued the novel with Johnson's name on the title page and a preface by Van Vechten. With a new audience for black literature the *Autobiography* had become "effectively a different book" (Lawson 98).[5] Despite this change, the *Autobiography* remains marked as a distinctly "coloured" text. Van Vechten's introduction functions much like the prefaces attached to slave narratives by white benefactors, attesting to the accuracy and veracity of authors presumed to be artistically, or even functionally, illiterate. Sherman, French had called the book an explanation of "the Negroes of the United States," who were "more or less a sphinx" to the firm's white readership (J. Johnson xii). For Johnson's (white) readers fifteen years later, for whom black experiences and communities—or at least a particular version of them—were becoming less mysterious thanks to novels like *Nigger Heaven*, Van Vechten affirms that the novel "reads like a composite autobiography of the Negro race in the United States in modern times" (vi). No detail of black life is omitted, Van Vechten assures Johnson's (white) audience: "Jim Crow cars, crap-shooting, and the cake-walk are inimitably described. Colour snobbery within the race is freely spoken of, together with the economic pressure from without which creates this false condition. There is a fine passage devoted to the celebration of the Negro spirituals and there is an excellent account of a Southern camp-meeting, together with a transcript of a typical oldtime Negro sermon. There is even a lynching" (vii–ix). While in 1912 this catalog of "authentic Negro life" had no perceived market, by 1927 the project of selling black narratives to white audiences was well underway, so the *Autobiography* passes once more, speaking anew to a much wider black readership in Harlem and beyond while also being marked for white readers as a composite account of an exoticized black experience.

This shift is nowhere more apparent than in Van Vechten's last line, "There is even a lynching." Still widespread enough in 1911 for a *Crisis* cartoon to call lynching "The National Pastime" (quoted in Allen et al. 26), and still common enough in the next decade to trigger episodes of terrible violence, such as the

1921 Tulsa massacre, the gruesome practice appeared in numerous postcards circulated throughout the South and other areas, as the extraordinary collection *Without Sanctuary* documents. Van Vechten's inclusion of "even a lynching" within his catalog of Negro life, then, expresses a sinister side of white commercial interest in the "authentic" black experience and, indeed, of cultural hybridity more broadly: to consume the "ex-coloured" author by name in 1927 implies *both* a greater interest in Negro fiction and a prurient curiosity about the violent cultural subtexts that marked the Harlem experience as ostensibly other than black life in the South. (And, of course, the Tulsa massacre exposes the fiction of this supposed geographical distinction.) While there is no doubt that writers like Johnson and Langston Hughes influenced the Knopf list, or that Reiss's illustrations indicate an atmosphere of interracial exchange for *The New Negro*, the underlying social power reinforcing racial systems is also an inescapable presence, one which operates either benignly or malignantly, but unavoidably.

As a more extended example of how publishers' constructions of whiteness pose inevitable questions for minority writers, I examine the publication history of Wright's revolutionary novel *Native Son*. Harper and Brothers had published Wright's first book, *Uncle Tom's Children*, in 1938. Wright came to feel this series of novellas was " 'a book which even bankers' daughters could read and feel good about,' " and so was determined that his next book " 'would be so hard and deep that they would have to face it without the consolation of tears' " (quoted in Rampersad xv). The manuscript Wright sent in 1939 to Edward Aswell, his Harper editor, included an early scene in which Bigger and Jack masturbate in a movie theater and then watch a newsreel featuring Mary Dalton consorting with a well-known radical while on vacation in Florida. After Harper sent the manuscript to the Book-of-the-Month Club, Aswell relayed the club's concerns to Wright: "And incidentally the Book Club wants to know whether, if they do choose *Native Son*, you would be willing to make some changes in that scene early in the book where Bigger and his friends are sitting in the moving picture theatre. I think you will recognize the scene I mean and will understand why the Book Club finds it objectionable. They are not a particularly squeamish crowd, but that scene, after all, is a bit on the raw side. I daresay you could revise it in a way to suggest what happens rather than to tell it explicitly" (quoted in Wright, *Native Son* 486).

Wright did revise the scene, eliminating all overt references to masturbation and replacing the newsreel with an extended discussion of a film entitled *The Gay Woman*, in which a Communist tries to kill the title character's husband with a bomb, not realizing the man she is with is actually her partner in an affair. In addition, Wright alters the relationship between Bigger and Mary, so that Mary's sexual interest in Bigger in the original manuscript is largely absent in the published version. The book club accepted the novel with Wright's changes, as did the British publisher Gollancz, which had "'turned it down flatly'" after reading the original manuscript (quoted in Wright, *Native Son* 486, 1998 reprint). Aswell also agreed to an introduction from Dorothy Canfield Fisher without first consulting Wright, which Keneth Kinnamon terms a "latter-day example of the process of white authentification" (123). As Barbara Johnson observes, "It is not surprising that the first edition of *Native Son* should have been preceded by an introduction by Dorothy Canfield Fisher. It is as though the envelope of Wright's letter had to be made to say 'The white woman is safe'" (*Feminist* 68). Harpers' initial advertisement for *Native Son* set the stage for its reception by white readers, quoting the book club's newsletter: "The finest novel yet written by an American Negro, adventurous, exciting. It is no tract or defense plea. Like *The Grapes of Wrath* it is a fully realized story of unfortunates, uncompromisingly realistic, and *quite as human as it is Negro*" (emphasis added). *Native Son* went on to sell 250,000 copies in its first year, making Wright "easily the most respected black writer in America, and the most prosperous by far," as Rampersad notes in his introduction to the 1993 edition, which follows Wright's original manuscript (xxi). This edition advertises itself as "The Restored Text Established by The Library of America" on the front cover just below Wright's name. (The 2003 reissue from HarperCollins, meanwhile, is labeled the "Abridged Edition" and "The Original 1940 Text," in a clear effort to use historical "authenticity" as a marketing tool.) Wright's composition seems to have proceeded with two contrasting goals: to confront white readers with the stark reality of black masculinity in ways that *Uncle Tom's Children* had not, but also to reflect his own transitions between black and white, southern and northern backgrounds. As Kinnamon notes, Wright changes "ofays" to "white folks" at one point in the novel's drafting and typically composes dialogue in "standard" English before switching it into dialect (116).[6]

From the novel's initial publication in 1940 until Rampersad's edition in the 1991 Library of American volume of Wright's *Early Works*, there was no masturbation scene in print. This deletion renders incomprehensible a later reference to it in Bigger's trial (Kinnamon 119) but, more importantly, reflects the charged racial politics surrounding the portrayal of black male sexuality and Wright's acquiescence to those politics in order to get his novel into print more profitably. Wright employs violent rhetoric in portraying Bigger's masturbation; at one point he tells Jack, " 'I'm polishing my night-stick,' " and after Jack asks if a passing woman has seen them, Bigger responds, " 'If she comes back I'll throw it in her.' " Jack's answer, " 'You a killer,' " foreshadows the complex of violence and sexuality for Bigger which dominates the novel (as well as Wright's own image of "bankers' daughters" as readers), but this early expression of such tensions disappears in the book club version. Such revisions also apply to Mary's sexual response to Bigger. As Hazel Rowley notes, Mary in Wright's manuscript "desired her black chauffeur every bit as much as he desired her—if not more so," while in the published version she becomes more stereotypically "passive, limp as a rag doll, scarcely conscious" (183). The revised portraits of Bigger and Mary thus reinforce racial and sexual stereotypes of the day, even while the narrative as a whole remains a daring challenge to these same cultural constraints.

Modernist literature is, of course, fraught with examples of publishers and courts seeking to mute frank portraits of sexuality, including such well-known cases as *The Well of Loneliness* trial in 1928 and the vexed publication history of almost all of D. H. Lawrence's novels. Interestingly, the chief magistrate overseeing Radclyffe Hall's case ruled that the novelists offering to testify on her behalf did not qualify as experts in "obscenity," only in "art" (Marshik 879). The manuscript versions of Lawrence's novels contain numerous instances of sexual scenes and details that were removed by Edward Garnett and others, with varying degrees of approval or attention from Lawrence himself. While representations of sexuality provoked editorial problems across the modernist spectrum, then, the depiction of Bigger Thomas and Mary Dalton in Wright's manuscript remains a particular instance of a broader dynamic. After all, the kinds of sexual relationships portrayed by Hall or Lawrence resulted in their books being banned and burned (as with *The Rainbow* in 1915) but were not the subtext for lynchings and other violence against black men and women throughout the United States.

Wright's correspondence on these matters has not survived, so we cannot judge precisely how he reacted to this editorial interference. Nevertheless, the material history in this case documents the cultural boundaries confronted by a revolutionary novel like *Native Son*. Of special interest to me is the fact that this version remained the only one in print for fifty-one years. Both the 1991 and 1993 editions include detailed textual notes explaining the presence of the "new" masturbation scene in the main text, along with a footnote printing the originally published version of the scene. By privileging the version of the novel from the page-proofs sent to the book club judges within the main body of the book, and relegating the edited version to the footnotes, Rampersad reverses this scene's textual history, allowing readers to encounter the novel as Wright originally wrote it, while juxtaposing the suppressed scene against its distorted reflection.

I draw two conclusions from this example: first, it indicates the aesthetic limits for African American writers created by the economic power of mainstream publishers and, in this case, by the Book-of-the-Month Club. Again, such a power imbalance affects almost all writers, but as the Wright example indicates, there is a particular difficulty in representing "the black experience" in terms which depart too far from the mythologized version most often reinforced by mainstream presses: just as the violent rhetoric of the masturbation scene makes it too "raw" for book club readers, a white woman's sexual desire for a black man has the opposite, but equally disturbing effect, transforming Bigger from a character who remains "safe" because his behavior follows prescribed lines to an object of white desire that unsettles the cultural logic upon which depends both the mythic image of the violent black male and, therefore, lynching itself. In this respect *Native Son* demonstrates how far—and no farther—it was possible for a black novelist to go in the period just after the New Negro Renaissance.[7] Additionally, the ensuing fifty-one years of editorial silence reveal the extent to which scholars and editors themselves have perpetuated the aesthetic effects of publishers' cultural circumscriptions. Similarly, William Andrews, the editor of Frederick Douglass's *My Bondage and My Freedom*, asks: "If a writer once considered as unassimilable as Dreiser can now be regarded as worthy of meticulous textual reconstruction and republication in massive scholarly tomes, why can't such classic writers of the African American tradition— Phyllis Wheatley, Charles W. Chesnutt, Langston Hughes, and Richard

Wright, for example—also qualify for complete textual editions in formats comparable to those that are sealing a hallowed place in American literary history for a Harold Frederic or a Charles Brockden Brown?" (49–50). The "restored text" for *Native Son* is certainly a step in this direction, but it still lacks the full scholarly apparatus and university press imprint of Andrews's examples. As Andrews maintains, "The more one learns about African American literature the more one sees ample need for targeted textual *editing*—if not all-encompassing textual editions—of central texts and representative phenomena that can help us understand the origin, evolution, and fate of minority texts in a 'majority' literature" (51, original emphasis). An academic construction of literary history that highlights white male writers therefore perpetuates an implicit connection between whiteness and aesthetic value, underwriting the continued neglect of minority literature as worth preserving with the imprimatur of the scholarly edition.

At the same time, the *Native Son* case demonstrates the tensions between ideas of individuality and hybridity that become apparent from a materialist approach to textuality. Examining the relationship between hybridity and other models of racial identity, Samira Kawash maintains that "the demands of fixity, knowability, identity, and authenticity given form in the figure of the color line are constantly exceeded by something else, by a force we might call hybridity. But . . . hybridity . . . is not another substance, however socially constructed, that would displace the essentially conceived notion of blackness. The individual is not hybrid; rather, hybridity constantly traverses the boundaries of the individual" (217). I cite Kawash's analysis here as both thoughtful and typical of contemporary approaches to racial identity, in her emphasis on the continuing and fluid interaction between the individual and the cultural. Considering the editorial decisions behind the publication of Wright's "restored" text from this perspective on hybridity and individuality, though, reveals the extent to which the implicit editorial choice between versions labeled "lost" and "restored," or "censored" and "unexpurgated," relies on the originary presence of a "pure" text—an individual with its boundaries intact. In contrast to this vision of authors and texts, many contemporary editorial theorists would privilege the first published version, rather than the "restored" text, as most expressive of the social circumstances in which the author worked. If the originally published version does not express the author's ideal version, that is precisely the point, from this editorial perspective, as publication almost never represents, historically, anything other than some level of compromise. Yet as I will argue, editorial theory in general has taken insufficient account of race as a social factor, and Kawash's notion of cultural hybridity always crossing through the "boundaries of the individual" importantly enriches the sense of the social underlying an editorial emphasis on authorship as a social process. In this sense, the most significant aspect of Rampersad's edition is the presence of both versions of the film scene within the same book, allowing readers to document the material outcomes of this historical interaction between the hybrid sphere of publication and the "individual" zone of composition (though, of course, Wright, or any author, already writes with various audiences in mind).

Such questions of audience return me to the historical and theoretical importance of white publishers' control of the means of production and distribution, control which demonstrates the difference race and ethnicity make for apparently universal descriptions of the relationship between author and public. In her introduction to the Modern Library edition of *Mrs. Dalloway*, for example, Virginia Woolf writes innocuously, "Once a book is printed and published it ceases to be the property of its author; he commits it to the care of other people" (*Essays* 549). But throughout the twentieth century, and especially in its first half, African American authors have not enjoyed this property relationship with their work (unlike Woolf, who owned her own press) and have often not been able to rely on the "care of other people," confronting instead what James Weldon Johnson calls "a special problem which the plain American author knows nothing about—the problem of the double audience" ("Dilemma" 267). This double audience derives from the same social forces that create Du Bois's double consciousness and make him conclude the "Forethought" to *The Souls of Black Folk* with a seemingly rhetorical question: "And, finally, need I add that I who speak here am bone of the bone and flesh of the flesh of them that live within the Veil?" (6). The double insistence here on bodily identification and knowledge at once plays on the typical white readerly desire for a speaker who knows the "flesh and bone" black experience, while also undercutting the strict distinctions upon which such desire depends through the permeability of the Veil, behind or beyond which Du Bois can speak in *Souls*.

Werner Sollors notes more broadly, "Ethnic writers in general confront an actual or imagined double audience, composed of 'insiders' and of readers, listeners, or spectators who are not part of the writer's ethnic group" (249). Sollors's focus is primarily on the aesthetic effects of this double audience, rather than on author-publisher interactions, though he notes in passing that a group of "rebellious and aggressive" Yiddish poets published a 1907 anthology by "self press," suggesting a need to work outside mainstream publishing systems (248).

Over the course of the twentieth century—and now into the twenty-first—authors' and publishers' responses to the problem of the double audience have ranged from a deliberate shielding of a writer's identity because of race, as in the first edition of Johnson's *Autobiography*; to a more engaged but still conflicted author-publisher relationship during the New Negro Renaissance, as in the *Cane* advertisements; to explicit distrust from Black Arts writers for the mainstream publishers issuing their books, as in LeRoi Jones's and Larry Neal's description of the "devils" at William Morrow who published the paperback *Black Fire* anthology; to the creation of several units within larger houses focusing specifically on African American books and readers, a development prompted in part by the extraordinary commercial success of Oprah's Book Club, which in its first incarnation focused frequently on African American authors.[8] (I return to these last two examples in chapters 3 and 4.) The historical progress demonstrated in these examples has shifted, but certainly not eliminated, the problem of the double audience, as evidenced recently by the best-selling legal thriller, *The Emperor of Ocean Park* (2002).

Lori Ween, citing the marketing of Yale law professor Stephen Carter's debut novel "as a mainstream, blockbuster, best-selling legal thriller, not as an African American novel per se" (90), suggests optimistically that future "authority to choose authentic images [of ethnic identity] belongs to the reading public, which will put its consumer dollars behind the vision that most appeals to it and spur certain publishers to move in the direction that seems to succeed in the marketplace" (100). It is too soon to tell, of course, but I would argue that the market and cultural forces at work in the publishing world do not always intersect or overlap and, indeed, that minority texts produced within a majority culture will continue to be marked as such, one way or another. Interestingly, while Knopf's ads for Carter's novel present it in nonracial terms, reviews and press coverage almost invariably emphasized the author's blackness, and the novel's "unique" portrait of a generally underrepresented segment of black life, the upper middle class. A full-page Knopf ad in the *New York Times* trumpets *Emperor* as "the thriller of the year!" and compares Carter to John Grisham and Tom Wolfe, concluding with an *Entertainment Weekly* blurb saying that the novel is " 'poised to become the biggest book of the summer.' " *Emperor* also garnered a cover article in the *New York Times Book Review*, with a subheading—"In Stephen L. Carter's thriller, what he calls 'the darker nation' and 'the paler nation' discover each other after a mysterious death"—above a drawing of a bespectacled black man looking out from a partially open window in the backseat of a car. This admixture of class and race carries over to Ward Just's review, headlined "How the Other Half Lives," which announces in its opening paragraph that "a hidden world is brought to life, a world with its own language and modes of behavior and domestic economy and myths and legends" (11). This "hidden world" is again that of the black upper middle class, which in Just's and other's readings has been concealed in plain sight, waiting for a portrait like Carter's to make it visible within the "known" white world. Like many reviewers, Just discounts Carter's mystery as a hackneyed thriller, but lauds its social portrait, declaring that "in Stephen Carter the black upper class has found its Dreiser" (11). *The Emperor of Ocean Park* thus figures as a window into the world of the black bourgeoisie—indeed, Just's review closes with that metaphor—in a paratext which is beyond Knopf's immediate control, but nonetheless reinforces the cultural pattern into which African American literature seems inevitably drawn. In order to illuminate the material traces of that cultural vortex, I turn now to the reasons for reading minority literature through the lens of editorial theory, as well as the revisions that critical focus produces for editorial theory itself.

BLACK RIDERS: RACIAL AND TEXTUAL TRUTHS

Reading texts, like reading races, involves complex negotiations between internal and external properties, in an attempt to understand the soul or identity beneath the skin, or the text inside the covers. Both interpretive systems, I argue in this section, rest on false foundations. While ostensibly biological systems impose cultural fictions onto raced bodies, seemingly natural notions of the text overlook the material forms on which the "inner" text depends. The ultimate unreliability of bodies as expressive of a "real" racial identity, as evidenced most prominently in social anxiety about passing, leads to ever more convoluted ways of seeing, culminating in the insistence on blood as the ultimate—though invisible—physical symptom. This cultural desire for physical confirmation of racial fantasies—which shifts through a Lacanian chain of shifting objects, never settling on a site that can satisfy the fantasy of the desire—derives from the fundamental fiction upon which American racial ideology has always depended. As the philosopher Charles W. Mills maintains, the American "Racial Contract" develops from a "particular hallucination" (18) among whites regarding the racial realities that have been perpetuated by white culture: "There will be white mythologies, invented Orients, invented Africas, with a correspondingly fabricated population, countries that never were, inhabited by people who never were—Calibans and Tontos, Man Fridays and Sambos—but who attain a virtual reality through their existence in travelers' tales, folk myth, popular and highbrow fiction, colonial reports, scholarly theory, Hollywood cinema, living in the white imagination and determinedly imposed on their alarmed real-life counterparts" (*Racial* 18–19). This paradox, in which race is a fiction with all-too-real consequences, maps onto editorial theory through an inverse focus on the relationship between the material forms of books and their immaterial contents, the stories and ideas which seem ultimately to reside in readers' minds, rather than in the book's material elements. The insistence on seeing racially marked bodies as black and unmarked bodies as white has perpetuated the mythology Mills outlines. Conversely, I will argue in this section, the historical tendency within textual scholarship to leave black texts unmarked—that is, not to see them as meriting bibliographical attention—has created a blind spot within the discipline that affects both how editors construct the literary past, through the new editions which are or are not produced, and how editorial theorists envision their own practice, by maintaining an implicitly "white" theory of textual editing.

Contemporary editorial theory focuses frequently on what McGann calls the "textual condition," an acknowledgment both of the particular historical circumstances that have contributed to the production of a particular text and of the alternative versions of that same text which could have been produced. The textual condition expresses contingency, illuminating through manuscripts, drafts, and different published editions the range of versions a particular book could have inhabited and the material record that explains which version(s) among a potentially limitless range actually have been published. Editorial scholarship is most often a study of the trace: the lingering elements of variants in published editions and the residue of the social processes through which texts pass on their way to publication. These artifacts—first editions, colophons, book jackets, title and copyright pages, drafts and manuscripts, and advertisements—make up what McGann terms the bibliographic code, an equally meaningful counterpart to a text's linguistic code. McGann argues, in an influential statement within the field, that "both linguistic and bibliographical texts are symbolic and signifying mechanisms. Each generates meaning, and while the bibliographical text commonly functions in a subordinate relation to the linguistic text, 'meaning' in literary works results from the exchanges these two great semiotic mechanisms work with each other" (*Condition* 67).[9]

The revolutionary theoretical import of McGann's account of textuality, along with the various responses it has generated, lies in the understanding of the linguistic and bibliographic codes as mutually constitutive of meaning. Most readers think almost automatically of the "inside" and "outside" of books, distinguishing the "words" from the cover, jacket, binding, and the various paratexts appearing on them. For these readers it makes little difference whether they buy a hardcover or a paperback, or one edition rather than another, because they intuitively understand the "text" to exist at some immaterial level which transcends the merely physical conveyor of words and ideas, the book as object. Editorial theorists, by insisting both on the interpretive importance of a text's particular physical manifestation and on the inherent instability of those physical forms, find the book-text relationship to be both fundamentally meaningful and unreliable at each level. A work exists in various documentary versions, but just as poststructuralist literary theory since Derrida has voided the concept of stable meaning in the authorial or textual sphere, editorial theory since McGann has demonstrated the impossibility of settling on a single, "correct" or "definitive" version. Instead, editorial theorists accept the multiple documentary states of Marianne Moore's "Poetry," Wordsworth's *Prelude*, or Shakespeare's

Lear—among many such examples—as limited and yet not reducible to a single form. As Bornstein explains, such textual histories "clearly dislodge the notion of one privileged form for a text exercising authority over all other forms and, indeed, constituting their teleological ground. Yet they provide a limit to *différance* by limiting the deferral to a finite sequence of versions constituting the bound of that particular text" ("Introduction" 7).

This attention to material meaningfulness, along with an amenability to material variance, situates editorial theory as the most illuminating way of seeing the traces of larger cultural systems through which minority texts pass. No author works as an isolated genius, as editorial theorists have emphasized since McGann's *Critique of Modern Textual Criticism* (1983), but because that pose has long been available only to white men, it is especially ahistorical to reinscribe such a cultural image for minority writers. While investigating relationships between white publishers and black authors, however, I am not suggesting that an "essential" black identity is lost or compromised by this social process. Indeed, literature produced through this intersection often destabilizes accepted notions of blackness and whiteness as defined in opposition to each other, while also revealing the social circumstances that reinforce such definitions. Even while *Passing* represents the arbitrariness of strict racial classifications—there is, after all, no biological reason that Irene Redfield and Clare Kendry should be categorized as only "black" or only "white"—Knopf included Larsen's novels on its list of the "Negro in Unusual Fiction," marking race as the exceptional category within modernist narrative, just as it already functions in these terms socially. Thus Larsen's agency as an author conflicts with the Knopfs' authority as a publisher: they produce and distribute her work, but do so ultimately according to the terms in which (black) texts are marketed to (white) audiences. Such specifically racialized intersections of intentions are largely indicative of the circumstances under which African American literature is produced.

Editorial theory can contribute most effectively to studies of minority literature by revealing these kinds of historical interactions through their material traces. By emphasizing the circumstances of textual production, editorial theory motivates revised histories of modernism, for instance, by examining simultaneously the various works produced by a particular publisher; similarly, a focus on material textuality recovers the social and cultural contexts in which authors, editors, and publishers worked together,

factors which often disappear in contemporary editions. McGann's editorial preference is therefore for a work's first edition, as the version most representative of the historical circumstances behind textual production. It is
worth noting here that McGann emphasizes a work's first edition not as a
way to privilege authorial intention, but rather to highlight the historical
circumstances of production, which, indeed, often limit authorial agency
within the influence of publishers, editors, and others reviewing prepublication manuscripts. This tendency follows from a historicist emphasis on
the inseparability between material documents and the texts they contain
(and yet which seem to exceed those physical boundaries), as related to the
impossibility of separating out individual creative activity from the social
process of authorship. McGann thus maintains that " 'final authority' for literary works rests neither with the author nor with his affiliated institution;
it resides in the actual structure of the agreements which these two cooperating authorities reach in specific cases" (*Critique* 54).[10] Applied to minority literature, for which these textual authorities are often not "cooperating,"
such historical recovery demonstrates the specific ways in which the fictionality of race has been mapped onto real bodies, both textual and anatom-
ical. Because the imaginative space of fiction both reflects and departs from
lived reality, its necessary existence in material versions creates a fundamental conflict between what is possible on the imaginative plane and what is
produced in actuality.

Henry Louis Gates makes a related point in his discussion of Ishmael
Reed's *Mumbo Jumbo* (1972), concluding, "There can be no transcendent
blackness, for it cannot and does not exist beyond manifestations of it in
specific figures. Put simply, Jes Grew cannot conjure its texts; texts, in the
broadest sense of the term (Parker's music, Ellison's fictions, Romare Bearden's collages, etc.), conjure Jes Grew" (*Signifying* 237). Yet what Gates overlooks, both at this point and in his larger discussion of "Signifyin(g)" as "the
figure of the double-voiced" black tradition (*Signifying* xxv)—and what a
critical perspective grounded in editorial theory restores—is a method for
historicizing the author-publisher (and author-reader or author-society)
interactions that give rise to that double-voiced tradition. Such material
scholarship restores the physical text itself and posits it as a Signifyin(g) site
expressing the tensions between authors and publisher, without necessarily
reducing that process to either party. While Gates examines intertextual

Signifyin(g) between Reed and Ellison, for example, he overlooks the different historical circumstances of production in each case. In Gates's account *Mumbo Jumbo* responds to the history of the African American novel by "repeating received tropes and narrative strategies with a difference. In Reed's differences lie[s] an extended commentary on the history of the black novel" (*Signifying* 217). As I demonstrate in detail in chapter 2, this "extended commentary" also takes shape through the physical features of *Mumbo Jumbo*'s first edition, most prominently a black copyright page with white type. This black page expresses Reed's productive relationship with his mainstream publisher, Doubleday, and his simultaneous resistance to the practical necessity (as Reed sees it) of relying on such firms to produce and distribute his novels. *Mumbo Jumbo* thus comments as well on the history of publication for black novels, Signifyin(g) on the financial structures that compel minority writers to remain with mainstream firms. Finally, the ensuing defamiliarization of black type on a white page exposes the otherwise unseen political implications for maintaining whiteness as the field on which reading occurs, extending the narrative's challenges to history and interpretation onto the physical constitution of the book itself. Without tracing *Mumbo Jumbo*'s textual history, though, such Signifyin(g) remains invisible for contemporary readers, whose editions omit the black copyright page.

Just as that page questions the way reading works, a focus on African American textual history importantly revises the scope and conceptual framework of editorial theory itself. By confronting the material book as residual evidence of the "white mythology" that has dictated the kinds of African American literature that could be published, editorial theory can realize its unique ability to investigate the social networks that motivate, shape, and often control textual production. While editorial theorists argue generally against authorial intention as a guiding principle for editing and interpretation, African American authorial agency has been systematically circumscribed and even ignored, so the bibliographic codes for minority texts are, indeed, the only possible demonstration of this historical silencing. That history thus redirects the study of social authorship onto the vexed relationship of whiteness and blackness that has largely defined Americanness.

An increased editorial focus on minority literature would first expand the historical scope of those works which have been seen as "meriting" scholarly editions, as William Andrews observes in an essay I have quoted earlier. Such editorial projects would provide African American authors with the imprimatur of canonicity derived from the scholarly edition and would recover, or even discover, for contemporary readers lost works of black literature, as in the famous recent case of Hannah Crafts's handwritten manuscript of *The Bondwoman's Narrative*, bought at auction and edited by Gates. The more new editions of minority texts that appear, whether academic or popular, the more the social dimension of much contemporary editorial theory should come into focus as expressly and importantly engaged with minority literature's material history. Up to this point, though, editorial theorists and textual scholars generally have marginalized minority literature, either by ignoring it altogether or by considering it superficially, in comparison to much more extensive examinations of white, canonical texts.[11]

For example, McGann's study of modernism's "visible language," *Black Riders* (the title refers to printed letters on a page), notes in the introduction that "from Yeats and Pound to Stein and Williams and the writers of the Harlem Renaissance, fine-printing work, the small press, and the decorated book fashioned the bibliographical face of the modernist world" (7). Except for one brief comment within a larger discussion of Pound's influence, though, *Black Riders* glosses over New Negro writers while focusing extensively on Dickinson, Stein, Pound, William Morris, Bob Brown, Jack Spicer, Laura (Riding) Jackson, and Yeats. "Many of the influential works of the Harlem Renaissance," McGann observes, "for instance Hughes's *The Weary Blues* (1926), various books by Countee Cullen, Alain Locke's anthology *The New Negro* (1925)—all display the profound effect produced by the graphic and bibliographic revolution at the end of the nineteenth century" (81). But from there the discussion turns immediately to Hardy's *Wessex Poems* and Yeats's editing of the *Oxford Book of Modern Verse*. Similarly, Cunard appears as Pound's publisher, but not in relation to the *Negro* anthology. McGann's peripheral attention to African American literature is indicative of a more widespread myopia within the field, which acknowledges New Negro literature among "other important records of the period" (81) but does not seek "to redraw the map of modernism" (179) along racial and ethnic lines. Indeed, D. C. Greetham notes that of "the three hundred-plus volumes awarded seals of approval" by the MLA's Committee on Scholarly Editions and its predecessor, the Center for Editions of American Authors, "only two were of texts by women (Woolf and Cather), and there were none by persons of color" ("Introduction" 1). Since McGann inaugurated the study of socialized authorship in his 1983 *Critique of Modern Textual Criticism*, five major collections of editorial theory and practice have appeared, with a total of fifty-one essays on individual authors or texts—McGann's *Textual Criticism and Literary Interpretation* (1985), Bornstein's *Representing Modernist Texts* (1991), Bornstein and Ralph Williams's *Palimpsest* (1993); Bornstein and Theresa Tinkle's *The Iconic Page in Manuscript, Print, and Digital Culture* (1998), and Alexander Pettit's *Textual Studies and the Common Reader* (2000). These include just one essay focusing primarily on minority authors or texts, Clayborne Carson's "Editing Martin Luther King, Jr." in *Palimpsest*. Even Greetham's collection *The Margins of the Text* (1997), which, he explains in the introduction, developed in response to the possibility that there is "something patriarchal, elitist, even racist, about the very construction of the traditional scholarly edition, with its approved clear text of accepted 'authorized' readings and its separate apparatus of 'rejected' readings" (1), includes only one essay oriented toward race, William Andrews's overview of the issue in "Editing 'Minority' Texts."

In McGann's case, this neglect results from the conceptual basis of his approach, which is ironically "both author-centric and dependent upon intention," as Bornstein points out in a review of *The Textual Condition* and *Black Riders* ("Beyond Words" 392). Shillingsburg and Bryant present related, but distinct, criticisms of this aspect of McGann's approach to socialized authorship. Granting that "the concept that physical books have integrity and meaning in themselves bears more thinking about," Shillingsburg maintains that "the meaning referred to can be not only in addition to the linguistic text but also separate from or unified with that text. They can be meanings of which the author was unconscious or meanings the author consciously exploits or manipulates" (136). Shillingsburg concludes, however, that "for the most part authors do not control these matters [the physical features of their books], and the 'meanings,' or implications, of the physical text, if anything, reveal unconsciously things about the author or publisher" (137).

Bryant, in a discussion of Melville's working draft for *Typee*, concludes, "Unfortunately, McGann's theory, which locates the beginnings of social text at the moment of publication (however broadly that may be defined), is not equipped to address the mixture of authorial intentions and social pressures" (58). I would echo both criticisms of McGann's theory and practice as they apply to editors and textual scholars focusing on African American literature: the "social pressures" Bryant cites clearly affect publishers as well, as Shillingsburg notes, and so the material texts in question display, whether consciously or not, the cultural environment in which they have been produced.

McGann's consistent focus on writers like Pound, Morris, Yeats, Dickinson, and D. G. Rossetti highlights authors who maintained an extraordinary degree of control over their works' production, thus leaving little conceptual space for writers like Wright, Larsen, Reed, and, indeed, almost every racially marginalized author whose relationship to textual production is characterized by a lack of control, both at the material and broader social levels. Yet that element of McGann's and others' accounts of socialized authorship—how to account for authors lacking a significant say in how their works would be produced—represents for me the untapped potential of contemporary textual scholarship: a chance to broaden the conception of the "social" to include not only minority writers themselves, but the cultural contexts in which their work develops. In a striking passage from *The Textual Condition*, McGann insists that "the most important 'collaboration' process is that which finds ways of marrying a linguistic to a bibliographical text. We confront such marriages most forcefully when we read texts which, while 'written by' certain writers, were never 'authorized' by them. The production of this kind of text is carried out under the authority, and by the final intentions, of persons other than the writer of the texts" (61). McGann's examples here are Faulkner and Byron, who, while certainly relevant, evoke only a faint echo of the "unauthorized collaboration" evidenced by Toomer, Wright, Reed, or, indeed, almost every African American writer working with mainstream publishers. McGann in *Black Riders* is ultimately interested in charting the philosophical and literary shifts from "the idea that poetry had a significant political function to perform" during the modernist period to a postmodern perspective on "poetry's social function" as a "more general examination of how we are to understand the relation of language and truth" (122, 123). These political and social functions, however, are particular to an implicitly unraced society and politics, as part of an argument that should apply conceptually to a universal condition but, in fact, operates only within particular histories.

The political and social truths that emerge from the intersection of (white) editorial theory and African American literature revise not only the objects of inquiry for textual scholarship, but the field's fundamental ways of seeing textuality itself. As Reed's black copyright page makes clear, "standard" or "natural" assumptions about the constitution of printed books are themselves grounded in oppositions between whiteness and blackness which can be reversed to expose the politics of print. This is a point that should emerge from McGann's title in *Black Riders*, but which is oddly silent throughout the book. Indeed, an explanation of the title appears only on the paperback's back-cover description: "Jerome McGann demonstrates the extraordinary degree to which modernist styles are related to graphic and typographic design, to printed letters—'black riders' on a blank page—that create language for the eye." The elevation of this metaphor to the book's title without an attendant discussion of its seemingly inescapable racial implications demonstrates the extent to which editorial theorists have repressed minority literature and the ways in which that repressed object returns in ways that may escape their conscious awareness. That the "black riders" here appear on a "blank" rather than "white" page reinforces this point, as "blank" glosses over the racial analogy haunting the book's central metaphor. In a further telling example of the book's bibliographic return of the repressed, the paperback's front cover features black letters on a blank (white) background for author and title, with the subtitle (*The Visible Language of Modernism*) in white type on a burnt orange background. The spine shifts to a black background, with "McGann" and the title now in white letters, except for the "B" in burnt orange. Even as the book's overall cover design recalls Morris's ornamental pages and typography, in keeping with McGann's decision to take Morris "as a point of departure for a study of modernism" (xiii), the juxtaposition of black type/white background and white type/black background conveys, however "unintentionally," the racial implications of this design.

Finally, the ambiguity of intentionality itself here is a key element of my critique. Though no designer is listed on the cover, it seems reasonable to assume that McGann would have enjoyed a considerable degree of input into the book's design, given both his professional stature and the book's (linguistic) content. The back-cover copy was either written or approved by McGann (or some combination thereof), presumably, putting McGann in a similar position of authorial agency to those writers on whom he has focused his scholarly investigations. Yet a bibliographic reading of the cover in terms of race seems clearly to exceed the intentions of either McGann or the editors and designers at Princeton University Press, in an example of Bornstein's observation that "conflicts or even differences between authorial intent and the inevitable bibliographic codes of publishers still await clarification" ("Beyond Words" 393). This issue, writ large, is the defining bibliographic situation for most African American literature, and so textual scholarship centering on these texts must shift away from even McGann's ultimately author-centered model of bibliographic inquiry, toward a more genuinely social version of socialized authorship.

To take race and ethnicity as a central editorial focus, then, could involve not only new principles determining which authors and texts need new editions, but also new editorial methodologies themselves. One such change might involve a reorientation of the page in terms of main text and peripheral text, such as footnotes, textual variants, and other marginalia. To transfer marginalized text to the center of the page, that is, would effect a textual reversal of historical marginalizations according to racial identity and transfer the presumed authority of the textual center toward the suppressed edges. While this maneuver would disrupt conventional ways of reading, that would, of course, be precisely the point; such an edition of Reed's *Flight to Canada* (1976), for instance, could extend the novel's own play with historical "correctness" in a way that would subvert traditional notions of textual structure as well. Such challenges to conventional models of textual authority could also develop beyond the page itself, as in Clayborne Carson's observation that while the editing of Martin Luther King's papers "would not exist if not for the widespread belief among American elites in the notion that Great Men and their ideas alter the course of history," such projects "can also become valuable sources of knowledge about the social forces that make possible the emergence of new leaders" (314).

A third implication of editing texts with racial and ethnic contexts in mind is a new and different emphasis on historical accuracy, this one in keeping with the effects of cultural history on what we can know—and cannot know—about the production of black texts. As I argue in chapter 1 in response to *Passing*'s editorial conundrum—the original last paragraph disappeared in the third printing, and no one knows why—the most ethically responsible edition might well be one that prints half its copies with the original last paragraph and half without, in order to signal a contemporary lack of knowledge, and the reasons for that lack. Similarly, I argue in chapter 5, on the mass of Ralph Ellison's manuscripts published as *Juneteenth*, that the imposition of order created by the conventional structure of a book belies both the fragmentary state of the drafts—Ellison's editor reduces more than two thousand manuscript pages into the shape of a regular novel—and by extension Ellison's fragmentary approach to the problem of racial identity.

Finally, an editorial emphasis on race raises important questions about who editors are. It hardly seems coincidental that a field that has been populated primarily by white men has focused its energies primarily on white, male authors. That tendency has recently begun to shift, as a growing number of women have occupied important positions within the field. Betty Bennett's work on Mary Shelley, Robin Schulze's on Marianne Moore, Marta Werner's on Dickinson, Ann Thompson's on Shakespeare, Julia Briggs's on Woolf, Susan Rosowski's on Willa Cather, and Elaine Forman Crane's on the eighteenth-century American diarist Elizabeth Drinker, among others, have all begun to change the face of textual scholarship, in ways that could also develop with increased attention to minority literature from editors and editorial theorists. As a white man myself, I am sensitive to the need for what might be called "editing across the lines," in an echo of Michael Awkward's notion of white critics "reading across the lines" (71). Awkward observes, "Even in self-reflexive critical acts, racial privilege may create interpretive obstacles or, more important, points of resistance that color, in racially motivated ways, the effects of an exploration of blackness. In other words, white reading can mean the adoption of a posture that can be demonstrated to be antithetical to black interests" (60). Such points of resistance certainly apply to self-reflexive white editing as well, and so that interpretive act would also require the vigilance Awkward calls for among white and black editors and readers. Greetham proposes one way to theorize this editorial situation, adopting Homi Bhabha's notion of "naming over time" as a way to enable genuinely critical editing across racial and ethnic lines. "If the editor or textual critic," Greetham writes, "of whatever ethnicity or displaced ethnicity, can hold faith to this 'interrogative' agency rather than to a simple conflation of interest with the text, then alterity, no longer constructed only around history but along any other axis of difference, can still operate as a discursive practice" (*Theories* 429).[12] Thus Greetham concludes that "while it would not be an accident that Arnold Rampersad should edit Richard Wright or that Susan Rosowski should edit Willa Cather, neither would it be assumed that a gender or race identification would obliterate the 'realm of otherness' that the social text must inhabit" (430). In writing this book I have sought to keep that "realm of otherness" alive in my attempts to inhabit the textual spaces of African American authors and readers, as well as their white editors and publishers, while also acknowledging the historical and social limits of this enterprise. Such problems of historical and cultural distance always confront editors and textual critics, so to trace the material manifestations of race on texts produced across the twentieth century means to acknowledge and preserve the historical mutability of race as well as its sometimes inescapable consequences.

The chapters that follow—on Larsen's *Passing*, Reed's *Mumbo Jumbo*, Brooks's collected poems and *Children Coming Home*, Morrison's novels selected for Oprah's Book Club, and Ellison's *Juneteenth*—examine various aspects of the author-publisher interaction as inflected by cultural constructions of race. In each case we see conflicts between authorial intention and authorial agency, that is, between versions of a text designed by authors versus those actually produced. Such interactions operate at the individual level of the author, the publisher, and the book, and at the broader levels of culture and the canon. The twentieth century has witnessed shifting balances of power, both economic and cultural, but has consistently maintained distinct racial categories in which literature marked as black could be produced and consumed. The preservation of a racial other, as Gates argues, can work not so much to challenge social and cultural hierarchies as to maintain them: "The threat to the margin comes not from assimilation or dissolution—from any attempt to denude it of its defiant alterity—but, on the contrary, from the center's attempts to *preserve* that alterity, which result in the homogenization of the other as, simply, other" ("African American" 315, original emphasis). In contrast to Gates's claim here, bell hooks's "oppositional gaze" of black female spectatorship takes up the margin as a productive site of resistance, what she terms "a way to know the present and invent the future" (131). In this project I have focused on the sites of material production of black literature, which has generally meant looking through the "center" of the (white) publishing world into the margins. Brooks's publications with black presses offer a compelling literary analog to the oppositional gaze which hooks traces in film. The material texts of twentieth-century African American literature demonstrate the literal markings of their otherness, as mainstream publishers seek to homogenize it—*Cane* is reduced to "black vaudeville"; *Passing* represents the "Negro in Unusual Fiction"—and as authors negotiate a more "authentic" alterity, as in Reed's black copyright page or Morrison's Oprah editions.

There is a certain historical progress implied by the sequence of these examples, but in charting the transition from modernism to postmodernism as part of this study, I will also examine the extent to which minority literature remains defined as inherently other, in ways that transcend historical and theoretical shifts over the last century. As Appiah suggests, "the binarism of Self and Other" represents "the last of the shibboleths of the modernizers that we must learn to live without" ("Is the Post-" 894). Distinctions between self and other ultimately reduce into each other, as Slavoj Žižek maintains, because one inevitably understands the other in terms of the self: the "very feature which seems to exclude the subject from the Other . . . is already a 'reflexive determination' of the Other; precisely as excluded from the Other, we are already part of its game" (66). For subjects defined already as other, the resulting double consciousness derives from this split image. Along these lines, the critical discourses employing notions of intentionality and agency merge in a study of twentieth-century African American material texts. Theorists of textuality and race both have responded to the demise of authorial intention as an arbiter of textual meaning: for editorial theorists, intentionality remains an important measure of an author's plans for the language, punctuation, and style of a work, even while this level of intentionality is framed within a larger disavowal of that concept as a larger authority, while for African Americanists agency has provided a useful description of the social and cultural power available to racially marginalized subjects.

The changed ending of *Passing* provides my opening example of such cultural negotiations and the problems they present for contemporary scholars: we cannot know even whether Larsen intended (in the narrow editorial sense) to remove the novel's original last paragraph, because the lack of intentionality (in the larger interpretive sense) historically associated with black writers has contributed to the absence of any significant archival record, either for Larsen or Knopf, that could address this question. Just this sort of historical archive, Alain Locke notes, is what "the Afro-American in this country needs in order to have a history; and the race, in order to have a culture" (quoted in Lott 147). My reading of Reed's *Mumbo Jumbo* in chapter 2 centers similarly on the role of the archive, both as a central feature of the novel's portrait of American racial history and in relation to Reed's own archive at the University of Delaware, which restores *Mumbo Jumbo*'s material history in ways that are impossible for *Passing*. While the Delaware archive enables us to ascribe intentionality and agency to Reed (and his editors at Doubleday), it also points to the historical loss of that record in contemporary editions of *Mumbo Jumbo*, which tilt the original edition's self-conscious balance between authenticity and commodification further toward a masked appearance for an implicitly white audience.

Gwendolyn Brooks's papers, unfortunately for this study, are not yet available for scholars at Berkeley's Bancroft Library. The same is true for Morrison's archive, which has not yet found a library home, and of the Ellison manuscripts for *Juneteenth*, in the Library of Congress, which will become available once the scholarly edition of that book appears. Without these materials to draw on, I have focused my bibliographical readings on these writers' published records. Brooks and Morrison chart opposite paths in their engagement with popular literary audiences. Brooks, after establishing her poetic career with Harper, abandoned the mainstream firm for independent black presses, first Broadside Press in Detroit, then Third World Press in Chicago, and finally her own David Company, also in her hometown. Morrison, meanwhile, worked within the mainstream publishing industry in the 1970s and '80s as an editor at Random House and one of the unnamed producers there of *The Black Book*, before aligning herself with the incredible commercial power of Oprah's Book Club in the early '90s. Whereas Brooks sees a return to her Chicago community as the natural outgrowth of her cultural awakening during the Black Arts movement, Morrison takes advantage of Winfrey's unprecedented business success to position her novels for new kinds of popular audiences, even while still publishing them with mainstream firms. Such a cultural revisioning was not possible for Brooks at Harper, of course, but the deliberately narrow focus on particular Chicago neighborhoods expressed in Brooks's last poetry collection, *Children Coming Home* (1991), would also not work within the very different dynamics of Winfrey's TV book club.

My final chapter, on the book published as *Juneteenth*, ties together this study's historical range by examining the 1999 publication of a novel on which Ellison had labored for most of the second half of the twentieth century. While I have no doubt that *Juneteenth* will eventually change scholarly conceptions of the modern and postmodern novel, the text that has this effect will pass itself off as a far more coherent narrative than the massive manuscript Ellison left behind. The editorial ethics involved in this case thus return me to the questions raised by *Passing*: while in *Juneteenth* we can clearly identify Ellison's authorial agency, we cannot ultimately ascribe to him an intention to publish *Juneteenth* (or, indeed, even to use that title). Just as I argue that we should acknowledge the historical impossibility of knowing which is the "correct" text of *Passing*, I conclude that in reading Ellison's "novel" we should keep alive its deeply fragmentary condition at the material level, and thus engage the necessarily fragmentary representations of racial identity produced by each text.

Finally, I should note those authors not covered in detail in this study but who would also reward an editorial focus: these include Hughes, Hurston, Wright, Charles Chesnutt, Toomer, Dunbar, Claude McKay, Cullen, Sterling Brown, Jessie Redmon Fauset, James Weldon Johnson, Georgia Douglas Johnson, Rudolph Fisher, and Wallace Thurman from the modernist period, loosely defined, and James Baldwin, Robert Hayden, Amiri Baraka, Rita Dove, Gayl Jones, Leon Forrest, and Octavia Butler, among postmodern writers. Wright's and McKay's periodical publications in *New Masses* and *The Liberator* merit further study for the contextual codes produced there, for example. A contextual code, according to Bornstein, "is bibliographic, in that it pertains to the physical constitution" of a work, and "linguistic, in that it is made up of words" ("What Is" 179). Also needing further study are Hayden's career-long association with smaller presses and the first edition of Butler's *Kindred* (1979), which interestingly resembles the original *Mumbo Jumbo* cover in its illustration of a Janus-faced woman looking ahead and behind. Broader bibliographic studies of ethnicity and whiteness are certainly needed as well, but also lie outside the scope of this volume. Through my primary focus on Larsen, Reed, Brooks, Morrison, and Ellison, I have tried to maintain a thematic coherence through a broad historical spectrum and to survey the bibliographic production of race across a range of gender and class positions. That this book could well consist of five entirely different chapters, though, should demonstrate the breadth and depth of critical inquiry that still lies ahead.

CHAPTER ONE

PASSING (ON) TEXTUAL HISTORY

The Ends of Nella Larsen's *Passing*

Nella Larsen's *Passing* has become one of the most widely read New Negro Renaissance novels in recent years, but no one really knows how it ends. By this I do not mean that critics have not determined how much guilt to assign Irene Redfield in Clare Kendry's fatal fall, or to what extent the narrative is actually a lesbian story "passing" as a racial one. I mean the ending is actually unknowable, because the original last paragraph disappeared from the first edition's third printing, and no extant evidence can explain this change. There is no conclusive answer to the question of presenting this textual crux "correctly"—despite assumptions to the contrary by Larsen's editors—but I will argue that this textual problem itself bears an important lesson: the best response to a gap in textual knowledge is to recognize the absence and its causes, not to produce editions that gloss over such gaps, thereby eliding the social and cultural elements of these textual histories and compelling Larsen's novel to pass as textually and historically stable.

In this chapter, I connect *Passing*'s incomplete material history to the circumstances of its production and reception, which I take to be indicative of the broader cultural tensions at work in the New Negro Renaissance between African American authors and their white publishers. As I argue in the introduction, the tensions in this period between the culturally hybrid circumstances of production and publishers' continued marketing of New Negro literature in racially marked terms reflect the unbalanced power dynamics that produced what Gilles Deleuze terms a "minor literature": "that which a minority constructs within a major language" (152). The record of that minor language lies in the material traces of its production history.

In this case, the primary material issue is the inclusion or omission of the original last paragraph. Knopf's first two 1929 printings of *Passing* ended with the following two paragraphs, after Clare Kendry has fallen to her death from an open window and Irene Redfield has descended from the party to the street:

Her [Irene's] quaking knees gave way under her. She moaned and sank down, moaned again. Through the great heaviness that submerged and drowned her she was dimly conscious of strong arms lifting her up. Then everything was dark.

Centuries after, she heard the strange man [a police officer, presumably] saying: "Death by misadventure, I'm inclined to believe. Let's go up and have another look at that window."

The second paragraph disappeared in the novel's third 1929 printing, so that "Then everything was dark" ends this version, not the police officer's remark. There is no archival evidence to explain whether Larsen requested that the "Centuries after" paragraph be omitted, or if she approved of this change as a revision initiated by Knopf, or even whether the omission was intended by either party. The extensive Alfred A. Knopf archive in the University of Texas's Harry Ransom Humanities Research Center contains no files on Larsen that resolve or even address this matter, and there is no Larsen archive as such. My discussion focuses first on the various editorial approaches to this problem. Of the four editions currently available, three include the second paragraph above, while the other does not (except in a footnote). The practical matter of choosing one version or the other, I argue, masks the deeper historical and cultural issues that generate this choice in the first place. After demonstrating the interpretive consequences of using a particular edition without taking account of the novel's full textual history, I turn to the pedagogical implications of this essentially unknowable ending. As Pamela Caughie contends, Larsen's novel is an especially effective vehicle for teaching the fluidity of cultural identity, for "we are always 'passing' in the classroom" (137). To edit or teach *Passing* without acknowledging its incomplete history, I conclude, forces the text to pass as stable, and thus erases the material and racial histories behind this textual mask.

PUBLISHING "NEW NEGROES"

Our lack of contemporary knowledge about Larsen's authorial agency echoes her own tenuous status as a new black novelist establishing herself within the New York literary scene. Beverly M. Haviland observes, "All of the writers of the Harlem Renaissance faced difficulties about how they would become authors in, and yet not in, the white world that controlled the traditions and the material means of publication. There were many issues to resolve: about the subject matter one chose, about the publisher one chose—or was chosen by" (305). Chidi Ikonné similarly distinguishes between a few early years characterized by an "essentially Negro self-possessing and Negro self-expressing" literature and the period after 1926, when New Negro literature became "publisher/audience-controlled, even if essentially Negro self-expressing" (xi). Larsen's brief novelistic career—essentially just the last two years of the 1920s—inhabits this transitional period in the New Negro Renaissance, just after Van Vechten had demonstrated the large, implicitly white audience for "inside" tales of Harlem life. Van Vechten's famous passage into Harlem culture also opens the possibility of inverting such racial spectatorship; as Lori Harrison-Kahan points out, "African Americans who passed in(to) the white world were able to gaze upon white in a reversal of the typical Harlem Renaissance scenario where whites sought out the spectacle of black life" (111).

While Van Vechten's descriptions of African American life now seem rooted as much in this kind of desire for the exoticized, Other as in more genuine racial awareness, his practical efforts to help black writers into print are clear. As Emily Bernard notes, Van Vechten's "most important contribution to the movement . . . was not material but symbolic" ("What" 533). The year after the Knopfs restored James Weldon Johnson as the author of *Ex-Coloured Man*, they brought into print another of Van Vechten's friends with Larsen's first novel, *Quicksand*. Larsen followed this debut the following year with *Passing*, dedicated to Van Vechten and his wife, Fania Marinoff. The addition of gender difference to passing narratives like Johnson's reflects the additional complications experienced by African American women in their encounters with the publishing system.

Knopf's bibliographical fields for *Passing* and *Nigger Heaven* demonstrate the cultural anxiety surrounding the publication of black authors by white publishers or white novels with black subjects. As Van Vechten's book was going to press, he requested an early advertising campaign from Knopf because, he said, "This book is different. It is necessary to prepare the mind not only of my own public, but of the new public which this book may possibly reach. . . . If they see the title, they will ask questions, or read 'The New Negro' or something, so that the kind of life I am writing about will not come as an actual shock" (quoted in Leuders 87). Van Vechten had also published several articles on New Negro literature prior to his novel's appearance, as part of his strategy for building a market for the book (Flora 75 n28). As I noted in the introduction, Van Vechten's novel became a literary sensation, at least among white readers, and Knopf marketed it accordingly. A Knopf advertisement for the "Latest BORZOI Novels" in the *Saturday Review of Literature*, for example, places *Nigger Heaven* at the top of the column, with an illustration of Van Vechten himself, rather than Harlem. Caricatures of Van Vechten by such well-known artists as Ralph Barton and Miguel Covarrubias were common during this period, as Bernard points out, so the ad's use of Van Vechten for its illustration also taps into the established popular cultural market for Van Vechten's image (*Remember* xiv). This figure, combined with the blurb from William Rose Benét— " 'Nigger Heaven' is a book you can't lay down. It positively crackles with energy"—clearly markets the novel to a white audience, who will identify with the racial perspectives of both Van Vechten as author and Benét as exemplary reader.

The white audience envisioned here is also reflected in both novels' colophons, each describing the Caslon typeface and its printing history. The *Nigger Heaven* colophon, which follows a "Glossary of Negro Words and Phrases," identifies William Caslon's place in printing history and notes that the "principal difference" between the eighteenth-century font and its modern adaptation "is a slight shortening of the ascending and descending letters." The *Passing* colophon provides a much fuller context: "An artistic, easily-read type, Caslon has had two centuries of ever-increasing popularity in our own country—it is of interest to note that the first copies of the

Declaration of Independence and the first paper currency distributed to the citizens of the new-born nation were printed in this type face." The political and economic history evoked by the *Passing* colophon returns America to a history in which full citizenship and independence were racially and sexually determined. At the same time, the "increasing popularity" of the typeface tacitly evokes the slow emergence of civil rights, based in the ideals, rather than the historical context, of the "Declaration," even while Caslon, as the typeface for the first paper currency, mediates the financial profits created for Knopf by Larsen's novel through a white commodification of a black text. While the colophon's ostensible aim is to relate Knopf's printed book to an American history of printing, the subtext here becomes a reassurance for Van Vechten's white audience that not everything is dark at Knopf. *Passing*'s (type)face is grounded in an implicitly white American history, even if its content challenges the racial assumptions growing out of that history. Just as passing narratives depend on a "double audience" in which "one audience [is] ignorant and another . . . knows the truth *and remains silent about it*" (Rabinowitz, "Betraying" 205, original emphasis), Knopf's publication of Larsen's passing story seeks out its own double audience, in which one group of readers will stay silent about the white commodification of black literature.

A more charitable reading of the *Passing* colophon might view the text there simply as an effort to locate Larsen's novel as quintessentially American, in a stable connection to the Declaration of Independence. To me, though, the colophon's emphasis on Caslon as a type which is "easily read" and "of ever-increasing popularity" and its historical connection to American currency speak to the fundamental questions of commodification generated by the New Negro Renaissance. Even if the colophon establishes an ostensibly affirmative connection between *Passing* and the Declaration, it does so in ways that are more about commerce than independence.

These issues also arise in the colophon for Knopf's edition of *Ex-Coloured Man*, which offers a rhetorically similar description of Caslon Old Face: "Caslon's types were made to read. Even their apparent imperfections contribute to this effect being, in fact, the result of a deliberate artistry which sought above all else for legibility in the printed page." As the publisher's "last word" in Johnson's novel, which was here finally made public *as* Johnson's novel, this colophon echoes Van Vechten's emphasis in the preface on the book's clear and comprehensive portrait of the modern black experience: the novel's "imperfections" aside, it has been "made to read," though in strikingly different ways by the preface than by the narrative itself. With the author's name on the title page, Johnson and Knopf themselves seek a different kind of legibility, one which will allow their new (white) audience to read (or reread) the novel in the specific terms of its production.

Throughout her brief career, Larsen seems to have been especially attuned to the ways in which her authorial identity might be commodified. Larsen's biography recently has become much more common scholarly knowledge, so I will mention only the essentials here: on the strength of her two novels, Larsen was quickly supplanting Jessie Redmon Fauset as the most recognized and significant female writer within the New Negro Renaissance. Although Knopf's sales records for Larsen have not survived, *Passing* went through three printings in 1929, so there is some evidence of Larsen's commercial success. Du Bois's unsigned review in *The Crisis* concludes: "If the American Negro renaissance gives us many more books like this, with its sincerity, its simplicity and charm, we can soon with equanimity drop the word 'Negro.' Meantime, your job is clear. Buy the book" (249). In 1930 Larsen became the first African American woman to win a Guggenheim fellowship, which was to support the research for and composition of her third novel. That book never went to press, in large part because Larsen was accused of plagiarizing a short story and so fell quickly from public grace and attention. As Haviland notes, Larsen continued writing, though not for publication, after this episode, but these manuscripts have not survived (297). Larsen did submit a third novel, titled *Mirage*, to Knopf in 1931, which Charles R. Larson speculates may have been what she called her "white novel" (107–8). A Knopf reader's report suggested substantial revision, but Larsen never seems to have returned to the novel and broke off contact with the Guggenheim Foundation at around this point (108–9).

But Larsen was also a victim of the New Negro Renaissance's fade from marketability. In both Larsen's novels the "race question" obscures themes of marriage, changing gender roles, and, in some critical estimations, suppressed lesbian desire, reflecting Hurston's complaint that with "only the fractional 'exceptional' and the 'quaint' portrayed, a true picture of Negro life in American cannot be" ("What White" 173).[1] Larsen's literary career from the 1930s on is a blank; she subsisted on alimony and other support for a few years and then began a nursing career in 1941. As Larson notes in his dual biography of Larsen and Toomer, it is "difficult to believe" that Larsen's later novels "were inferior to *Quicksand* and *Passing*. It is impossible to believe that they were of lesser merit than the hurricane of undistinguished novels published every season. . . . Publishers no longer wanted books about black life. Readers had lost interest in black subjects. Rather than face obscurity, she tried to write to their dictates, to adjust to the changing market. There is one novel that she refers to as her 'white' novel. No one knows how long she kept writing and sending out manuscripts before she gave in to the humiliation of constant rejection" (210). Larson's historical case is somewhat overstated here, as the commercial success of Wright's *Uncle Tom's Children* and especially *Native Son* demonstrate a continued mainstream audience for African American fiction in the years just after Larsen's public career ended. Still, a dwindling market was certainly in place, as demonstrated by the paucity of novels from the 1930s in Alain Locke's catalog of New Negro fiction for the decade: only four other works of fiction before Wright's *Children* appear (*Critical* 270).

Larsen's first public texts bore a different countenance, as she published two stories in 1926 under the pseudonym "Allen Semi," an anagram of her married name, Nella Imes. By reversing her husband's name, Larsen entered the public sphere of authorship with her name, her gender, and her race veiled; as Larsen biographer Thadious M. Davis notes, "the unusual name lacked a clear ethnic or racial association" (174). When she did become a published novelist under her own gender, Imes, like so many modernist women writers, chose a different identity for her literary career than for her personal life, which, as Cheryl A. Wall notes, "constitutes a form of passing" (88).[2] Larsen also fabricated portions of her author's biography for Knopf, including the date of her birth and her parents' identities, leading to inaccurate jacket copy for *Passing* (Larson xviii–xix; T. Davis 22). The only place Larsen's alternate identity exists publicly, it is important to remember, is in print: in her personal life she remained Mrs. Nella Imes, but by changing her signature for publication Larsen begins to write herself out of the dilemma Nancy Miller posits for women's public identity. In response to Foucault's question, "What matter who's speaking," Miller responds, "I would answer it matters, for example, to women who have lost and still routinely lose their proper name in marriage, and whose signature—not merely their voice—has not been worth the paper it was written on; women for whom the signature—by virtue of its power in the world of circulation—is *not* immaterial. Only those who have it can play with not having it" (75). The literary power of the signature, in Miller's terms, gives Larsen a measure of authorial autonomy; she can control the name on her books if not the other terms under which they are distributed.

While she had mixed feelings about submitting her work to Knopf after the firm had rejected Fauset's 1924 novel *There Is Confusion* (eventually published by Boni and Liveright), Larsen "understood well the power of white males in the New York literary establishment, and she knew that as a female and a woman of color in search of a major publisher, she needed support from within their ranks" (T. Davis 186). Knopf's first edition of *Quicksand* includes a list of the "Negro in Unusual Fiction," implicitly designating Larsen within this category. So while in her two novels Larsen critiques the ideological dependence on a strict racial separation, her publisher reinscribes this constructed divide, even while stepping outside mainstream publishing trends by marketing minority texts in the first place. Like her protagonists, Helga Crane and Clare Kendry, Larsen bore a mixed racial heritage, as she explained in her author's statement for *Quicksand*.[3] In another example of the interaction between the hybrid and the particular, then, we can see here Larsen marked not as of mixed race but as only and exceptionally "Negro," at the same time that her novels appear within the broader aesthetic category of "Unusual Fiction" and, indeed, implicitly reconfigure the narrative elements and social boundaries of that genre.

TEXTUAL AND NARRATIVE INSTABILITIES IN *PASSING*

Turning from the novel's original production and reception to current scholarly reaction, I outline in this section the main editorial responses to the last paragraph(s) and the interpretive costs of neglecting the novel's material history. Since the appearance of Deborah McDowell's 1986 Rutgers University Press edition of Larsen's two novels, they have been analyzed widely in studies of race, gender, sexuality, and modernism. Claudia Tate, McDowell,

Cheryl Wall, Pamela Caughie, Peter Rabinowitz, and Judith Butler, among several other scholars, have traced the novel's elusive interpretive status, paying particular attention to the subtextual lesbian narrative (more or less as articulated by McDowell) that works alongside (or against, depending on one's critical perspective) the more apparent story of racial passing.[4] As I will argue here, an important parallel adheres between these kinds of narrative instabilities and the textual instability produced by the insoluble problem of the last paragraph. (For an interesting discussion of this edition's typography and its effects on interpretation, see McCoy.) To read *Passing's* narrative instabilities while ignoring its textual instability transfers the narrative dynamics out of their original context of production and therefore passes off the text as a stable document, even while a productive ambiguity operates at both the narrative and material levels.

That narrative ambiguity develops primarily from Irene's increasingly unreliable point of view, which corresponds both to Clare's growing desire to leave white society behind and Irene's fears that toward this end Clare is having an affair with her husband. Harrison-Kahan notes that Larsen has "taken away Irene's 'I' by giving us a narrative from Irene's point of view that is in the third person instead of the first person" (110). When Clare falls out an open window at a mixed-race party in the novel's final scene, it is not clear whether Irene or Clare's husband, who discovers her "true" identity at the party, pushes her out the window, or whether she falls out herself, either deliberately or inadvertently. There is no critical consensus on exactly what happens in this scene, but Larson makes the strongest case for Irene as Clare's murderer (86); see also Kawash (164–66) and Claudia Tate ("Nella Larsen's *Passing*"). It seems clear to me that Irene at least wishes for Clare's death and that mostly likely she causes it. I am most concerned, however, with the impact of the final paragraph, in both versions, on readers' conclusions.

In considering here the editorial and interpretive problems of *Passing's* ending, I should emphasize that these are *not* two discrete processes, for to edit is inherently to interpret. As Bornstein notes, editorial decisions often "seem natural and inevitable rather than contingent and constructed," when, in fact, all editorial choices entail specific textual, and therefore interpretive, consequences ("Introduction" 2). Given the evidentiary lack for *Passing*, it is not surprising that Larsen scholars have reached various conclusions about how to explain this situation. As I hope the ensuing discussion will show, these different approaches have created something of an editorial muddle, perhaps because none of Larsen's editors so far have been textual scholars per se. While the publication of a new edition requires a particular editorial decision, I will conclude that the most faithful contemporary edition of *Passing* would, ironically, refuse to choose either ending.

McDowell's Rutgers edition ends with "Then everything was dark," with a footnote that includes the original last paragraph. There McDowell writes, "In 1971 Macmillan issued an edition of *Passing* that ended with the following final paragraph, which was not included in the original 1929 Knopf edition . . . [quotes 'Centuries after' paragraph]. This closing paragraph does not seem to alter the spirit of the original in any way" (246 n10). McDowell's first sentence is historically inaccurate, of course; the "Centuries after" paragraph was included in the "original 1929 Knopf edition," in the first two printings. The 1971 Macmillan edition is a paperback reprint of the first printing, but because McDowell does not distinguish between different printings of the original Knopf edition, she misrecognizes the Macmillan reprint in relation to the original Knopf text. McDowell's statement that the original last paragraph "does not seem to alter the spirit of the original in any way" is equally wrong-headed. As I discuss below, the switch from one paragraph to the other as the novel's last word, in fact, carries substantial interpretive consequences.

Mark J. Madigan, the first scholar to offer a thorough discussion of *Passing*'s textual history, also recommends an edition ending with "Then everything was dark," but he does so more judiciously than McDowell. Madigan concludes: "Since there is no evidence that Larsen opposed the substantive change of dropping the final paragraph, I contend that the definitive edition of *Passing* should end with the sentence 'Then everything was dark' as it does in the third printing. In light of the uncertainty concerning the reason for the change in ending, and the confusion caused by reprintings, though, I would also recommend that editors of the novel discuss the final paragraph in a textual note recounting its enigmatic history, a history which underscores the difficulty of establishing authorial intentions" (523). Madigan opts for an editorial compromise, allowing the omission to stand while still directing readers toward its ambiguous textual status. Madigan effectively follows Larsen's final authorial intentions, the policy pursued most famously by G. Thomas Tanselle, among contemporary editorial theorists. Tanselle argues, "If we grant that authors have intentions and therefore that the intentions of past authors are historical facts, we require further justification for the attempt to recover those intentions and to reconstruct texts reflecting them, whatever our chances of success may be" ("Editorial Problem" 76). Madigan's approach leans toward the omission of the "Centuries after" paragraph as reflecting Larsen's final intentions, while acknowledging that the "chances of success" in ascertaining those intentions are low in this case. The particular problem is that we cannot conclude that the omission of the "Centuries after" paragraph was Larsen's *intention*, only that, as Madigan notes, "there is no evidence that Larsen opposed the substantive change." But again, this is not the more common case of an author letting a change stand because he or she does not disagree with it. Or rather, that *could* be the case with *Passing*, but there is no extant record to lead us to any clear conclusion, and so we can only speculate in one direction or another.

Indeed, this evidentiary lack has led Thadious Davis to support two opposite conclusions. In her 1994 biography, Davis writes, "Larsen herself was not satisfied with the ending of her novel. . . . Although she does not say so, she may well have been responsible for dropping the final paragraph of the novel after the second printing in order to suspend the action before a verdict is reached on Clare's death and Irene's fate. She concludes the text of the revised third printing of *Passing* with a sentence doubly evocative of female unconsciousness: 'Then everything was dark'" (322). But in her Penguin edition of *Passing* three years later, Davis does not end with the line "Then everything was dark," explaining her decision in "A Note on the Text": "The text of this edition is based on the first edition, first printing of *Passing*, which was published by Alfred A. Knopf in 1929. . . . Although it is possible that the revised ending conformed to the author's sense of her novel, there is no indication that Nella Larsen herself recommended, sought, or approved the excision of the final paragraph. The text of this edition, therefore, follows the original Knopf first printing" (xxxv). While Davis does not explain this switch, I would surmise that it derived from the lack of material evidence, which led her to reverse her original hypothesis: not that Larsen dropped the last paragraph in order to create a more artfully ambiguous ending, but that Larsen was cut out of the decision-making process, unable to "recommend, seek, or approve the excision of the final paragraph." Davis's rhetoric interestingly attributes a level of agency to

Larsen in keeping with Davis's particular editorial decision. The Larsen of the biography is probably responsible for "dropping" the original last paragraph, and thus "concludes" the novel on a different note. The "excision" of the "Centuries after" paragraph, as Davis terms it in the Penguin edition, infers both a change in her view of Larsen's agency as well as of the social ramifications for that lessened authorial control, as we now read that Larsen probably had not "recommended, sought, or approved" this change. Losing editorial control over the "Centuries after" paragraph, that is, ironically forecasts Larsen's lack of control over the future of the novel and of her career. Davis's interpretation of this textual conundrum changes hand in hand with her approach to its editing.

The Modern Library's edition also ends with the "Centuries after" paragraph, without comment in the hardcover, but with a note from editor Mae Henderson in the paperback. Henderson offers a fuller textual history and a discussion of her own editorial preferences:

Two different endings to the novel were published by Alfred A. Knopf in 1929. . . . Later editions, including those published by The Arno Press (1969), Negro Universities Press (1969), Ayer Publishing Company (1985), and Rutgers University Press (1986), close with the abridged version. In contrast, the 1971 Collier Books edition (Macmillan) and the 1997 Penguin Books edition conclude with the extended ending. The Modern Library edition also contains the original extended ending. Interestingly, editor Deborah McDowell states in her introduction to the Rutgers edition that "[t]his closing paragraph does not seem to alter the spirit of the original in any way." I am inclined to believe that the ending does make a difference, in that the amended conclusion enhances its status as a "writerly" text—in the sense that French critic Roland Barthes defines as "writerly" an open-ended text that requires the reader to collaborate in producing its meaning. (204)

While Henderson charts which last paragraph has appeared in which edition,[5] she does not explain the Modern Library's editorial decision, simply noting that it "contains the original extended ending." Her partial agreement with McDowell—on the preference for the "Then everything was dark" ending if not on McDowell's dismissal of its interpretive ramifications—indirectly applies an aesthetic, rather than historical, standard to editing *Passing*, with the argument that the text becomes more writerly with a more open-ended conclusion. I certainly agree with Henderson that the last paragraph "requires the reader to collaborate in producing its ending" (204), but this is even more powerfully true with a full knowledge of that paragraph's history: it is not just the linguistic text itself that makes *Passing* a writerly text, but also the work's open-ended material status. As readers we must collaborate with the text by acknowledging its two possible endings, but because there is no clear intention with which to collaborate here, authorial or otherwise, this readerly engagement with the text at a material level finds the physical book itself to be "writerly," in Barthes's terms.

Finally, Charles R. Larson's recent edition of Larsen's *Complete Fiction* includes the "Centuries after" paragraph, based on Larson's supposition that its omission in the 1929 third printing was the result of a mechanical error. In *Invisible Darkness*, his biography of Larsen and Toomer, Larson notes: "The Rutgers edition of Larsen's novels was apparently based upon the Ayer Company's reprint of *Passing*, published in 1985. That edition, a photo reproduction of the third printing of Larsen's novel, omits the final paragraph of the novel. I am unable to determine if the ending of the Knopf third printing of Larsen's novel is an alteration suggested by Larsen or—as I suspect more likely—a matter of a dropped plate" (218 n129). Larson does not explain here his reasons for thinking a dropped plate "more likely," nor in his textual note to the *Complete Fiction*: "This is the only complete edition of Larsen's fiction, including her three published stories and the correct ending for *Passing*. Deborah E. McDowell argues erroneously for omitting the final paragraph of *Passing* because the second printing of the 1929 Knopf edition inadvertently omitted it. McDowell argues that Larsen was a perfectionist and decided to change the ending of her novel. Perfectionist she may have been, but there is no evidence for this conjecture. Rather, the missing final paragraph of the second printing would appear to be the result of a dropped printer's plate" (xxii). Oddly, Larson here confuses the novel's original second and third printings, an error he had not made in his earlier biography. (The book's original copyright page notes that the first and second printings were produced "before publication," indicating that Knopf's advance orders had exceeded the first printing run, and so a second printing occurred in advance of the book's initial publication. In this case, therefore, there should be no material differences between the first and second

> **PASSING**
>
> Bellew was not in the little group shivering in the small hallway. What did that mean? As she began to work it out in her numbed mind, she was shaken with another hideous trembling. Not that! Oh, not that!
>
> "No, no!" she protested. "I'm quite certain that he didn't. I was there, too. As close as he was. She just fell, before anybody could stop her. I—"
>
> Her quaking knees gave way under her. She moaned and sank down, moaned again. Through the great heaviness that submerged and drowned her she was dimly conscious of strong arms lifting her up. Then everything was dark.
>
> Centuries after, she heard the strange man saying: "Death by misadventure, I'm inclined to believe. Let's go up and have another look at that window."

Fig. 1. Last page from Nella Larsen's *Passing* (1929), with the "Centuries after…" paragraph included

printings.) Additionally, McDowell makes no argument about Larsen being a perfectionist in the Rutgers edition. Finally, Larson again offers no explanation of his dropped-plate hypothesis, which the textual evidence, in my opinion, does not support. The last page in the novel's first two printings begins before the original last paragraph, with nineteen lines of text, and the colophon reads in part, "Set up, electrotyped, printed, and bound by the Vail-Ballou Press" (see fig. 1). If my understanding of the electrotype process is correct, this colophon would indicate that the dropped paragraph could not be a "matter of a dropped plate," as Larson suggests, because the last page would have been printed from a plate carrying more type than just the final paragraph; the omission would therefore have to represent a deliberate decision by someone, whether author, publisher, printer, or some combination thereof.[6]

Ultimately, I am less interested in the question of which is the correct or definitive edition. Various editorial theorists have argued for what Richard Finneran terms the "fundamental impossibility of arriving at a 'Definitive Edition'" (39), in the sense of an absolutely stable text, thanks to the inevitable textual questions arising from the series of social interactions leading to any textual production. In this particular case, we might privilege either the third printing as the last revision published during Larsen's lifetime, or the first two printings as representative of Larsen's original intentions. The problem lies, of course, in not being able to know whether the omitted paragraph represented any intention at all, authorial or otherwise. The lack of either a relevant author's or publisher's archive makes it impossible to prefer one printing versus the other on the basis of intentionality.[7] What is important theoretically for me about this problem is, instead, the larger cultural lesson borne out by this bottom-line textual instability.

The presence or absence of the "Centuries after" paragraph has two main interpretive effects: the now more ambiguous question of how Irene's role in Clare's death will be perceived and the removal of the police officer as a closing voice of white male authority, in contrast to the final line, "Everything was dark." A careful review of the novel's previous pages, following the arrival of Clare's white, racist husband and thus the discovery of her secret, seems to establish that Irene has pushed Clare out the window, or at the very least has wished for her death in this manner. This evidence includes, for example, such passages as these: "It was that smile that maddened Irene. She ran across the room, her terror tinged with ferocity, and laid a hand on Clare's bare arm. One thought possessed her. She couldn't have Clare Kendry cast aside by Bellew. She couldn't have her free"; "What happened next, Irene Redfield never afterwards allowed herself to remember. Never clearly"; and "Irene wasn't sorry. She was amazed, incredulous almost. What would the others think? That Clare had fallen? That she had deliberately leaned backward? Certainly one or the other. Not—" (all 111, in the Penguin edition). The critical consensus largely supports the reading that Irene is responsible for Clare's death.[8]

So the penultimate (or closing) paragraph thus ends with a clear sense of Irene's guilt, but without a definite resolution of the plot, at least as far the legal consequences of her guilt are concerned. (*Black's Law Dictionary* defines "misadventure" as "an accident by which an injury occurs to another." By terming the incident "death by misadventure," the officer may be holding no one directly responsible or may be suggesting that someone, presumably Clare's white, racist husband, Jack Bellew, has accidentally caused her death.) The (perhaps) final line, "Then everything was dark," also echoes the novel's return to an overtly black community (Bellew is absent in the final scene), and so "dark" bears the additional connotations of Irene's wish for Clare's death: the restoration of a racially "pure" identity, along with the return, Irene hopes, of a stable marriage, enabled by Clare's absence as an object of attraction for both Brian Redfield and his wife.

Aside from their specific effects on these narrative questions, the final paragraph(s) bear special weight by virtue of their position. Rabinowitz observes, "The ending of a text is not only to be noticed; there is also a widely applicable interpretive convention that permits us to read it in a special way, as a conclusion, as a summing up of the work's meaning. . . . [R]eaders *assume* that authors put their best thoughts last, and thus *assign* a special value to the final pages of a text" (*Before Reading* 160, original emphasis). To be fair to McDowell, the novel's close would have this same general effect with either last paragraph; Rabinowitz points to the final pages of a novel, after all, and certainly Rutgers readers would still respond to the ending in the same general ways. All the same, to ignore this textual crux risks short-circuiting the careful narrative dynamics that do change significantly, depending on which paragraph holds the privileged final position.

Indeed, two recent, insightful readings of *Passing* depend on the absence of the "Centuries after" paragraph to reach their conclusions. Samira Kawash observes: "The novel opens and closes with Clare, beginning with Clare's letter to Irene and ending with Clare's death. When Clare dies, Irene loses consciousness, and the novel ends with her blackout: '. . . Then everything was dark.' I would suggest that Irene's loss of consciousness is not simply tidy narrative closure: it is the necessary result of the foreclosure of desire marked by Clare's death" (165). Kawash's analysis relies on the last paragraph ending "Then everything was dark," without the "official and authoritative" presence of the police officer. Not only would *that* last paragraph prevent the symmetry that Kawash reads as more than "tidy narrative closure," but the male voice would shift the novel's closing focus away from Irene's consciousness and desire (what Kawash terms "not only the consciousness *of* desire," but "consciousness *as* desire" [165]). Kawash uses the Rutgers edition of *Passing*, but does not cite McDowell's (erroneous) footnote on the "Centuries after" paragraph.

Turning to a critic who does note the novel's textual history, albeit mis-
leadingly, Neil Sullivan provides a Lacanian reading in which "Irene becomes
an image of Clare's self" (375). When Clare dies, Sullivan writes, "Irene
replicates Clare's death in a fainting spell mirroring the one that eventually
led to her reunion with Clare two years earlier" (382). (In the novel's opening scene, Irene is faint from heat and passes for white in a white hotel bar,
where she meets Clare.) Sullivan concludes that Irene's aphanisis is manifested in the final "everything was dark" paragraph: "The narrative ends
here, since Irene's consciousness—the one that drives the narrative—dims
and then fades completely" (382). Interestingly, Sullivan then cites Madigan's
discussion of the novel's textual history, claiming that the "Centuries after"
paragraph "was omitted from the third printing *in accordance with Larsen's
instructions*, apparently to add ambiguity and suspense to the ending. Larsen's
crucial revision allows Irene's fainting to be aligned more closely with
Clare's death" (383, emphasis added). Sullivan strikingly misreads Madigan
here. Madigan writes simply, "In the third printing of *Passing*, however, the
final paragraph is dropped," a sentence which, through its passive construction, ascribes no agency to Larsen or anyone else (522). In a closing passage
I have cited previously, Madigan observes that "there is no evidence that
Larsen opposed the substantive change of dropping the final paragraph" (523),
but this is as close as he comes to suggesting that Larsen instructed Knopf
to make this change. Whether consciously or unconsciously—though for
Lacan the two are more or less indistinguishable—Sullivan posits two "subjects presumed to know," in Lacanian terms: Madigan and Larsen herself.
While Madigan, as a scholar, does occupy the structural position of the knowing subject, he carefully avoids any claims of definitive knowledge. Sullivan's
misreading of Madigan in order to impute intentionality to Larsen is a particularly interesting slip, however, as it suggests Sullivan's knowledge of *Passing*'s
textual instability and also his desire to erase that instability by imagining it to
be the product of Larsen's intention "to add ambiguity." In fact, the ambiguity
is there at the material level, but this kind of ambiguity may be more unsettling than one which can be explained as a conscious decision rather than as
a result with an unknowable cause. The material instability challenges
many readers' fundamental, and often unexpressed, assumptions about textuality itself. By addressing the insolubility of the novel's ending, that is, we
see material documents themselves as "texts presumed to know" their own

stability, when, in fact, the Lacanian recognition of this structural assumption reveals the true, productive lack of definite textual "knowledge."

Two other recent, prominent articles interestingly misread or overlook the novel's material history. Harrison-Kahan, though she cites McDowell's Rutgers edition without the original last paragraph, concludes her analysis by noting that Irene has "avoided interpellation by the law, in the form of the police officer" (135). Irene's avoidance of the law manifests itself most clearly in the original closing paragraph, while Irene's response to the police officer's questions, which Harrison-Kahan reads as evidence that Irene "is a subject without a voice who simply fades into darkness" (135), take on a different tone when the novel's last line is "Then everything was dark," as in the Rutgers edition. By leaving the final pronouncement from the voice of the law outside the narrative proper, Harrison-Kahan effectively refuses interpellation from McDowell as an editor by omitting any mention of the final paragraph's disputed status and McDowell's position on this question. Thus Harrison-Kahan's reading of Irene's subjectivity and of passing more broadly—she argues that as "a figure who defies both realness and readability," the passer signifies "identity's ultimate illegibility" (122)—concludes by attributing that illegibility to a text which is also "mobile, rather than static" (122). But without acknowledging that textual fluidity, Harrison-Kahan acts as if *Passing* is a stable narrative which depicts passing and subjectivity in these terms, rather than the more radical reality that the text itself is ultimately "illegible," and thus an even "deeper" shadow of its fictional content.

Similarly, Brian Carr focuses only on the surface of the narrative, overlooking the material instability in the process. Carr concludes his intriguing psychoanalytic analysis with Irene upstairs at the party, worried that Clare may not be dead, before even the last paragraph in the Rutgers edition, which he also uses and in which Irene descends to the crowd surrounding Clare's body on the street. In his closing argument that "the problem Clare represents for Irene and for readers never quite dies," Carr insists, "In its interpretation of desire's nonobject, *Passing* comes to know something we frequently refuse to know: because knowledge is tethered to desire, we cannot kill knowledge or possess it all, since there is no all—no full knowledge or permanently satisfiable desire" (294). The striking personification of the text here indirectly reveals Carr's apparent desire not to know the novel's textual history, a history that is similarly "undead," in Carr's terms. That is, Carr's desire to know *Passing* as unknowable leads him, however unconsciously, to McDowell's edition, where the adumbrated ending supports his emphasis on Irene's hesitant response to Clare's death, rather than her more deliberate and focused answers to the police officer's questions. As Carr himself points out, reading objects is "predicated on the intervallic relation between desire and language" (290). By collapsing the historical time and space between our contemporary readings and the novel's production, Carr follows his desire for a particular version of the narrative into a false reliance on the text itself as knowable, even when desire is not.

I have selected these examples as highly visible work within the profession—Carr's essay appears in *PMLA*, and Harrison-Kahan's was a prize-winning paper in *Modern Language Studies*—in order to point out the inattention to textual history that remains the scholarly norm, both for *Passing* and more broadly.

The ironically "dark" clarity advanced and then undermined in the novel's closing paragraphs is itself founded on the larger illusion of racial identity in 1920s America. "It is not precisely that Clare's race is 'exposed,'" Butler writes, "but [that] blackness itself is produced as marked and marred, a public sign of particularity in the service of the dissimulated universality of whiteness" (183). That is, the racial ideology that leads to passing as a cultural practice depends on whiteness as an artificial norm, and Clare's "discovery" as black locates her outside this norm. But to read, edit, or teach *Passing* without drawing attention to its textual history, I would argue, presents a similarly false norm: using either edition without editorial comment compels the text to pass as stable, belying its authentic instability. Thus the text's most powerful ambiguity—which inheres at both the interpretive *and* the material levels—disappears as the payoff of this combined reading.

More broadly, *Passing* raises the editorial and interpretive issues inherent in what Greetham terms "multi-cultural biography," in which editors would seek to preserve a "realm of otherness" (*Theories* 430). The limit for this model of editing lies in its elision of material histories like *Passing*'s, in which one important part of the "realm of otherness" is a lost textual record, which, of course, connects importantly with a broader American cultural and social history. That history has not always privileged the archival records of writers like Larsen as worth preserving. Similarly, there is no surviving manuscript of Zora Neale Hurston's classic work of folk anthropology, *Mules and Men* (Hemenway 355), and the original works and papers of African American artist Nancy Elizabeth Prophet have been lost, as have most of Augusta Savage's original sculptures (Leininger-Miller 17, 162). I do not mean to suggest here that a lack of archival material is a defining feature of African American literature generally; witness, for example, the Ellison and Hughes archives at the Library of Congress, or the James Weldon Johnson Memorial Collection at the Beinecke Library. But still, the cultural impetus to preserve intersects with the particular invisibility of black modernist women, as evidenced by my examples above. That we cannot recover an accurate material record of Larsen's or Knopf's intention(s) speaks ultimately to the construction of literary history, and to editors' roles in either perpetuating or revising the historical conception of minority literature, in particular. What editorial theorists can learn from a case like *Passing*'s, then, is how to represent editorially the social networks of authorship which actively work against the privileging of the author, both in the material processes of textual production and in the preservation of that textual record as an expression of cultural significance.

In keeping with Greetham's "genuinely *critical* posture" (*Theories* 430), the most effective editorial strategy for future editions of *Passing* might well be for a single press to issue some editions with the final paragraph and some without, as the most faithful representation of the historical record (however unlikely actual publishers might be to agree to such a scheme). Whatever practical decisions might be made, the most accurate edition of the novel would, ironically, gesture only to the insolubility of its closing crux, because the most ethical editorial strategy would be the preservation of our lack of knowledge. Not to acknowledge this lack risks displacing a genuine understanding of the novel's instability with an unquestioning assumption, or unthinking neglect, of its material history.[9] That is, to make any editorial decision about *Passing*'s last paragraph risks passing the text off as falsely stable and passing over its incomplete history. Editing Larsen's novel in terms of that material history would bring readers face to face with questions we cannot answer, and with a history we cannot write, thus directing them to confront such gaps in the literary past and to address them directly in the future.

TEACHING *PASSING* AND TEXTUAL AUTHENTICITY

With an eye toward the future, then, I turn to the classroom, where discussions of race and textuality can complement each other in their attention to the fluid identities that inhere in both areas. Inquiries into a given text's material history raise a host of questions about the seemingly straightforward process of reading a book. As Jacqueline Foertsch explains, "That students may be required to buy and study and even be tested on not one but *two* versions of the 'same' novel can lead them to questions that their teachers ask as well: Is there only one 'right' text? If so, how did the 'wrong' one get into print? Can there be two 'right' versions of the same story? What else am I reading 'out there' for which a radically different version exists?" (698). Questions about the "right" and "wrong" version of a work, I would add, take on a more highly charged meaning from the interactions of white, male publishers and writers who have been marginalized along gender or race lines (or both).

Passing serves as a particularly effective classroom application of textual scholarship: because the textual discrepancy in question is confined to a small section of the novel, this crux is easily accessible.[10] Reading one edition of the novel or the other does not require complex distinctions between genetic and synoptic editions (as in Hans Walter Gabler's edition of *Ulysses*) or of sequential printings of variants (as in the three major versions of Wordsworth's *Prelude*) or of extensive apparati appearing at the end of a volume or even in a separate volume sometimes published years later (as has been the case for several medieval works and will be as well for the scholarly edition of *Juneteenth*). Admittedly, students reading *Passing* lose much of the complexity produced by such examples, but the same basic theoretical point holds for Larsen's novel and can thus be extended clearly to its more far-reaching cousins.

For my courses I ask the campus bookstore to order equal numbers of the Rutgers and Penguin editions, in order to take advantage of the different endings currently in print. Half the class reads each edition, and I advise students on the first day of the semester only that we will discuss later the difference it makes to read a particular copy. On the second or third day of our *Passing* discussion, we reach the novel's end, and I ask someone to read the last paragraph aloud. Puzzled expressions soon appear on half the students' faces, along with questions and comments about either the missing or extra paragraph. I also assign a brief response for this day, "What you think happens at the end of the book?" a question that deals on its surface with Irene's role in Clare's death, but also leads usefully into the text's other closing ambiguity.

Following a quick determination of the textual facts at hand, I ask students to evaluate McDowell's claim, with a specific explanation of why the last paragraph would or would not affect interpretation. These classroom conversations about the end of *Passing* help to clear up obscure readings— for instance, a student once took the line "Everything was dark" to mean that *Irene* has died—but, more importantly, such discussions encourage student-centered awareness of the novel's textual contingency. Another student remarked that she had come to class already aware of the closing discrepancy, after comparing notes with a colleague the night before, and now felt that she could no longer "take for granted that what you read in a book is what the author meant to be there." This displaced faith in authorial intention at the material level shifted quickly to a broader discussion of authorship as an inherently social process, which both makes authorial intention (as a final and stable entity) unrecoverable and converts traditional conceptions of authorship into more nuanced appreciations of the social and cultural forces at work in any textual production.

Classroom discussions of *Passing*'s textual history also intersect with issues of interpretive authority between white teachers and students of multiple racial and ethnic backgrounds. As Pamela Caughie observes, this pedagogical dynamic creates "questions about how to teach for diversity without treating texts only in terms of their racial, ethnic, or gender identity while acknowledging that their identity as such is precisely why we are teaching them—that is, in response to our recognition of the racial, ethnic, and gender bias of our traditional curriculum" (125). Caughie's thoughtful response to this dilemma is to emphasize first that while "we are always 'passing' in the classroom . . . we must realize that 'passing' functions differently for differently positioned subjects" (137). Caughie's use of "we," though, risks eliding the specific historical connotations of passing if late-twentieth-century white professors can "pass" in structurally similar ways as light-skinned African Americans did earlier in the century. Caughie is very much aware of this issue; she goes on to write, "If as teachers we are always 'passing' in the classroom because our authority is positional, and if we are multiply positioned in the multicultural classroom, still, race may intervene in some of our classrooms to expose not simply the illusion of authority but the illusion of whiteness as well" (137). But this is one of the points at which Caughie's larger discussion of "passing" as an analogue to "performativity" intersects with a specifically racial context. Caughie seeks to employ "passing" generally as part of an "ethical practice" (25) which is "both the problem and the solution" to the "binary logic of identity" (22), and she explicitly distinguishes between "passing" in her sense and "passing as" another subject position, or assuming another cultural heritage. I would argue that by transferring "passing" out of its historical context, Caughie is still implicitly engaged in the practice of "passing as," for her to distinguish between the earlier use of "passing" and her own reinscription of the term implies her ability to understand "passing" from both points of view, to inhabit both subject positions, in order to be able to tell the difference.

Caughie's "passing" teaching aims to demonstrate the limits of heretofore stable bodies of knowledge because of the positionality inherent in any classroom discussion of multicultural literature. Seeking to disrupt classroom structures in which the teacher alone functions as the subject-presumed-to-know, Caughie instead opens textual analysis to the process of different readers assuming different subject positions. Toward this end, she cautions against uncritical assumptions that Larsen's novel contains specific, systemic meanings, finding *Passing*'s lesson instead to be "that we cannot always rely on tangible evidence and that desiring certainty and coherence in our interpretations may lead us to project the absence of such traits onto the craft or craftiness of the other—the text, the passer, or the teacher or student who has had a different racial, ethnic, or gender experience" (139). Interestingly, Sarah Chinn reports that her students, "whatever their race or ethnicity, are always taken aback" by the discovery of Irene's racial identity (53). "Irene's inability (or refusal) to see the world around her accurately is at the center of the novel," Chinn continues, "and as she is the central consciousness of the text, it is not surprising that readers fall into that same mode of perception" (54). Chinn uses the Rutgers edition (188 n13) and so misreads "everything was dark" as the text's definitive statement on Bellew's "logic of all-or-nothing blackness" (65), when the alternative ending might reinscribe Irene within the police officer's presumably similar racial outlook, but in a way that would work to Irene's advantage. (If the officer perceives Clare to be black, that is—she has been at a Harlem party, and her white husband has apparently vanished—he will presumably be more likely to attribute Clare's death to "misadventure" and avoid a more prolonged investigation.)

As Caughie points out, the desire for narrative certainty negates a recognition of its absence, as readers attribute a craftily hidden coherence even to those entities which seem to lack it. As a textual scholar, I am particularly struck by Caughie's equation of texts with people, whether teacher, student, or passer. By not attending to *Passing*'s particular textual history—Caughie's chapter in *Passing & Pedagogy* makes no mention of the final paragraph's omission—Caughie ultimately assumes a textual certainty that is, in fact, absent. Rather than attributing this discrepancy to the text's presumed craftiness, Caughie simply ignores the matter altogether. Thus Caughie implicitly locates the material text in the "structural position of authority" too easily credited to "white teachers of nonwhite literature" (137). The interpretive and pedagogical effects of this oversight are structurally similar to those Caughie diagnoses for the complex interplay between *Passing* and the multicultural classroom. Caughie argues that Larsen's novel "enacts the tensions involved in reading and teaching narratives that focus on multiple differences, and to this extent it can reveal the difficulties and resistances that ensue whenever we attempt to read, interpret, or teach in terms of *one* privileged reference point, whether sexual politics or racial politics, the authority of experience or the authority of theory" (134, original emphasis). I agree with Caughie's point as far as it goes; despite *Passing*'s status as what Rabinowitz terms a "fragile text," its demonstration of the limitations Caughie describes can only develop through active discussions of the novel. Yet by leaving an unstated faith in textual stability in operation as the single "privileged reference point" still left unchallenged, Caughie indirectly invites students to pursue the text's "politics of (dis)placement" (135) without displacing the material text itself.

Were Caughie to incorporate the kind of textual history I have outlined above, the result would be a more firmly rooted sense of its uncertainty and incoherence. That we cannot know which version of *Passing* is "correct" demonstrates much about the politics of (dis)placement when it comes to the historical preservation of New Negro Renaissance textual records.

That is, by dislodging students' and teachers' unquestioning reliance on falsely stable texts, we might both amplify our understanding of *Passing*'s historical condition and expand our "open" sense of interpretation. Because reactions to the novel's conclusions vary according to which is the last paragraph, and because this unresolvable crux mirrors the text's more abstract ambiguities, teaching this text materially takes the book itself out of the structural position of authority, instead placing alternative versions of the novel into different "subject" positions in relation to its readers.

This move away from the text's presumed stability also impacts discussions of its submerged lesbian narrative. Rabinowitz and Caughie, in the two most sustained pedagogical treatments of *Passing*, disagree over the centrality of this theme. Rabinowitz begins by explaining, "I treated *Passing* as an exemplification of its subject: a novel about lesbians passing as heterosexuals that passes as a novel about racial passing" ("Betraying" 201). His subsequent discussion of the novel in terms of its "gullible" and "knowledgeable" audiences depends on this double-edged reading: the second group of readers may not wish to disclose the novel's hidden story, because to do so would require "shattering" the "fragile" text. "Rhetorical passing," Rabinowitz explains, "requires *two* audiences: one audience that's ignorant and another that knows the truth *and remains silent about it*" (205, original emphasis). Caughie challenges the premise that the lesbian and racial lines of the narrative can supersede each other, contending that "the two issues brought together, those of race and sex, are not substitutable" (136). Seeking not to reduce *Passing* to one kind of narrative or another, Caughie concludes instead that the fragility Rabinowitz finds is the product of the changing classroom itself, not an inherent textual feature. "I would say these ethical issues *arise from* our teaching of multicultural issues," Caughie writes; "what the teaching of multicultural literatures and cultural criticism has brought to literary studies is a new ethical dynamic that could never have been conceptualized in terms of canonical literatures and the formalist and expressivist pedagogies" that supported the traditional canon (143, original emphasis).

Before turning to the effects of the novel's material history on this debate, I would like to add a brief account of my own teaching experience, because my student population differs from both Rabinowitz's and Caughie's. I have taught *Passing* most recently in an upper-level course on the twentieth-century novel to a group of mostly white, Appalachian students, many of whom are first-generation college students. This particular pedagogical context interestingly complicates the ethical issues Rabinowitz and Caughie outline, as my students have been almost uniformly resistant to the idea of a submerged lesbian narrative (even after I have provided them with Rabinowitz's article or McDowell's introduction to the Rutgers edition, and my own list of passages especially amenable to this interpretation). The desire that Rabinowitz postulates among homosexual students to keep this fragile narrative unexposed would be felt even more strongly, I would guess, among my student population, where open acknowledgement of a gay or lesbian lifestyle is relatively rare and the risks attendant on agreeing with a lesbian interpretation might well be too great to engage in such a discussion. On the other hand, not to present such a reading would carry its own risks of perpetuating the heterosexist bias that might be keeping some students silent in the first place. So in this particular pedagogical environment, I have concluded, the costs of keeping the lesbian narrative publicly unread outweigh the potential costs to individual students. Furthermore, a classroom discussion of *Passing* as a text which lacks in conventional authority—because there is no "right" or "wrong" ending—might help challenge broader attempts to require stable sexual identities, suggesting that there is also no right or wrong answer there.

A material reading of *Passing* is also important to this discussion because neither Rabinowitz nor Caughie (nor any other Larsen critic, for that matter) confronts the problem of *which* version of the work to consider within this ethical framework. The most authentic representation of Larsen's novel would not presume to know which version is correct—or indeed, that any version is correct—and would instead represent the absence of historical knowledge. Imagining a hypothetical future, even if a long-lost note from Larsen or Knopf were to surface in a misplaced library folder or in a distant relative's attic, clarifying exactly what happened to the novel's third printing, the history of editorial uncertainty still would remain as a vital part of the work's representation for future readers. Along with the new questions such a discovery would raise about why Larsen or Knopf had made a particular editorial decision, there would remain difficult issues concerning how best to convey this decision within its historical context. If Larsen opted to drop the final paragraph, was she responding to pressures from Knopf, effectively censoring herself? Or was she altering the novel's first published version for other reasons, perhaps seeking to represent differently a fictional world in which "everything was dark" (as Sullivan imagines)? Or, if the decision to drop the paragraph was Knopf's, was Larsen further removed from her publisher's power over her work than has been previously realized? The particular nature of textual instability might vary according to the terms of the hypothetical, but the work's basic character as materially unstable would remain a significant issue for editors to represent.

Absent such new information, any future edition will still have to make a practical choice about whether and where to print the original final paragraph, along with some explanation of the text's historical uncertainties. The best solution—if the least commercially viable—would be to maintain the current textual situation under the banner of a single press, which would issue some copies ending with "Then everything was dark" and others ending with the "Centuries after" paragraph. A detailed textual note would of course have to explain the absence or supplement for each edition, but as I have found in my classrooms, the most effective way to call attention to this insoluble textual crux is for readers to encounter it directly, and thus experience for themselves how it affects their interpretations.

Passing is in this way a different kind of fragile text from that which Rabinowitz describes. Here the gullible audience becomes those readers who do not question its textual status, and the knowledgeable audience those who recognize its material uncertainties. *Passing* is fragile in this second sense when encountered by gullible readers because an inauthentic sense of textual stability belies a historical attitude that has not privileged the archival records of writers like Larsen as worth preserving. Not to acknowledge this lack risks displacing, in Caughie's terms, a genuine understanding of the novel's instability with an unquestioning assumption, or unthinking neglect, of its material history. The question of how best to represent *Passing* in a contemporary edition demonstrates the broader need to teach texts materially, as a means of remaking the classroom into a site for more historically accurate encounters with the uncertainties of textual production. Rather than perpetuating a view of literary history in which every material thing is "dark," this pedagogical approach would illuminate the social networks of authorship that often mirror the cultural and political biases and lacunae of the surrounding society.

In the next chapter I turn from a metaphorical textual darkness to a literal one, focusing on the black copyright page in the first edition of Reed's *Mumbo Jumbo*. Unlike the Larsen case, there is a substantial archive for Reed available at the University of Delaware, and so I read *Mumbo Jumbo* in light of both its own textual history and the American history on which the novel signifies throughout. While this archive does not explain the precise origin of the black page, it does demonstrate in detail Reed's negotiations, both productive and uneasy, with the white cultural power he has associated with mainstream presses.

CHAPTER TWO

BLACK PAGE, WHITE COPYRIGHT

The Politics of Print in Ishmael Reed's
Mumbo Jumbo

In *Mumbo Jumbo* (1972), Ishmael Reed implicitly parallels the New Negro and Black Arts movements, two brief periods in literary history which witnessed both collaborative and uneasy exchanges between white publishing houses and black authors. Just as Larsen occupied a sometimes tenuous relationship with her white benefactors, the Knopfs and Carl Van Vechten, so too did Reed negotiate a tentative partnership with Doubleday, his mainstream publisher during the late 1960s and early '70s. The first edition of *Mumbo Jumbo* strikingly responds to this cultural tension with a black copyright page, foregrounding the issues of literary property and artistic authenticity that might otherwise lie dormant. Because the paperback reprint restores the copyright page to its "normal" color, only a material history can recover the text's original intervention into the cultural politics of the Second Renaissance. As I argue in this chapter, a material reading complicates the novel's already complex and self-conscious representation of material textuality. Just as Jes Grew is "*seeking its words. Its text*" (6, original emphasis), *Mumbo Jumbo* seeks a subversion of traditional textuality by figuring Jes Grew as immaterial, without a physical manifestation. This fundamental aesthetic tension between the desire for a fixed textual form and the need for an African American textuality to remain "unprintable" is nowhere more clearly and powerfully manifested than in the black copyright page, a moment of textual stability that fades into a trace by its absence from the paperback reprints.[1]

The black copyright page expresses this textual play between the material and the immaterial by pointing us both forward to the paperback version and back to Reed's archive, with its documentary record of the social, material processes through which *Mumbo Jumbo* passed on its way to its initial publication. As McGann insists, "the circumstances of production *always* bear upon literary meaning" ("What Difference" 190, original emphasis). In this case the production circumstances bear especially on Reed's efforts to subvert the normal processes of literary meaning, which is to say, for Reed's purposes, "white" meaning. With Jes Grew functioning as a kind of absent structure, or what Patrick McGee calls "the black hole at the center of *Mumbo Jumbo*," the narrative (or anti-narrative, just as Jes Grew is an "*anti-plague*" [6]) issues "a direct challenge to and critical subversion of the hegemony of white culture" (McGee 114).[2] From a materialist standpoint, this "black hole" within the text's linguistic code parallels the text's material fluidity. Additionally, the historical elements that give rise to this fluidity juxtapose the narrative's jumbled historical attitude against specific production decisions. We can thus read American racial history as refracted through Reed's Neo-Hoodoo perspective with and against the cultural history that forms the specific context for the novel's publication.

Most black-owned presses during the Black Arts movement and Second Renaissance were financially incapable of competing with mainstream firms and, indeed, "were not interested in making money, but in publishing what needed to be published," as Broadside's Dudley Randall writes in a 1975 article (34). Except for the poets and pamphleteers who found homes with Broadside, Third World, or Jihad Productions, then, African American writers in the 1960s and '70s "were dependent on white publishers" (Bigsby 50). While the underlying economic realities of the white publisher—black writer relationship were essentially unchanged between the 1930s and the 1970s, authors in the later period were much more vocal about their lack of power, in response to the civil rights movement that gave rise to the Black Arts aesthetic. The 1969 paperback reprint of the *Black Fire* anthology, for example, includes an editors' note by LeRoi Jones and Larry Neal in which they list the additional contributors who could have appeared in the new edition. Jones and Neal explain: "Various accidents kept this work from appearing in the 1st edition. We hoped it wd be in the paperback, but these devils claim it costs too much to reprint. Hopefully, the 2nd edition of the paperback will have all the people we cd think of. The frustration of working thru these bullshit white people should be obvious" (xvi).³ The rhetorical strategy adopted by Jones and Neal exposes the problems attendant on this dependence. (In retrospect, it is striking that William Morrow authorized this note, something that would be difficult to imagine in today's far more corporatized publishing environment.) Aimed at a wide audience, the paperback *Black Fire* carries the potential for a greater financial return for William Morrow, especially without the added expense of new material. For Jones and Neal, the paperback anthology bears the same promise of a wider audience, which presumably justified their decision to go along with its reprint, however reluctantly. Furthermore, the editors' note establishes their resistance against (white) power as manifested in the publishing industry. By inveighing against the financial "claims" of William Morrow's "devils" and "bullshit white people," Jones and Neal mark themselves as independent agents from their publisher, even as they are economically dependent on these same devils. (The use of contracted auxiliary verbs and Arabic numerals emphasizes this cultural split.) Faced with a choice between wider distribution (and greater profit) versus creative independence, Jones and Neal attempt a compromise in the paperback edition of *Black Fire*, which itself aims at a wider commercial audience.

While the *Black Fire* and *Mumbo Jumbo* copyright pages position themselves as resistant to the publishing industry's white power structure, the Reed archive also demonstrates the compromises required to produce the novel, from both Reed and Doubleday. The three main textual records—the archive, the first edition, and the current paperback reprint—follow a progression of public/private relationships. As Jacques Derrida maintains in *Archive Fever* (*Mal d'archive*), the archive aims conceptually at the future, rather than the past: "the technical structure of the *archiving* archive also determines the structure of the *archivable* content even in its very coming into existence and in its relationship to the future. The archivization produces as much as it records the event" (17, original emphasis). That is, the terms of the archive's creation and organization influence its reception; rather than functioning in a passive relationship to the text and its interpretation, the archive's structure sets the terms under which genetic textual criticism—and, more broadly, the future of memory—can proceed.

The archive's future directedness takes on a particular significance for African American authors, I would argue, because their cultural pasts are already under erasure. As *Flight to Canada*, Reed's fifth novel, makes clear, the past of slavery and the present (and future) of "freedom" inform each other at every turn, in a kind of double-sided palimpsest. The use of contemporary technology—telephones, airplanes, television, radio, etc.—within the historical context of the Civil War argues implicitly for a perspective on the future which is grounded in the inescapable, if culturally repressed, realities of the past. The politics of cultural memory thus take on special importance in an African American context. As Derrida insists, "there is no political power without control of the archive, if not of memory" (4 n1). By its very presence, an African American archive signifies a political power over the past—and thus over the future—which stands in opposition to the historical denial of memory and community from the earliest days of slavery. Just as Reed's novels compel an understanding of the past, present, and future as always interconnected, Reed's archive enables a specific, material reconstruction of a textual past that importantly informs our approach to the interpretive future.

Of course, Reed's archive, like any other, is inherently incomplete. Our documentary history is always limited by access to those materials that have survived and are publicly available, and the idea of a "complete" archive is a fantasy from the start. As Paul J. Voss and Marta Werner observe, "Even if the historical winds never destabilized the archives, their ultimate stability would not be guaranteed; the archive's dream of perfect order is disturbed by the nightmare of its random, heterogeneous, and often unruly contents" (i–ii). For the purposes of my argument here, the most important missing document in Reed's archive is one that would explain the precise origins of the black copyright page in *Mumbo Jumbo*'s first edition. The galleys direct the printer to produce a "SOLID BLACK PAGE," but the details behind this decision remain unclear. In its three incarnations—as galley, first-edition copyright page, and absent trace in the paperback edition—the black page signifies triply, expressing the social network of textual production, a subtle resistance to conventional power structures, and finally an elision of that resistance in the most commercially accessible version. Because the *Mumbo Jumbo* paperback does not carry a note like Jones and Neal's, Reed's contemporary (and presumably future) audience will most likely remain unaware of this buried textual history, as a new generation of readers fall outside the community of (textual) history. The black copyright page replaces the normal—and normative—whiteness of the standard page with a black field for the book's expression of itself as literary property, and subsequent editions cover over this material challenge to "regular" textuality with white pages that, as usual, do not give rise to questions about their color.

DOUBLE(DAY) CONSCIOUSNESS

By the time *Mumbo Jumbo* appeared, Reed had established himself as a satiric, and relatively marketable, novelist with *The Free-Lance Pallbearers* (1967) and *Yellow Back Radio Broke-Down* (1969). In 1971 he became a publisher as well through Yardbird, which produced *Yardbird* magazine and various anthologies, focusing primarily on minority writers who might well have failed to find mainstream acceptance. (Reed has worked on a number of such ventures, including Reed & Cannon, Inc., and the Before Columbus Foundation, and has published such authors as Amiri Baraka, Mei-Mei Berssenbrugge, Victor Cruz, William Demby, Bill Gunn, Joy Harjo, and Shawn Wong.) Reed acknowledges that the publishing industry is "dominated by white males" and that he has therefore been "a prominent token" (quoted in Burns and Sugnet 135, 136), but he continues to publish his own books under these terms. In an interview conducted a few years after *Mumbo Jumbo*'s appearance, Reed explains that he relies on mainstream presses for his own books because "they can put out a hardcover book, which I can't do" (quoted in Dick and Singh 123). Though Reed answered, "Yeah. Definitely," when asked in 1975 if he planned to publish his own books, he has remained with mainstream firms since then (quoted in Dick and Singh 93). Reed implicitly justifies this decision in another interview, explaining, "I demand the whole thing, as much as I can possibly get. I can get this from big publishers more so than I can do for myself or from a small publisher. Why not use everything you can possibly get if you have this kind of desire?" (quoted in Dick and Singh 52–53).[4]

As both a writer and publisher, Reed occupies a liminal position, publishing works that would almost certainly be rejected by the presses accepting his own novels. The Reed archive illustrates this tension most clearly through Reed's various efforts to involve himself in all phases of production with Doubleday, from cover design to ad copy. Reed was principally responsible for *Mumbo Jumbo*'s cover design, sending Doubleday editor Anne Freedgood in February 1970 "an excellent, to my knowledge rarely shown photo of Josephine Baker i [*sic*] would like to use for a cover. . . . It is a beautiful metaphor for what i [*sic*] set out to do in the book Erzulie Isis Procreation, you know" (Ishmael Reed Papers).[5] In this letter Reed also asks Freedgood, "Gimme some 1920's typeface for title." It is worth noting here the Doubleday contributors to these aspects of the book: the inside jacket copy also credits Allen Weinberg for the cover's design, and Ken McCormick, who replaced Freedgood as Reed's editor at Doubleday, wrote to Reed in April 1971 to suggest a switch from curved to straight type for the title.[6] "Your design conception was inspired and very good, but in execution we found that many people were not reading the title correctly," McCormick explains. "Their eyes simply didn't move in that curve. Enclosed is a layout that is not quite as witty as yours but with more clarity. Which do you prefer? I'm all for amusing design but never at the expense of clarity. Do you agree with me that the straight lines of MUMBO JUMBO punch at the reader in a way that the curved line doesn't?" (Ishmael Reed Papers). After Reed had agreed to this change, McCormick wrote back in November: "The last thing I want to do is interfere with your own design, but we both know that readability is essential. Speaking of readability—I'm preparing my notes for sales conference and it has been an absolute joy to reread your book with an eye to telling the salesmen what an exciting sales prospect they have" (Ishmael Reed Papers). Finally, Reed responds in March 1972: "Was very glad to receive the Mumbo Jumbo cover. It is beautiful!! Again, I am very appreciative of the way the jacket was handled; the care and responsibility given" (Ishmael Reed Papers).

Gates's reading of the original cover juxtaposes the "complex yet cryptic *vé vé*" at its center—the doubled image of Josephine Baker and the rose, both symbols of Erzulie—with the medallion in the corner, representing the Knights Templar. "The opposition between the *vé vé* and the medallion represents two distinct warring forces, two mutually exclusive modes of reading" Gates remarks. "Not only are two distinct and conflicting metaphysical systems here represented and invoked, but Reed's cover also serves as an overture to the critique of dualism and binary opposition which gives a major thrust to the text of *Mumbo Jumbo*" (*Signifying* 221, 222). From the standpoint of textual scholarship, Gates himself invokes a dualism and binary opposition between author and publisher through his reference to "Reed's cover," when, in fact, the cover is the product of a mutual interaction among Reed, Weinberg, McCormick, and the designers and typesetters at Doubleday who were responsible for its physical production. The idea for the cover originates with Reed, certainly, but passes from there through a social network which it ultimately represents. To refer to this bibliographic code as "Reed's cover," then, not only misstates the historical facts, but maintains an outmoded hierarchy of authorship which ignores the actual socialized process. By recovering this textual history, we might read the cover as representing two other distinct and conflicting systems for conceptualizing authorship, the "Knights Templar" mode in which the author remains the isolated genius and the "Legba" mode which places authorship at the crossroads of the private and the public. Read in this way, the cover gestures both toward the dissolution of Western traditions of textual interpretation and toward a more historically accurate view of authorship as an essential form of cultural hybridity.

Reed's letters also demonstrate his concern for the book's marketing, another important space of cross-cultural negotiation. In a July 1970 letter to Freedgood and her assistant Helen Jackson, for example, Reed writes of the forthcoming *19 Necromancers from Now*: "Thank you for preparing the announcement concerning the book. I am most anxious to see it. In the future however I would like to be consulted on these matters; I feel that as much thinking should go into these auxiliary projects as the book itself. I would also like to be consulted on the Ads" (Ishmael Reed Papers). In figuring the "auxiliary" marketing plans as equally important to the book itself (and capitalizing "Ads"), Reed displays a keen awareness for the book business. Similarly, Reed explains in an interview, "I write the jacket notes, and get something tantamount to editorial control on this, because I have a good lawyer and the clause where it says it has to be satisfactory to them was struck out" (Northouse 36). Elsewhere in the Delaware archive, Reed writes to McCormick to agree with Doubleday's decision to delay *Mumbo Jumbo*'s paperback edition and to discuss television and print promotions. A March 1972 letter, for example, declares, "Only a Today Show or [Dick] Cavett would justify my returning to the east in August," while a letter in September of that year states, "I hope that allusions to people like Burroughs,

Golding and Vonnegut in ad copy cease. I have nothing in common with the gentlemen; it is made to look as if they are masters and I their apprentice— I tried to make my influences clear by publishing [*sic*] the biblio. at the back of the book" (Ishmael Reed Papers).

Both these requests demonstrate Reed's desire to reach a particular audience in a particular way. While *Today Show* or *The Dick Cavett Show* viewers would have been predominantly white and middle-class, Reed also would have retained more direct control over his promotional image, in contrast to the ads connecting his work to contemporary white "masters." McCormick's replies oblige Reed on both counts: he notes that among various TV shows, "for some inexplicable reason there are no takers. I have satisfied myself that this is not racial," and later writes, "Sorry you don't care for the references to Burroughs, Golding and Vonnegut. Obviously we won't do this anymore if it bothers you" (Ishmael Reed Papers). For all the uneasiness that remains between black authors and white publishers during the Second Renaissance, McCormick's correspondence with Reed still takes a strikingly different tone than was common fifty years before. A September 24 advertisement, with no references to Golding or Vonnegut, does include a blurb from *Time*, declaring that "the outrageousness of Reed's comic vision and the sinister coils of his prose beg comparisons with William Burroughs." Similarly, the *New York Times Book Review* cover article on *Mumbo Jumbo* aligned Reed with Burroughs against Golding and Vonnegut, explaining that in *Lord of the Flies* and *Cat's Cradle*, "we are led to believe in the fantasy by a persuasive context," while *Mumbo Jumbo*, like *Naked Lunch*, "avoids persuasion, invites disbelief" (Friedman 1). A one-paragraph notice in *Esquire*, under the headline "August Futures," also makes a Burroughs connection, proclaiming, "What we'd like to see is Reed and Burroughs in a write-down, and the winner gets a free dinner at Nedick's— with Irving Wallace" ("August").[7]

The problem that Reed articulates with such reviews is essentially that they erase an African American lineage from his work, effectively marketing it to a single white audience. As the inside jacket notes in *Mumbo Jumbo*'s first edition maintain, "The Big Lie concerning Afro-American culture is that it lacks a tradition." Ads citing Burroughs or Vonnegut, as Reed argued to Doubleday, implicitly perpetuate this "Big Lie" by omitting a black cultural tradition, even as they represent a significant financial investment from Doubleday's marketing department.[8] *Naked Lunch* is certainly the most bitingly satiric and controversial American novel to precede Reed's; its 1966 Grove paperback edition includes excerpts from the Massachusetts obscenity trial that had finally allowed for its sale there. In his testimony, Norman Mailer connects Burroughs to Joyce, a comparison also made in the back cover's *Newsweek* blurb: "*Naked Lunch* comes off the presses carrying a heavier burden of literary laudations than any piece of fiction since *Ulysses*." While such reviews serve only to enhance Burroughs's reputation, the cultural politics in Reed's case effectively yield the contemporary equivalent of a white editor's authentication of a slave narrative, locating Reed's satire within a specifically white, male tradition. To explore the cultural politics of such canonical associations, consider contemporaneous ads for a white novelist, John Barth, whose *Chimera* appeared from Random House a few weeks after *Mumbo Jumbo*'s publication. By 1972 Barth was a more established novelist than Reed, both critically and commercially, primarily on the strength of *The Sot-Weed Factor* and *Giles Goat-Boy*. An ad published in the *New York Times Book Review* two weeks after the *Mumbo Jumbo* ad discussed above is strikingly similar in its visual construction, with two symmetrical black curves balancing the figure of the chimera itself. The top blurb, from a review in *Life*, declares, "Like Joyce and Nabokov, like Burgess and Borges, John Barth is a writer who writes about writing. . . . [Barth's] skill and ambition are well-nigh heroic." The ad also marks *Chimera* as a valuable piece of literary property, noting that a $15 limited, signed edition is available "Now at your bookstore" in addition to the regular $6.95 version. A *Times* ad from earlier that week balances a photo of Barth himself, in the lower right corner, against the chimera illustration, in the upper left corner. To me, Barth's disappearance from the larger Sunday ad is a striking indication of Random House's marketing strategy, as the figure of the author himself appears once to signify literary celebrity, but then drops away in the second ad, which now identifies Barth in the Joyce-Nabokov-Burgess-Borges line. The earlier ad includes a different blurb from the same *Life* review, but once Barth's canonical status becomes a selling point, an image of the man seems to become aesthetically distasteful, just as we would not want to imagine Joyce or Nabokov or Burgess or Borges in anything as common as an advertisement (although Joyce did once appear on the cover of *Time*, as did Eliot and Woolf).

My point here is not that this particular literary tradition should not include Barth; he is, of course, a wonderfully imaginative, self-reflexive novelist (as is Reed). Rather, my argument is that the *Chimera* ad sells that book by appealing to consumers who will want to read (or at least own) the latest Joycean, Borgesian novel, and may pay as much as $15 (in 1972) to do so. Ads that locate Reed in relation to Burroughs and Vonnegut, by contrast, do not market *Mumbo Jumbo* to consumers interested in the latest satire of American racial hypocrisy; rather they reduce Reed's multiple audiences to a single, implicitly white readership. In order to counter this dynamic, Reed cites four other blurbs in a September 27 letter to McCormick (written three days after the *Times* ad cited above):

Will it be possible to change the ad copy in future ads for "Mumbo Jumbo"?

I would like to see, for example:

"Reed has written a visionary comic myth here. The novel, oddly enough, works as comedy, even while its incantatory method is cloaking it in enigma; as myth the writing is locked in hoodoo hieroglyphics."—Boston Globe—

"Reed is at heart a satirist, unquestionably the funniest and finest satirist writing in America today." —Chicago Daily News

"Ishmael Reed by now must be, hands down, the most original poet-novelist working in the American language." San Fran Chronicle

"Reed's vision is clear. He has, like an 'anti-Freud,' begun renaming things." The Washington Post (Ishmael Reed Papers)

These efforts to set the terms of the novel's marketing extend, of course, to its reception and interpretation. The remainder of McCormick's letters to Reed in the Delaware archive, however, focus only on marketing and sales matters. McCormick reassures Reed of the novel's marketability on several occasions, at one point declaring, "This is no runaway bestseller by any means, but we are not discouraged. William Faulkner, at this point in his career, had to be satisfied with much lower sales than you have" (Ishmael Reed Papers). McCormick's correspondence is generally more concerned than Freedgood's with marketing and sales, indicating a striking level of concern for the commercialism of a revolutionary black novel in 1972. While McCormick focuses primarily on sales figures, Reed keeps the method of marketing—the politics of literary advertisement—at the center of his discussion. This portion of the archive, then, charts the circumstances under which *Mumbo Jumbo* was made public, implicitly tracing as well the cultural background for the novel's distribution and reception. This complicated historicism manifests itself both in a more detailed understanding of the novel's production and in the complex terms under which Reed and Doubleday negotiated its representation to an audience of both black and white readers. Whereas Knopf advertised Van Vechten's *Nigger Heaven* as a "book you [the white reader] can't put down," Doubleday markets *Mumbo Jumbo*, following Reed's intervention, no longer as a novel emerging from a distinctly white tradition, but instead as a "visionary comic myth" that has "begun renaming things." Such advertising involvement would not have been possible for modernist writers like Larsen or Toomer, who saw their work promoted as "Negro" even while its content expressly challenged rigid racial distinctions.

The prepublication portions of the archive juxtapose Reed's efforts to control the novel's marketing against his collaboration with the Doubleday editors, who propose several changes to the book's organization and structure. Freedgood, for example, suggests that the placement of three epigraphs (from Hurston, James Weldon Johnson, and the American Heritage definition of "mumbo jumbo") "all go on one page." After Reed agrees, Freedgood's assistant Mary Dick responds, "I had an idea which would hoke things up a bit and wondered what you thought: Instead of having a half-title page (the very first page, which is blank except for the title), why not use the 'definition' of 'Mumbo Jumbo'—it seems that it would look one cut different than the average Dday book and might also get people to look a little further in. It's just an idea, but please let us know what you think" (Ishmael Reed Papers). The published book does not precisely follow either of these plans—the dictionary definition appears on a later page with a Louis Armstrong quotation, replaced as the middle epigraph with the line "The earliest Ragtime songs, like Topsy, 'jes' grew,' " and with the title page still otherwise "blank" —but they still indicate Reed's engagement with the Doubleday editorial staff. The need to "get people to look a little further in" manifests itself in the published version through the movie-like structure of the opening pages, with the novel's opening scene preceding the "credits" of the copyright and title pages. As Reed notes in a style sheet for Doubleday's compositors, "Most of the book is in *present tense*, like a film script. (See in this connection position of front matter)" (Ishmael Reed Papers). I return to this cinematic effect below, in a fuller discussion of its relation to the black copyright page, but I would emphasize here that this kind of stylistic visual device seems to derive from Reed's active collaboration with his Doubleday editors, who share his interest in "hoking things up a bit" and producing a text which "would look one cut different than the average Dday book." Reed is not an isolated genius author, of course (for neither is any other writer), but his work with the Doubleday staff indicates an interesting cultural hybridity at the material level of textual production, even if this dynamic is sometimes in tension with the politics of the narrative's linguistic code.

This correspondence about the appearance of the book's early pages extends from Reed's own textual manipulations in the novel's drafts. Several manuscript copies use the title "Mumbo Jumbo Kathedral," with the "K" reversed. This typographical symbol presumably alludes to the common commercial practice in the 1920s of spelling a store's or company's name with a "K" rather than "C," as a way of signifying Klan membership, or at least support. The backwards "K" both refers to this history and reverses it, just as the narrative as a whole alludes to and redirects racial history, from ancient Egypt, to the Crusades, to the 1920s and finally 1960s in America. Another early draft begins with this title page, and a following page legend, "A NeoHooDoo WhoDunIt/With 22 Basic Clues" (Ishmael Reed Papers). These "Basic Clues" are inserted throughout the narrative (structurally paralleling the "Situation Reports" of the published novel), in a pattern that would highlight *Mumbo Jumbo* as a "NeoHooDoo" detective novel.

The decision to drop both these stylistic devices in the published version speaks interestingly to the text's status as a commercial product, a matter in which both Reed and his editors, especially McCormick, display a clear interest. That is, this portion of the archive implicitly locates *Mumbo Jumbo* as already a commodified work, even at the ostensibly private draft stage. As McGann insists, "as soon as a person begins writing for publication, he or she becomes an author, and this means—by (historical) definition—to have entered the world of all those who belong to the literary institution" (*Critique* 53). By extension, as the *Mumbo Jumbo* draft makes clear, to become an author is this sense is also to become a commodified author, as among those who "belong to the literary institution" are the buyers and sellers of literature. The omission of "Kathedral" broadens the title's field of reference, shifting away from a more particular designation of PaPa LaBas's "office" toward a wider reference to the various levels of "mumbo jumbo" represented stylistically, structurally, and thematically. At the same time, the absent Klan allusion makes the title less politically direct, and therefore more commercially accessible. The removal of the "Basic Clues" has essentially an opposite effect; *Mumbo Jumbo* becomes less overtly a detective novel, although the original dust jacket still explains that, "In this HooDoo detective novel, extra-mundane Private Eyes PaPa LaBas and Black Herman investigate questions which have long plagued mankind and New Yorkers too."[9] The inclusion of the "Basic Clues" within the narrative proper would remark frequently on the text's allusion to and subversion of the mystery formula, an emphasis which Reed or his editors, or both, may have felt was finally too didactic to be effective. I write "may" here because the archival material includes no document which would explain this particular editorial decision. Faced with this evidentiary lack, I would speculate that both omissions signal an interest in greater commercial accessibility, in addition to their revisions to the narrative "proper" (though, of course, these two realms are never wholly separate).

In reading *Mumbo Jumbo* alongside its archive, then, we can see the traces of these drafts within the published versions. Such textual interpolation conflates draft and published novel as private and public states of the text, just as the presence of multiple drafts changes our approach to the text as a whole. As John Bryant observes, "we gravitate toward revision in ways different from our gravitation toward genesis. This is true because revision always reveals *an intention to change meaning*, and we sense that a text with a history of revision is always more deeply interpretable than if that same text were known to us only as an act of genesis" (96, original emphasis). Viewing *Mumbo Jumbo* in particular as this kind of fluid text emphasizes its complex tensions between materiality and immateriality, expressed in the narrative through the unrealized need for Jes Grew's physical text, and manifested in the draft versions in the various thematic and stylistic techniques and strategies that eventually coalesce into a published novel, but even then into two different published versions. This textual condition neatly parallels Reed's fictional representations of race; as Gates observes, "Reed's fictions argue that the so-called black experience cannot be thought of as a fluid content to be poured into received and static containers" (*Signifying* 218).

On various levels, the published text represents a permeable boundary between the private and public stages of composition, perhaps most notably in the handwritten letter from Abdul Hamid that explains his decision to destroy the physical text of Jes Grew (200–3). Hamid's handwriting is, literally, Reed's. A production memo in the archive reads: "Attached are photos of a letter which appears in MUMBO JUMBO by Ishmael Reed. He has decided that he would like this letter to appear in book in long hand." The same folder contains two copies (one photostatic) of Hamid's letter. This portion of the novel is thus both autographic and allographic, according to the distinction Gérard Genette draws *pace* Nelson Goodman. As Genette explains, "in certain arts, the notion of *authenticity* is meaningful, and is defined by a work's *history of production*, while it is meaningless in others, in which all correct copies of a work constitute so many valid *instances* of it" (*Work* 16, original emphasis). To copy a handwritten letter for a forgery, in other words, would entail viewing the text as autographic, while to copy the letter for a record of its content would require an allographic view. The Abdul Hamid letter, written by hand by Reed and then photographed and copied into the published novel, appears as a copy of an original text in a way that the rest of the novel does not. All printed books, designed for mechanical reproduction, are copies without originals, in the sense that we cannot refer to the "authentic" *Hamlet* as we could the authentic *Mona Lisa*. *Mumbo Jumbo* takes this textual condition a step further, centering around a fictional textual object, Jes Grew, which is itself a simulacrum. As McGee maintains, "Reed's novel operates as the simulacrum of the process Jes Grew. It is not simply a copy of an original process but a trace (or veve) inseparable from the process of its own becoming. The process has no being apart from its trace: Jes Grew itself is a simulacrum" (103). Even while the narrative allows for no meaningful reference to an "original" text of Jes Grew, that is, the narrative itself develops in the same way, according to McGee's reading: the act of recovering the text of Jes Grew or of interpreting the text of *Mumbo Jumbo* encounters only a trace (or veve).

Hamid's handwritten letter parallels yet complicates this textual dynamic. At the narrative level, the letter justifies Hamid's destruction of the physical text which LaBas has been seeking, because "black people could never have been involved in such a lewd, nasty, decadent thing as is depicted here. This material is obviously a fabrication by the infernal fiend himself!" (202). Hamid only reaches this judgment after several readings, and so the letter also comments ironically on the lack of white commercial interest in the text which Hamid has originally taken to be sacred: "They say they can no longer find a market for this work. Isn't that incredible!! A sacred black work, if it came along today, would go unpublished!" (200). Reed's decision to include this letter as "handwritten" (that is, as a copy of an originally handwritten document) extends the irony of the letter's content. Just as Hamid laments the impossibility of publishing important African American texts while simultaneously naming himself as the sole cultural arbiter for African American readers, so the letter as (reproduced) handwriting recalls an original scene of writing while simultaneously transferring that physical document into a mechanically reproducible condition. Once Doubleday has photographed and copied the original handwritten letter, it becomes, in the printed book, a simulacrum, directing us toward an original that lies outside the bounds of the printed book. We perceive the letter in different physical, textual terms, that is, because it looks like "original" handwriting, and yet the particular "handwritten" pages of any single copy of *Mumbo Jumbo* are merely one in a potentially endless series of copies.[10] The letter as printed on pages 200 to 203 of *Mumbo Jumbo* is thus an example of what Genette terms "*mixed* works, since they simultaneously call on the resources of language and on those (figurative, decorative, connotational) of the graphic arts" (*Work* 128).

It is important to note here how this reading of Hamid's letter changes with access to Reed's archive, where we can see the letter's actual original (or at least a particular handwritten copy which Reed sent to Doubleday). By reading the published novel in conjunction with the archive, we can view the letter both in its original, autographic state and in its published, allographic (or rather, mixed) condition. Because we could speak of forging the letter in the archive in a way we could not of the letter in the novel—for part of the letter's integrity within the archive relies on its physical authenticity— we can juxtapose the text's published immateriality against its original materiality. This is a different case from the usual encounter with handwritten manuscripts, which are themselves designed for reproducibility as printed documents; to read other handwritten portions of the *Mumbo Jumbo* manuscripts at Delaware entails a different relation to the printed novel, because the Hamid letter is written in order to be copied directly, not to be reproduced via typesetting. The particular orthographic features of Reed's other handwritten works do not bear the same relationship to the printed text, that is, because their function is to be "translated" into print in a different manner from the Hamid letter. Their handwritten origins are designed to disappear in the print version, whereas the photographed handwritten letter preserves the appearance of its original "reality." Yet as Jean Baudrillard notes, *pace* Benjamin and McLuhan, "all the forms change once they are not so much mechanically reproduced but even *conceived from the point-of-view of their very reproducibility*" (100, original emphasis). Considering the reproduced "original" of the Reed/Hamid letter as an example of Baudrillard's third-order simulacra, we see this linguistic/bibliographic, autographic/allographic, verbal/visual device gesturing toward its own hand-crafted production, while simultaneously acknowledging the erasure of that origin as a mechanically reproduced object within a mechanically reproduced book.

The textual irony becomes powerful here as well, if we recall that Hamid's letter seeks to restore African American culture to its own "lost" origins by containing the spread of Jes Grew but, of course, fails in this doomed effort at cultural homogenization. Just as Hinckle terms the dispersed text of Jes Grew "Untogether," Abdul Hamid advises PaPa LaBas that the black community needs not works like his translated "Book of Thoth," but "works of reform. Works, which will assist these backward, untogether niggers in getting themselves together" (200–1). The frequent disruption of "normal" textual appearance renders *Mumbo Jumbo* itself an "untogether" work, but this surface disorder both masks and points toward a different system of order, just as the Hamid/Reed letter, read in relation to both the archive and the printed book, gestures ironically toward the dissolution of originary authorship, when the appearance of the author's own handwriting in a printed book would seem to point toward precisely the opposite effect. The photographed, mechanically reproduced letter, originally written by Reed, calls for a monolithic black culture within a novel that itself disrupts the originary fantasies of American traditions and literature and culture. There is a "real" source by an original African American writer to recover, the archival/printed letter suggests on this level, but that marginalized origin can become visible only through the mechanics of mainstream cultural production that have rendered it invisible in the first place. That is, we can only access Reed's critique of the contemporary American literary marketplace and its representation of black culture through a linguistically and bibliographically subversive book published by a mainstream New York firm.

MUMBO JUMBO'S MATERIAL TEXTUALITY

Like a Brechtian performance, in which the house lights stay on and the stage curtain remains open to prevent the willful illusion that is an unspoken premise of most theater, *Mumbo Jumbo* calls attention throughout to the mechanics of its own consumption. The novel's pages are full of such devices as photographs, drawings, charts, quotations and "Situation Reports" in different typefaces, yin-yang symbols, gray squares for the text of placards and other signs, a handwritten letter, and a "Partial Bibliography." (For a fuller list of the text's non-linguistic devices, see Gates, *Signifying* 223.) In an eloquent merger of form and function, these breaks from the novel's "usual" appearance mirror its narrative content. The postmodern mystery plot follows the investigations of PaPa LaBas, "astrodetective" (64), into the progress of Jes Grew, the "anti-plague" (6) from New Orleans to New York. Both LaBas and the narrator provide frequent discussions of the various historical conspiracies through which the Atonists have sought to maintain racial control, all the way from Set's betrayal of Osiris in ancient Egypt to the installation of Warren Harding as a puppet president. As Gates notes, the complex narrative becomes "an allegory of the act of reading itself" (*Signifying* 229), just as the book's disruptive structure "is a version of 'gumbo,' a parody of form itself" (223). The readerly self-consciousness required by *Mumbo Jumbo* foregrounds the text's consumption, both economic and aesthetic, by constantly recalling readers' attention to the process of reading, which cannot proceed "normally" when confronted by the variety of non-linguistic signifiers coupled with the non-linear progression of the narrative. This montage of generally nonlinguistic intrusions forces the reader to consider *Mumbo Jumbo* in a material way, to think anew about what it means to see words and images on a page, just as *Tristram Shandy* does in a very different context.[11] There are limits to what the printed word can say, Reed suggests through this panoply of non-novelistic forms, especially when the history of the novel's production reflects American racial history.

Similarly, Reed uses Arabic numerals throughout *Mumbo Jumbo*, a decision which first becomes apparent on the second page of text—"1 man approaches the Mayor" (4)—and is perhaps nowhere more visible than in PaPa LaBas's explanation that Abdul Hamid has burned the text of Jes Grew because, in his attempt to censor this secret document, "He couldn't stop the influences coming in on 1 people. Multitudinous, individual—the 1000 1000000000 stars of a galaxy" (204). This stylistic decision works in part to disrupt readers' standard perception of print, just as the black copyright page has. Commenting on her own use of numerals for the Bluestone address in *Beloved*, Morrison points to a hidden orality there as well: "there is something about numerals that makes them spoken, heard, in this context, because one expects words to read in a book, not numbers to say, or hear" ("Unspeakable" 31). In Reed's case the substitution of Arabic numerals for English words also reveals Western civilization's generally forgotten debt to Indian and Arabic mathematics. (The Arab mathematician Muhammad Ibn Musa al-Khwarazmi appears to have introduced the Indian decimal system, via Chinese Buddhist missionaries, into Baghdad in the ninth century ACE, and the English word "algebra" derives from the Arabic *al-jabr*, meaning "adjustment.") Reed's readers—that is, Doubleday's readers—would not pause at reading "one man" or "one billion stars," but the Arabic numerals compel a reconsideration of the tools employed by "standard" language and the political histories that lie behind them. In a "'Style' Sheet" Reed prepared for Doubleday's compositors, he explains that "*Numbers*, whether cardinal or ordinal, are NOT spelled out. . . . Numbers so expressed are vital to book's 'mystique'" (Ishmael Reed Papers). (Reed's examples of Arabic numerals here appear in red, for additional emphasis.) The first edition's inside jacket copy calls the reader's attention to this device, noting, "MUMBO JUMBO is a chilling night number in which the numerals are written in Arabic for those who would like to box them or play them straight." The distinction here between "number" (the "mystery" narrative itself) and "numeral" (a linguistic tool of the narrative) foregrounds the text's typographical disruptions for both camps of potential readers, those who would struggle with the book's resistance to "normal" appearance and textual mechanics and those who would engage this textual play "straight."

Indeed, Reed takes up this question—how to represent African American culture to different racial audiences—throughout *Mumbo Jumbo*. As a highly self-conscious text, *Mumbo Jumbo* foregrounds the issue of who is reading it and how, both through its physical appearance and in its frequent references to the publishing industry itself. Woodrow Jefferson Wilson consistently refers to Hinckle Von Vampton as "Publisher," for example, conferring through the capital letter a heightened level of cultural authority (which Von Vampton also attaches to the role, as it supports his hidden Atonist agenda).[12] Similarly, the rejection letter Abdul receives for his initial translation of the Jes Grew document explains, "*I was almost attracted to the strange almost mystical writing. But the market is overwrought with this kind of book. The 'Negro Awakening' fad seems to have reached its peak and once more people are returning to serious writing, Mark Twain and Stephen Crane*" (98, original italics). Not only does this letter parody the fading white interest in the New Negro Renaissance, it further subverts the idea of a distinctly white literary tradition, for as Shelly Fisher Fishkin has famously demonstrated, Twain traces some of his own literary roots to the African American oral tradition. To reject Jes Grew in favor of Twain, then, is to mask the racial origins of an American literary icon, just as the White House urgently suppresses stories of President Harding's black ancestry. Yet the rejection letter's next lines—"*A Negro editor here said it lacked 'soul' and wasn't 'Nation' enough. He suggested you read Claude McKay's* If We Must Die *and perhaps pick up some pointers*" (98, original italics)—point to the artificial aesthetic standards imposed on the New Negro movement from within, in response to the larger social structure. Similarly, when Von Vampton and "Safecracker" Gould visit Buddy Jackson's cabaret to recruit "authentic" black poets for the *Benign Monster*, Major Young rejects the cultural conflation on which their journal depends: "Is it necessary for us to write the same way? I am not Wallace Thurman, Thurman is not Fauset and Fauset is not Claude McKay, McKay isn't Horne. We all have our unique styles" (102).

Mumbo Jumbo further thematizes these linked cultural and commercial issues through such references as the rare book *Warren Harding, President of the United States*, which, because it posits Harding's African American heritage, has become worth $200,000 and is held only by the New York

Public Library after Woodrow Wilson orders its 250,000 copies destroyed (146). For the Harding biography, its political danger yields both its secrecy and thus its value, while the opposite cultural/commercial relationship appears in LaBas's retelling of the Set/Osiris story. Once Moses thinks he has mastered the secrets of Jethro's song, he rides away: "He dropped 'a couple of bucks' on old Jethro. Here's the copyright fee for the junk you taught me, he said sarcastically" (179). This moment serves as the genesis, of course, for white culture's continuing theft of black art forms, as will happen with the appropriation of ragtime into popular dance music by white performers. Just after Reed's middle epigraph from James Weldon Johnson's preface to his *Book of American Negro Poetry*, Johnson writes, "Some of these earliest songs were taken down by white men, the words slightly altered or changed, and published under the names of the strangers. They sprang into immediate popularity and earned small fortunes" (12–13).

Such attempts to control or appropriate black culture and history connect to a series of moments in which Jes Grew appears as either stable or fluid, controllable by its editors and translators or asserting its own textual independence. During his interrogation by the Hierophant, for example, Hinckle explains that he has distributed Jes Grew's physical text to "14 J.G.C. individuals scattered throughout Harlem. Only I can call it in and anthologize it. Janitors, Pullman porters, shoeshine boys, dropouts from Harvard, musicians, jazz musicians. Its carbons are in New York, Kansas City, Oakland, California, Chattanooga Tennessee, Detroit, Mobile, Raleigh. It's dispersed. Untogether. I sent it out as a chain book" (69).[13] By scattering the remnants of Jes Grew's physical text among this group of Carriers, who each represent the kind of occupations open to African Americans in the 1920s, along with the sites of growing black communities, Hinckle figures Jes Grew as powerless, illegible, except when gathered together into an anthology. The particular choice of genre is striking here, for even as a complete text Jes Grew would represent multiple writings and viewpoints, gathered together from their "dispersed" state. As Gates observes, Jes Grew also needs physical texts to remain culturally current: "The power of Jes Grew was allowed to peter out in the 1890s, Reed argues, because it found no literary texts to contain, define, interpret and thereby will it to subsequent black cultures" (*Signifying* 224).

In contrast, LaBas's explanation of Jes Grew as a translated text ascribes independent agency to Jes Grew itself. Hinckle has agreed to return the book to the Wallflower Order, LaBas states, "if indeed this is what Jes Grew craved. . . . The Text became stationary as Abdul began to translate The Work and this is when Jes Grew brought it on up and started to move toward Manhattan" (190). In this formulation, Jes Grew operates as an independent cultural force that can be distilled into a "stationary" physical form under certain conditions, but even then continues to move on a metaphysical, non-textual level. As McGee maintains, "Reed appeals to the subversive core of vodun when he transforms its symbolic practice, which resists writing, into writing—a writing against writing as the medium of Western metaphysics and ideology, a text against text, a quest for truth that subverts the very principle of truth as origin and end" (84). This tension inherent to the writing of vodun manifests itself as well in the novel's last words (before the bibliography): "*Jan. 31st, 1971 3:00* P.M. / *Berkeley, California*" (218, original italics). Such a precise compositional moment parodies the textual odyssey signified at the end of *Ulysses*, in the closing words "Trieste-Zurich-Paris, 1914–1921," but it also subverts the idea of completion itself for a work like *Mumbo Jumbo* (or Jes Grew). Reed inserts such playful "signatures" into several of his novels, with this parodic device most fully extended in *Flight to Canada*, which ends, "12:01 A.M. / Tamanaca Hotel, Room 127 / Fat Tuesday / March 2, 1976 / New Orleans" (179). This precise reference to a celebration which has its roots both in Christianity and in polytheistic "ancient origins" (Reed, *Shrovetide* 11), and to America's bicentennial year, is particularly appropriate for a novel that has conflated historical periods to suggest that the past is always the present. Such insistent locations of the text in specific times and places, however, run counter to *Mumbo Jumbo*'s depiction of textuality as an unfixed, fluid energy. A similar tension inheres, as Barbara Browning notes, in *Mumbo Jumbo*'s efforts to inscribe a lost African tradition within an American literary structure. "Reed seems to be making ironic a notion of a textual, nonliterate African cultural tradition by suggesting that the tradition has always been textual," Browning writes, "yet the text of the tradition has been suppressed and ultimately destroyed. Pan-African textuality, however, might be recuperated by the book itself" (77). This is indeed *Mumbo Jumbo*'s central paradox: how to subvert Western cultural traditions within the framework of conventional literary structures, in order to open those traditions and structures to a pan-African textuality, thus creating a new, hybrid textual method.

BLACK PAGE, WHITE PRINT

This fundamental tension applies, then, to the act of reading itself, for to transpose an originally oral text into a printed form requires a self-conscious challenge to standard reading practices, to the politics of print. *Mumbo Jumbo* twice figures Jes Grew as "unprintable," suggesting that its immaterial text cannot be contained within any material text, although the physical text always remains necessary to access the immaterial level.[14] The third epigraph, from Johnson's *Book of American Negro Poetry*, an anthology he edited for Harcourt Brace in 1922, reads: " '. . . we appropriated about the last one of the 'jes' grew' songs. It was a song which had been sung for years all through the South. The words were unprintable, but the tune was irresistible, and belonged to nobody" (11, original ellipsis). Hinckle and Hamid repeat Johnson's description after Von Vampton and Gould have learned of the Jes Grew anthology's existence from W. W. Jefferson. "What do you mean you don't have it," Hinckle demands:

I mean just that the words were unprintable.
  But the tune was irresistible. . . .
I don't think so. I don't like the lyricism. That kind at least. No, I don't have it. (95)

This repetition and reversal expresses the two tensions at work in Jes Grew's recovery. In Johnson's formulation, there is no original author of the "jes' grew" song; it sprung from a southern oral tradition and so "belonged to nobody," but then Johnson's version is fixed into a stable, printed song once he and his band have "appropriated" it. (These songs are then transferred into new cultural forms once they are appropriated and commodified further by white performers.) Abdul Hamid, in contrast, constructs the "unprintable" anthology but then determines it unfit for public circulation (as if the editors of the unauthorized Harding biography, rather than the White House, had ordered that book destroyed). The words are "unprintable" in both contexts because they would be unacceptable in "polite" society, but their trace remains, first, in Johnson's music, and then in his discussion of it in his poetry anthology, and later in Hamid's destruction of his anthology, which ultimately succeeds only in deferring Jes Grew's physical, textual manifestation.

Jes Grew is an inherently organic phenomenon: it "Jes Grew." It is also, as Gates argues, "the novel's central character," even though Jes Grew "never speaks and is never seen in its 'abstract essence,' only in discrete manifestations, or 'outbreaks.' Jes Grew is the supraforce which sets the text of *Mumbo Jumbo* in motion, as Jes Grew and Reed seek their texts, as all characters and events define themselves against this omnipresent, compelling force" (*Signifying* 222). In this concluding section, I read the original black copyright page as one more textual manifestation of Jes Grew, both as an ironic attempt to literalize the "black self" in the blackness of the page and, in this page's disappearance from the paperback editions, as a differently ironic expression of Jes Grew's disappearing textual stability.

By remaking the copyright page as black, Reed in his collaboration with Doubleday insists on marking the text as "his" even as he transfers it economically and legally to a publishing system within which he may function as a racial token. Readers of *Mumbo Jumbo*'s original edition find all the expected information in its conventional order: ISBN number, Library of Congress catalog card number, copyright, printing runs, etc. Yet the page itself reverses the field for this most mundane information: *Mumbo Jumbo* begins with a black page and white type, a "negative" image, as it were, of the standard white page with black type (see fig. 2). In a startling visual display, Reed's book inverts the white-black structure of all printed books, a structure so fundamental as otherwise to be overlooked entirely. By blackening the page that identifies *Mumbo Jumbo*, first, through its ISBN number, second, through its Library of Congress catalog card number, and, third, as Reed's literary property by virtue of his copyright, Reed adds race to the capitalist literary equation, using the color often associated with obscurity to illustrate ironically the operating assumptions of textual ownership on which the white page depends.[15]

The copyright page as a visual field reminds us when we reach the gray page of the Johnson and Hurston epigraphs that, while the words of the ragtime songs "belonged to nobody," in part because they were "unprintable," the book in which Johnson cites them did belong to several people, including Johnson himself, his readers, and, legally, Harcourt Brace, a firm

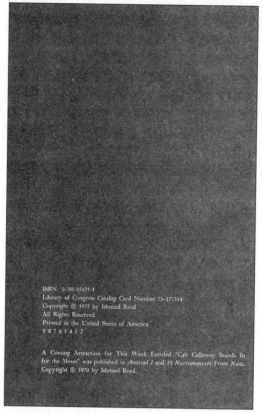

ISBN: 0-385-05675-5
Library of Congress Catalog Card Number 73-171314
Copyright © 1972 by Ishmael Reed
All Rights Reserved
Printed in the United States of America
9 8 7 6 5 4 3 2

A Coming Attraction for This Work Entitled "Cab Calloway Stands In for the Moon" was published in *Amistad 1* and *19 Necromancers From Now.* Copyright © 1970 by Ishmael Reed.

Fig. 2. Black copyright page in Ishmael Reed's *Mumbo Jumbo,* first edition (1972)

that realized early on the newfound marketability of black literature. *Mumbo Jumbo*'s own status as the product of a mainstream press becomes visible in the text a few pages after the first copyright page. After five white pages with black type, the reversal of the copyright page returns, with two black pages, one for the publisher and place and date of publication, and another for the title and author. We then find another copyright page, this one black-on-white, with a lengthy list of acknowledgments for illustrations. Finally, before the main text of the novel begins, there are two gray pages with black printing for Reed's epigraphs and dedications, a visual field that returns to standard print color but now on a mixed background. Here we see the white and black pages coming together as a kind of "mixed" text.

In their play with the black and white structure of printing, the opening pages of *Mumbo Jumbo* signify on (in Gates's use of the phrase) the interaction between white publishers and black writers in America, marking Reed's own text as one that works within this system while also calling attention to the racial hierarchy operating behind it. Reed's novel organizes itself around the genre and structure of the detective novel when the book's central mystery, in fact, becomes how to represent African American culture. Just as *Mumbo Jumbo*'s parody of the detective novel turns that genre inside out, so, too, do its opening pages turn the conventions of printing inside out, in a crucial mirroring framework.

The sense of a false start generated by the second appearance of a title page and copyright information deepens *Mumbo Jumbo*'s interrogation of the politics of print. For readers who have overlooked the first black copyright page, the intrusion of additional copyright information and other acknowledgments compels a return to the first such page—Haven't I already skipped this information once? we might imagine Reed's readers thinking.[16] Toward the end of what initially appears to be the beginning of the novel proper, we read the oft-quoted line, "*So Jes Grew is seeking its words. Its text*" (6). Once *Mumbo Jumbo* then re-announces its conflicted status as literary property through the second, white, copyright page, this search for genuine words and a genuine text takes on a new urgency: Reed, within the very book that we would ordinarily refer to as "his," is himself seeking his words and his text, seeking, that is, to mark *Mumbo Jumbo* as not wholly his and yet still more self-consciously not his publisher's, as his initial pages are powerfully not white. Of course, in this context, as in social and cultural settings, blackness appears as non-whiteness, as the page's blackness is especially visible in contrast to the whiteness of normal printing.

In this way the black copyright page importantly augments and complicates readings of the novel's subversion of stable racial narratives, advanced most effectively by Gates and McGee. Gates takes the text's fluid representations of Jes Grew to signify, ultimately, that "there can be no transcendent blackness, for it cannot and does not exist beyond manifestations of it in specific figures. Put simply, Jes Grew cannot conjure its texts: texts, in the broadest sense of the term (Parker's music, Ellison's fictions, Romare Bearden's collages, etc.), conjure Jes Grew" (*Signifying* 237). McGee reaches a similar conclusion, though through an emphasis on Jes Grew as a frustration of the desire for a (false) sense of completeness and stability: "*Mumbo Jumbo* is both a narrative, though an unconventional one, and a commentary on narrative, a text about desire as a function of narrative, about the quest for meaning and value through the mediation of language as the support of desire. It suggests that we can know desire not from a transcendent position outside the text but only from within the text by playing it in reverse, by bringing to readerly consciousness, if you will, the second narration within the first, that is, the story of writing as desire that secretly drives the first narrative toward an impossible culture" (109). Only by recognizing the impossibility of this stable, legible narrative of race, McGee argues, can readers of *Mumbo Jumbo* understand the cultural tensions that motivate the narrative; the text necessarily exposes conventional readings of both race and fiction as premised on false desires for transcendence.

A material approach to *Mumbo Jumbo* revises Gates's and McGee's readings through an understanding of the black page as a particular embodiment both of Reed's uneasy negotiations with the white commodification of black texts and of the text's frustration of the desire for the stability or transcendence even at a material level. First, the precise origins of the black copyright page are unclear within the archive. No extant correspondence identifies Reed or his editors, or some combination thereof, as responsible for this decision. The galley for this page bears a circled note reading, "SOLID / BLACK PAGE / BLEED 4 SIDES / TYPE WHITE." This handwriting is not Reed's (nor would one expect it to be at this stage of production), but it could, of course, reflect any number of decision-making processes behind this instruction. The device of the black page fits both Reed's interest in the opening pages' cinematic structure and, certainly, his concern for publishing this particular novel with a major white firm, but it also matches his editors' interest in producing a striking visual effect in the opening pages, to "get people to look a little further in." The black copyright page, like the cover, responds both to the problem of fixing an African American textuality within a marketable, essentially white form and to the necessary collaboration between Reed and his editors in order to produce the material book from which this immaterial effect will develop.

At this point the historical record behind the black copyright page remains murky, as with the omission of *Passing*'s last paragraph.[17] But I would argue that it is reasonable to conclude that Reed was involved in this decision in some capacity, whether the idea began with him or he approved the suggestion of a Doubleday editor. Correspondence from both Freedgood and McCormick indicates a consistent willingness to involve Reed in editorial (and advertising) matters. Whether initiated by Reed or one of his editors, then, the black page represents a productive relationship between author and publisher, even as it challenges the broader cultural assumptions reinforced by white copyright pages and books. From Brooks's perspective after 1967, Reed's decision to publish *Mumbo Jumbo* with Doubleday, even with the novel's material foregrounding of the politics of print, may still represent a compromise which privileges publishers' economic and cultural power over a black nationalist bibliographical environment. It is more financially viable for small presses to issue poetry broadsides than novels, of course, especially novels with numerous illustrations. Nevertheless, Brooks's association with the Broadside and Third World presses, and then her own imprints, locates Reed's material subversiveness as an ultimately less powerful critique of the cultural realities reinforced by commercial publishers.

Finally, *Mumbo Jumbo*'s black copyright page becomes a trace, in its absence from the paperback reprints. Doubleday first sold the paperback rights to Avon (which reprinted Reed's early novels, including a boxed set in 1984 [Dick and Singh 231]). There the original cover changes to a male and female dancer, with flowers superimposed over their heads, and the first copyright page is white, along with the title and epigraph/dedication pages. The current Atheneum reprint maintains the white copyright page, but restores the black title page and gray epigraphs and dedications. The Avon edition was a cheaper production than the Atheneum, priced at $2.25 and designed for a mass paperback audience. The switch to a white copyright page similarly suggests a shift toward greater commercial accessibility. As Reed complained in a 1976 interview with Stanley Crouch, his hardcover publications tended to struggle commercially, while the paperback reprints had been commercially popular. "I'm a big seller in paperback," Reed remarks. "You know, *Mumbo Jumbo*, *Yellow Back*, *Flight to Canada*, *The Last Days of Louisiana Red*, have all been brought out by Avon and I'm a big seller in their paperback, but in hard cover I don't think my books are advertised. And I think if you're trying to sell something, you have to advertise. You just can't let a book lie around the warehouse" (quoted in Dick and Singh 107). Reed often comments on what he feels to be insufficient marketing campaigns from his mainstream publishers (a sentiment shared by many authors, of course, regardless of race), but his paperbacks' commercial success itself requires comment. Just as the paperback *Black Fire* signifies its commodification through the omission of additional contributors, the paperback editions of *Mumbo Jumbo* express their enhanced commercial status by returning to a regular white copyright page, re-marking the paperback's white ownership by Avon and then Atheneum. At the same time, Reed profits more handsomely from these more commercial editions (as did Baraka and Neal, presumably, with the paperback *Black Fire*), in what would seem to be a classic case of sacrificing artistic (bibliographic) integrity for a lower cost of production and the larger markets and profits produced thereby.

Viewed once more as part of the fluid text comprising the manuscripts and other archival materials, the first edition, and the paperback reprints, the black-white copyright page expresses finally *Mumbo Jumbo*'s shifting relationship to the histories of its production; the "darkening" or "whitening" of this insignia of property relations connotes the changing economic and cultural circumstances of production for postmodern black literature. As Jameson argues, *pace* Althusser, "each system—better still, every 'mode of production'—produces a temporality that is specific to it" (*Cultural* 58). The erasure of textual history in the Avon and Atheneum reprints thus reflects the neglected interest in "authentic" African American literature manifesting itself, however problematically, during the Black Arts and Second Renaissance periods. As the politics of literary publishing shift during the late 1970s and into the '80s, the now white copyright page neatly signifies a greater emphasis on new profit than on historical critique, and on *Mumbo Jumbo*'s marketing by its new publishers to new audiences in cheaper formats. As with the paperback *Black Fire*, these reprints still serve an important economic and cultural purpose; they keep Reed and other experimental minority writers in print, after all, and keep discussions of their work current for new generations of readers. But by reading these contemporary editions of *Mumbo Jumbo* without juxtaposing them against the first edition and the archive, we risk perpetuating a textual orientation that is dislocated from the history of textual production. Linking Jameson's response to postmodernism— "an attempt to think the present historically in an age that has forgotten how to think historically in the first place"

(*Postmodernism* ix)—with Reed's insistence on the palimpsest of America's racial past and present, we can engage *Mumbo Jumbo*'s archive as a material record of these textual and cultural histories' erasure and recovery.

From Reed's critique of his publishers' advertising practices and cultural influence, I turn to Gwendolyn Brooks, who produced not just black copyright pages, but entire "black" books through her association with Broadside, Third World, and her own imprints. There is no need for a black copyright page in Brooks's later books, that is, precisely because the circumstances of textual production have shifted to a black publisher—black writer dynamic. The question of broader audiences remains for these works, though, both because of the ways in which Brooks has been anthologized and published (by HarperCollins) since then as a "safe" black poet and because of the encounters with white and other readers already envisioned within Brooks's bibliographically black texts themselves.

CHAPTER THREE

GWENDOLYN BROOKS'S BIBLIOGRAPHICAL BLACKNESS

In 1967, Gwendolyn Brooks famously became a black nationalist poet. At a Fisk University conference, Brooks explained to Claudia Tate, she encountered poets who "felt that black poets should write as blacks, about blacks, and address themselves *to* blacks" (40, original emphasis). Brooks had published her first six books with Harper and Brothers (later Harper and Row): *A Street to Bronzeville* (1945), *Annie Allen* (1949), *Maud Martha* (1953), *Bronzeville Boys and Girls* (1956), *The Bean Eaters* (1960), and *Selected Poems* (1963). The appearance of *In the Mecca* in 1968, over Harper's initial objections, inaugurated what has become known as the "second period" of Brooks's career, although, as Joanne Gabbin notes, such a distinction risks eliding "the political assertiveness and protest in her earlier poems" (255).[1] I agree with Gabbin and other contemporary critics who have seen the content and focus of Brooks's work as more of a political piece. The turn derives rather, as Zofia Burr argues, from Brooks's decision to publish her books only with black presses: "there is a 'shift' after 1968, but it consists more of a newly emphatic gesture of address (to black audiences) than it does of the discovery of a new (black) audience" (136). In this chapter I examine the bibliographic environment produced by that "newly emphatic gesture of address," arguing that Brooks's books with Broadside Press, Third World Press, and her own David Company express their circumstances of textual production in new ways of defining blackness, both for Brooks's local black audiences and for white readers approaching her later work in these forms. At the same time, the black image Brooks constructs through her small-press publications conflicts with the authorial portrait constructed by mainstream anthologies and the contemporary reprint of *Selected Poems*. These texts perpetuate a pre-*Mecca* image of Brooks, with her own anthology *Blacks* and other late works haunting *Selected Poems* as the ghosts of Brooks's "black" career.

While critics have focused extensively on Brooks's work during the Black Arts period, especially *In the Mecca* and *Riot*, published with Broadside in 1969, her career for many readers effectively ends in 1963, because that year's *Selected Poems* remains most widely in print. After outlining the historical factors motivating Brooks's departure from Harper and Row, I examine the contemporary paperback reprint of *Selected Poems*—reissued most recently in 1999 as part of HarperCollins's Perennial Classics series—in contrast to the much more extensive collection *Blacks*, as well as the dozen other books forming Brooks's small-press corpus. To read Brooks only through *Selected Poems* or contemporary anthologies is to misread the nature of her career after 1967, though that is also a crucial element of Brooks's decision to leave Harper: her willingness to abandon an established New York firm for small black presses in Detroit and Chicago signals her efforts to opt out of the cultural systems of market and canon. In a 1974 interview with Haki Madhubuti for *Black Books Bulletin*, Brooks declares, "I think that Black writers, for the time being at least, will have to give up the idea of becoming millionaires, and famous and profiting at any level. They may even have to let go of a few dollars that they have to aid these presses so that they can attract future writers" (quoted in Gayles 76). Given this emphasis on "brotherhood" (Gayles 76) rather than profit and fame, reading—or rather, rereading—Brooks's small-press volumes outside of their historical context runs counter to her bibliographic agenda of supporting such firms in word and deed. My aim in this chapter, then, is both to demonstrate the ways in which Brooks's popularly available poems maintain a corporate, effectively "white" image of her as a safe black poet and to argue for a necessary caution in transferring such books as *Children Coming Home* away from their original social, cultural, and bibliographic contexts. There Brooks revises standard notions of "black" and "home," overlaying a broader audience on the book's local network of composition, production, and reception. Whereas New York had become a publishing site from which Brooks could no longer be produced as a genuinely "black" poet, Detroit and Chicago were recognizably local sites of production, allowing Brooks not to be constructed for an implicitly white readership with her black audience marginalized, but to contribute directly to her own engagement with black readers, with an implicitly white audience now left to read Brooks's late books from the unfamiliar cultural position of exteriority.

OUT OF THE "HARPER HARBOR"

Knopf was the first mainstream publisher to express interest in Brooks's work, after she won a prize at the 1943 Midwest Writers Conference, but out of the forty poems Brooks submitted, Knopf was interested only in the nineteen "Negro" selections (Kent 62). Harper and Brothers, on the basis of a strong recommendation from Richard Wright, accepted the manuscript that would become *A Street to Bronzeville*, and Brooks began an effective and "somewhat maternal" collaboration with editor Elizabeth Lawrence (Kent 62, 64). When Lawrence announced her retirement in 1964, Brooks wrote, "You have made each of my books a little work of art, with I believe, not a single error in the twenty years of our association. It is not strange, therefore, that I regard your departure with bleakness and a sense of personal loss" (quoted in Kent 176). Brooks presumably benefited from working with a sympathetic woman as her editor, whom Brooks biographer George Kent calls "the creative engineer of her publishing career" (177). Following Lawrence's departure, Brooks continued to work with women editors at Harper, first Genevieve Young and then Ann Harris. While Brooks's relationships with her Harper editors, especially Lawrence, was "always productive" (Kent 177), it was unavoidably affected by the racial context surrounding all black writers in the decades after World War II. Kent notes of Brooks and Lawrence: "Despite the integrationist script from which both read their lines, the two represented black and white worlds, and the structure of their relationship would later arouse in Gwendolyn ambivalence. Thankful for having been prevented from disastrous plunges, she would still wonder whether this young chicken-mother hen relationship had not persisted too long. Such a response would also mean that she had effected a different relationship with the white liberal climate" (177). Kent's biography illustrates several points at which Lawrence effectively served as a barometer of Brooks's (and Harper's) white readership. Lawrence initially sought the removal of two poems from *Annie Allen*, "downtown vaudeville" and "I love those little booths at Benvenutti's," before Brooks convinced her otherwise, though "downtown vaudeville" was later cut from *Selected Poems*. (For a more detailed discussion of these examples, see Burr 114–15 and 123–30). After the initial *Mecca* manuscript, consisting only of the title poem, had "startled" its Harper reader, Harper asked to send the poem to the retired Lawrence, who agreed with the need for a longer volume and felt that in the title poem "the artifice overwhelmed the content" (Kent 212). While an editor's requests for revisions or additions to a manuscript are hardly unusual, in this case they illuminate what Burr calls "the complicated cross-cultural negotiation that must take place as a preface to the mainstream publication of any poetic text by a 'marginalized' writer'" (114). Particularly for a work like *In the Mecca*, which portrays for Harper's implicitly white audience the physical and textual space of black urban poverty, editorial exchanges cannot help but reinforce the aesthetic and political issues behind white consumption of black texts.

Harper did not learn of Brooks's 1969 decision to leave the firm until reading about it in a *New York Times* article (Kent 232). Brooks explained her interest in the Broadside Press to interviewer B. Denise Hawkins: "Dudley Randall at that time was giving a platform to young Black poets, people that Macmillan and Harper wouldn't accept. I thought joining Broadside Press was the right thing for me to do. Instead of staying in the 'Harper harbor' I decided to go with a Black publisher and give some assistance to them" (Hawkins 280). From the first, Brooks expressed her commitment to Broadside, and later to Haki Madhubuti's Third World Press as well as her own imprints, both through her interest in publishing her work with these small firms and through her direct financial support. Indeed, Brooks and Don Lee (before becoming Madhubuti) often paid Broadside's expenses for their own books and helped to cover costs for other titles as well (Kent 224). Similarly, Dudley Randall often forwarded manuscripts submitted to Broadside to Brooks for her opinion, and Brooks "worked diligently as an advocate of the younger writers, giving book parties and writing generous introductions" (M. Boyd 167).

Madhubuti explains Brooks's decision in more overtly political terms: "Naturally, she had a certain affection and dedication to Harper and Row, even though Harper's never, and I mean that literally, pushed the work of Gwendolyn Brooks. But the decision that was to be made in regard to Harper's was not either/or, but: what is best for black people" (91).[2] Randall himself, however, takes a softer line on this issue, explaining in a 1975 essay that he did not "expect or require" prominent black authors to follow Brooks's example. "Since Black publishers can't publish all Black writers," Randall explains, "perhaps it's the writers who have the courage to pioneer, experiment, cooperate, and perhaps sacrifice in determining who should publish with Black publishers. I don't think that Black writers should feel any guilt about publishing with white publishers. There are more than enough authors to go around" (35). As one of those pioneers, Brooks could see publishing with Broadside as "best for black people" because it shifted a well-known and commercially successful poet—Brooks won the Pulitzer Prize for *Annie Allen*, and *Selected Poems* sold particularly well, especially in Chicago—to small firms with lists emphasizing both contemporary and modernist African American writers. In addition to his own works, Randall included among the early Broadside volumes Robert Hayden's *Gabriel (Hanged for Leading a Slave Revolt)*, Margaret Walker's *The Ballad of the Free*, Melvin B. Tolson's *The Sea-Turtle and the Shark*, LeRoi Jones's *A Poem for Black Hearts*, Langston Hughes's *The Backlash Blues*, Jean Toomer's *Song of the Son*, and Etheridge Knight's *2 Poems for Black Relocation Centers*. Brooks's early broadsides, *We Real Cool* in 1966 and *The Wall* in 1967, thus orient themselves within a distinct cultural moment. *The Wall*, which appeared the next year in *In the Mecca*, is dated August 27, 1967, marking the poem's precise temporal point, while *We Real Cool* was initially issued in *The Bean Eaters* seven years before its Broadside version. The Broadside bibliographic environment emphasizes these poems' political content in ways that their original Harper volumes could not. As Melba Joyce Boyd notes, "the Black Arts movement in general worked through a renewed emphasis on writers' and publishers' hometowns: Randall establishing himself in Detroit, LeRoi Jones moving first from Greenwich Village to Harlem, and then to Newark, and of course Brooks moving bibliographically from New York to Detroit to Chicago" (124). The copyright notices identifying Brooks's books as published in Detroit or Chicago, then, signify a politics of place, just as the colophon for a Cuala Press edition of Yeats "stresses both the nationalist and feminist orientation of the press" (Bornstein, *Material* 24). Writing of Brooks's Broadside publications, James D. Sullivan observes similarly, "Publishing with Broadside places *Riot* in a specifically African American context. This was not a publisher's representation of a black poet's work (black art, white artifact), but a work written, published, and distributed in a black context. It had to be read as culturally specific rather than as universal" (560).

Brooks engaged with the mainstream publishing industry in a way that virtually no other black writer has before or since, reversing the usual career trajectory from small press to mainstream firm. LeRoi Jones, for example, published his own early poetry, along with works by other Beat and black writers, in the magazine *Yūgen*, with his Totem Press, and in the journal *The Floating Bear*, but simultaneously issued many of his own plays and essays with Morrow, beginning with *The Dutchman* and *The Slave* in 1964. Similarly, Ishmael Reed, as I discussed in chapter 2, has been involved with several independent publishing firms, while consistently publishing his own fiction with Doubleday and St. Martin's. So while Brooks's shift from a mainstream firm to small black-owned presses was consistent with the political impulses of the time, it also set her apart from most of her contemporaries. As Madhubuti tells Kent, "I knew deep down inside that very few people in the movement would be making that type of commitment" (232).

Brooks's new bibliographical environment, especially that generated by her own labels, is importantly distinct from another major twentieth-century woman writer who published herself, Virginia Woolf. Thanks to her co-ownership of the Hogarth Press with her husband, Leonard, Woolf was famously "the only woman in England free to write what [she] like[d]" (*Diary* 43). Hogarth began as a small handpress, issuing books by the Woolfs and their friends in limited runs, and eventually expanded into a mainstream, commercial press, producing bestsellers by Woolf and Vita Sackville-West, along with popular mysteries like *The Death of My Aunt* (1929). For Woolf, a direct correlation applied between financial profit and aesthetic freedom: along with other popular titles on Hogarth's list, Woolf's own more commercial titles (such as *Flush*, a biography of Elizabeth Barrett Browning's dog, which helped Woolf earn nearly £2,500 herself in 1933) paid for her experimental fiction and cultural critique. Brooks, in contrast, began her career with Harper and could not have afforded to do otherwise.

But the commercial success Brooks enjoyed there, especially after her 1950 Pulitzer, eventually restricted her aesthetic freedom. Only by sacrificing an appeal to a mainstream market could Brooks produce the kind of work that would speak freely to a contemporary black readership. At a time when no Oprah's Book Club was available to bridge the economic divide reinforcing the cultural tensions attendant on white-published black literature, Brooks collaborated on entire black books, not just black copyright pages. The *Riot* cover, for example, carries white type on a black background, as does the epigraph page (with a quotation from Henry Miller).[3]

Priced at $1.00 in paper and $3.00 in cloth, Brooks's broadsides were clearly produced with commercial accessibility in mind. This format also allowed for aesthetic choices that derive from the circumstances of material production. *Aloneness*, for example, at eighteen pages and just more than pocket size, appeared in 1971 with prominent illustrations of a young African American boy on almost every page and the poem's type in a font resembling handwriting. On the facing page is an epigraph from Brooks's daughter, Nora, then 20: "I like aloneness, but I/don't like loneliness./Aloneness is different/from loneliness." This maternal emphasis continues through to the book's last page, which features the poem's closing line below a large drawing of the young boy in a woman's arms (presumably his mother's), and the back cover's full-page photograph of Brooks, smiling and looking down, as if toward a child. *Aloneness* thus aims at children as its readers, both in content and format, to a much more significant extent than would have been possible with a mainstream firm. Even while Brooks often focused on representations of childhood in her Harper books, as part of what Richard Flynn calls her attempt "to negotiate a complex poetic strategy that explores 'childhood' as a position from which to critique prevailing constructs of class and race" (484), such critiques were often limited, rather than reinforced, by the bibliographical environments produced at Harper. In Brooks's first "childhood" book, *Bronzeville Boys and Girls* (1956), for example, the Harper illustrator's drawings depict the Bronzeville children "sometimes with stylized Black facial characteristics, but all with white faces" (Flynn 491). The cultural resistance of this volume is thus purely linguistic, as the poems disrupt the conventional nostalgia associated with adult readers of children's literature and "seem calculated to point out the dangers of a nostalgia that obscures the actual conditions of children. Given the relationship between

Brooks and her editors at Harper, and the cultural climate of the mid-'50s, Brooks is quietly subversive in these poems, which prefigure the powerful children's monologues in *Children Coming Home*" (Flynn 492). In that book, which I examine in this chapter's closing section, Brooks finally combines linguistic and bibliographic critiques in a marked departure from her role in Harper's production system.

The feminist ethic of care that derives from such images also bears interesting connections to Brooks's shift toward black nationalism, given her determination to "give some assistance" to Dudley Randall's broadsides. First, the illustrator for *Aloneness* was Leroy Foster, who had earlier contributed a mural of the Harpers Ferry conspirators to the courtroom of Judge George Crockett, a progressive black judge in Detroit whose defiance of the local police contributed to the atmosphere in which Coleman Young would be elected mayor in 1977 (M. Boyd 27). Broadside and Third World thus played key roles in "creating a mass and working-class black readership," as Bill V. Mullen notes (156). Foster's presence as Brooks's illustrator both associates this book with a specific sense of place and history and shifts a book about children from an ostensibly neutral into a more overtly political atmosphere. The *Aloneness* copyright page also marks Brooks as a distinctly black nationalist poet, including only her other Broadside titles except for *The World of Gwendolyn Brooks*, her last publication with Harper and Row. That title bears a particular significance in this context as well, as, unlike *Selected Poems*, this 1971 collection included *In the Mecca*. In negotiations with Harper, Brooks and her agent Roslyn Targ agreed to a lower advance in order to keep the book's cost at a reasonable $8.50 (as it contains five previous publications in one volume). Brooks also saw the inclusion of the *Mecca* poems as vital to this volume, writing to Targ, "Conceivably, the 'Omnibus' [the book's original title] will be in print for many years—but my work is changing and is going to continue to change, and the first hints of the change are in the Mecca book. The 'Omnibus' as they are planning it would NOT stamp me as part of this eruptive time, which I AM" (quoted in Kent 233). Within the bibliographical environment of the *Aloneness* copyright page, then, the appearance of *World* as Brooks's only commercial title indicates her ongoing concern for advertising her career beginning with *In the Mecca*, and continuing through her other six Broadside titles then in print (including two anthologies she had edited).[4]

But that careful emphasis on Brooks's post-Harper career as its own bibliographic sphere disappears in the two venues through which her poems are most accessible today: anthologies and the paperback reprint of her 1963 *Selected Poems*. From the standpoint of a text's material history, anthologies are inherently ahistorical, as all original bibliographical context disappears in the sea of the anthology's identical pages. As Bornstein observes of Brooks's sonnet "my dreams, my works, must wait till after hell" in the Norton poetry anthology, the poem loses contact with the rest of the sonnet sequence "Gay Chaps at the Bar" and, more importantly, appears without the original dedication to Brooks's brother Raymond, who was serving in the armed forces when the poem first appeared in the 1945 volume *A Street in Bronzeville*.[5] While this dedication was dropped from the sonnet sequence in *Selected Poems*, Brooks ensured its return for *Blacks*, leading Bornstein to conclude, "Tracking the poem to its earlier sites, then, allows personal, racial, and historical meanings to emerge that would otherwise be lost in transfer of the words of the isolated sonnet to an anthology" (*Material* 31).

This sort of historical myopia is a particular problem for Brooks in anthologies, I would argue, precisely because of the unusual progression of her career. Anthologies privilege her earlier work, at least in part because the post-Harper poems are either out of print or less easily accessible. McGraw Hill's *American Tradition in Literature* (tenth edition), for example, includes five of Brooks's poems, but only one published after 1960 ("Horses Graze," which first appeared in the 1975 Third World Press volume *Beckonings*). Similarly, Norton's American literature anthology includes three poems, out of twelve total, from Brooks's later career ("The Blackstone Rangers" from *In the Mecca*, "To the Diaspora" from the book of that title, and "The Coora Flower" from *Children Coming Home*). Norton's African American literature anthology features twenty Brooks poems, plus *Maud Martha* in its entirety. Although Brooks appears in the section titled "Realism, Naturalism, Modernism: 1940–1960," there are five poems originally published outside of this period, from *In the Mecca* (1968), *Riot* (1969), and *Family Pictures* (1970). Heath's American literature anthology (fourth edition) includes one selection from *Children Coming Home* alongside five poems first published between 1945 and 1960, thus offering at least a hint of Brooks's later career. McGraw Hill's biographical note discusses the importance of the 1967 Fisk conference in Brooks's decision to switch to black publishers, and the textual note observes that "most of her verse is collected in *Blacks*, 1987" (Perkins and Perkins 1402). But because the anthology's selections are heavily weighted toward the earlier periods of Brooks's career, the important shifts that occur through the later 1970s and through the '80s remain all but invisible. Such oversights, of course, affect both students and critics. As Brooks herself complains in the Hawkins interview:

There are many people writing about my poetry who have read "A Song in the Front Yard," "We Real Cool," and "The Bean Eaters." Then they're through. They know nothing about my book *Winnie*, which marks a very significant change in my writing. They know nothing about *In the Mecca*. They know nothing about *Children Coming Home*. . . . They are satisfied with trying to give the public the impression that I'm an "old-fashioned" writer, simplistic and outmoded. They want to use "A Song in the Front Yard" to represent my entire output and intent. I have been changing all along. None of my books is exactly like the other. (Hawkins 275)

Winnie (1988) and *Children Coming Home* (1991) were the last two books Brooks published with the David Company, and in this juxtaposition of poems about Winnie Mandela and Chicago children we see the range of topics and styles through which Brooks moved at the end of her career. While it is striking that two major anthologies of American literature, the Norton and Heath, each include one selection from *Children Coming Home*, the bibliographical codes for that book are so significant that the poems' anthologized appearances erase important elements of the texts' original environment and meaning. I return to this point in an extended reading of Brooks's last book at the end of this chapter, but first examine the competing bibliographic and linguistic codes of the current *Selected Poems* and *Blacks* reprints.

GAPS IN *SELECTED POEMS*

Other than anthologized misrepresentations (both linguistic and bibliographic) of Brooks's work, *Selected Poems* remains the most widely available venue for casual readers. Reprinted in paperback by HarperCollins for the Perennial Classics series in 1999, *Selected Poems* stands in opposition to *Blacks*, the collection Brooks issued through the David Company in 1987, and which is now in print from the Third World Press. In this section I examine the significant textual and paratextual differences between these two volumes, concluding that *Selected Poems* carefully packages Brooks as a safer and more distant poet than does *Blacks*, from its title on. To be sure, Brooks's version of her collected poems is itself also incomplete; as Henry Taylor notes, only nineteen of the poems Brooks published between 1968 and 1987 appear in *Blacks*. Still, the title alone sets this volume apart from *Selected Poems*, its "stark inclusiveness" suggesting that "Brooks perceives unity as well as variety in the range of her concerns and voices" (Taylor 255). *Selected Poems*, both through its contents and through the afterword attached to the contemporary reprint, steers readers away from Brooks's post-*Mecca* career, privileging her earlier, more canonical work as representative of what the back jacket calls "her compassionate and illuminating response to a world that is both special and universal."

This assessment echoes the more or less standard response to Brooks's work during the 1950s and '60s, and the *Selected Poems* paratextual elements consistently reinforce that circumscribed view of her career. The legend beneath a small back-cover photograph states simply: "Gwendolyn Brooks was born in 1917. Her books include *A Street in Bronzeville, Annie Allen, The Bean Eaters, Maud Martha*, and *In the Mecca*." While the list of "Books by Gwendolyn Brooks" opposite the title page includes all of her books published after leaving Harper and Row—though oddly placing *Blacks* last, out of chronological order—the afterword by Hal Hager, "About Gwendolyn Brooks," makes no mention at all of her self-published titles and figures her switch to black publishers in gentler terms than have Brooks and her associates. Although Hager's biographical sketch first appeared in the 1999 Perennial Classics edition, it discusses Brooks's career in terms that are strikingly similar to those of her mid-century critics and reviewers. Describing the "intensified emphasis on the problems of racism and injustice" in *In the Mecca*, for example, Hager reassures readers that "there is nothing bitter or explicitly vengeful about the poems themselves. Brooks's poetry remained—and remains—a poetry of clear vision, compassion, and artistic command" (133–34). The inference here, that "bitter" or "vengeful" poetry would lack clarity and command, backhandedly introduces the question of artistic "control," which has historically worried white readers of black texts. Don Jaffe writes in his famous 1969 essay "Gwendolyn Brooks: An Appreciation from the White Suburbs," published the year after *Mecca*: "Gwen Brooks leads us to a sense of the ghetto and the black man. . . . She has fashioned a style, developed a virtuosity, that makes it possible for her to grab big chunks of the American reality, moments of its hopefulness, portions of its resentments, and *give them cohesiveness and shape*" (58, emphasis added). Thirty-five years later, Jaffe's remarks seem clearly to respond to the white anxiety about race, generally, in the late 1960s and about black art, in particular: would it represent the black world to white readers in terms that would be cohesive and clear?

Such questions emerge from a much longer history of aesthetics, which, as Simon Gikandi observes, depends from the beginning on a mutually opposing (and therefore sustaining) relationship between art and race. "We are caught, on one hand," Gikandi explains, "in the idealistic claim that it is in the universal realm of art and aesthetic judgment that we come to a sense of ourselves as free, self-reflective subjects; on the other hand, however, we are trapped in the powerful modern claim that questions of identity or moral orientation cannot be solved in universal terms, that the terms of our identity depend on our recognition of the other" (347). Having examined the historical moment which gave rise to this aesthetic ideology—in which John Locke was a major shareholder in a slave-trading company and Immanuel Kant dabbled in racist anthropology—Gikandi concludes: "It is precisely because of this conjuncture between the necessity for universality in identity and the imperative for difference that questions about art and race have been kept apart for so long. This is why, in social epistemology, art has been made the custodian of universal identity while race has become the phenomenological sign of difference" (347). Returning to the rhetorical terms in which Brooks's poetry is figured to an implicitly white audience, we see the continuing effects of this ideological opposition between art and race motivating questions of Brooks's clarity. Poetry which is focused so clearly on the black experience, in other words, risks losing any claim to a universal identity, and thus to being art. Hager's efforts to reassure readers on this point echo the back cover of *Selected Poems*, where we find that this volume "represents [Brooks's] technical mastery, her compassionate and illuminating response to a world that is both special and universal, and her warm humanity." In contrast to what Gikandi describes as the eighteenth-century "slave aesthetic," which "was sustained by an underground symbolic order that spoke a cabalistic language, unintelligible or inaccessible to the dominant culture" (346–47), Brooks's poetry appears here to speak reassuringly to that dominant culture, in terms which "illuminate" the "special" black world for white readers and thus make it part of the "universal" whole.

Hager's afterword thus echoes the other paratextual element setting the rhetorical tone at the back of the book: three blurbs identifying Brooks and her poetry in similarly racialist terms. The Perennial Classics reprint includes excerpts from the *New York Times* 1950 review of *Annie Allen*, a 1953 *Christian Science Monitor* review of *Maud Martha*, and Harvey Curtis Webster's 1962 essay, "A Critical Reassessment," which aided significantly in elevating Brooks's critical reputation and confirmed Harper's interest in issuing *Selected Poems* (Kent 157). The emended Webster blurb carefully glosses over dated elements of his praise, which had been included on the back cover for the previous paperback reprint, issued through Harper and Row's Perennial Library. (The title for this line became Perennial Classics following Harper's takeover by Rupert Murdoch's NewsCorp.) The earlier reprint features two long paragraphs from Webster as the back cover's only blurb. The excerpt concludes: "Like all good writers she acknowledges Now by vivifying it accepts herself [*sic*] and the distinguishing background that is part of her distinction. But she refuses to let Negroness limit her humanity. . . . She is a very good poet, the only superlative I dare use in our time of misusage; compared to other Negro poets or other women poets but to the best of modern poets, she ranks high" (original ellipsis).

Kent finds that Webster's "remarks comprise the standard script inscribed by the white liberal critical consensus on the test sheets of those blacks about to be admitted into the company of true writers. But Webster also improves upon the script" (156). I see Webster's "improvement" as marginal at best. He writes condescendingly, for example: "Of course she writes of Emmett Till, of Little Rock, of Dorie Miller, of a white maid [*sic*] disgusted to see her child embrace the Negro maid. Of course she uses (less frequently and less successfully than Langston Hughes) blues rhythms, writes of the blessing-curse, the accident of color" (quoted in Kent 156). The rhetorical conflict in Webster's account, between Brooks "of course" writing about contemporary racial issues and in traditional African American tones while also "refus[ing] to let Negro-ness limit her humanity," demonstrates the extent to which racialist discourse, in Morrison's terms, controls his entire approach to Brooks's work. (Webster's review is reprinted in S. Wright, *On Gwendolyn Brooks*.)

The contemporary reprint sanitizes Webster's remarks by omitting the claim that "Negroness" might limit Brooks's humanity, and by deleting the comparison to "other Negro poets or other women poets," which in the original implicitly identifies the "best of modern poets" as white and male. Despite these cosmetic changes, the back of the book—which Gerald Graff identifies as a key element of unofficial interpretive culture—freezes Brooks's career in the 1950s and '60s. This was the historical context for the initial publication of *Selected Poems* in 1963, of course, but its reprint at the cusp of the twenty-first century offers a clear opportunity to update the volume in terms of Brooks's entire career, a marketing strategy which would seem to coincide with the presumed goal of introducing new readers to Brooks's work at the end of her life. That HarperCollins presents Brooks instead as a "safe" black poet of the 1950s speaks powerfully to some mainstream publishers' continuing efforts to offer racialist portraits of black writers to white audiences.

This kind of rhetorical fashioning is, of course, precisely what Brooks spent the last thirty years of her career working against, so the paratextual portrait that emerges from *Selected Poems* stands in stark contrast to Brooks's own work from 1967 on. In a 1971 interview with Ida Lewis, for example, Brooks notes that her early audiences were predominantly white.

It was whites who were reading and listening to us, salving their consciences—our accusations didn't hurt too much. But I was repeatedly called bitter. White people would come up after a reading and say, "Why are you so bitter? Don't you think things are improving?"

That's the glorious thing about today: we aren't concerned what whites think of our work. In one of Horace Bond's African rhetoric classes at Kansas University [*sic*], one man, a young teacher there, asked me, "What have you got to say about these critics who tell us we're not writing universally and we don't know how to put our words together?"

I said, "What do you care? We don't care about these notions anymore. Whites are not going to understand what is happening in black literature today. Even those

who want to sympathize with it still are not equipped to be proper critics."
(Brooks, *Report* 176–77)

That this interview originally appeared in *Essence*, before its reprinting in Broadside's *Report from Part One*, underscores bibliographically Brooks's rejection of even a "sympathetic" white audience.

In keeping with its contrasting bibliographical environment, *Selected Poems* presents Brooks's departure from her white publisher in muted terms. Hager's afterword quotes Brooks's explanation from the Hawkins interview: "'Dudley Randall . . . was giving a platform to young Black poets, people that the larger publishers wouldn't accept. I thought it was the right thing for me to do. . . . I decided to go with a Black publisher and give some assistance to them'" (134). Hager's ellipses and emendations are striking; here is Brooks's original answer, a portion of which I have quoted earlier: "I was with Harper, my first publisher, from 1945 to 1969. That's quite a while to stay with one publishing house. Dudley Randall at that time was giving a platform to young Black poets, people that Macmillan and Harper wouldn't accept. I thought joining Broadside Press was the right thing for me to do. Instead of staying in the 'Harper harbor' I decided to go with a Black publisher and give some assistance to them. It has been thirty years since I published with Harper. My publisher is now Third World Press of Chicago" (Hawkins 280). The version of this quotation which appears in *Selected Poems* omits all references to specific publishers by inserting ellipses and emending "Macmillan and Harper" to a looser reference to "the larger publishers." The *Selected Poems* afterword also erases "the 'Harper harbor'" from Brooks's answer, as well as the fact that Brooks had not published with Harper for thirty years, a particularly inconvenient fact for HarperCollins to acknowledge in its reprint of this volume. This subtle manipulation of Brooks's publishing history figures her departure for Broadside largely as an altruistic gesture, a desire to "give some assistance" to black presses which would not also entail a firm rejection of white publishers. Finally, the omission of Brooks's current publisher, Third World Press, steers readers away from the alternative collection of Brooks's work now in print, *Blacks*.

The *Blacks* paperback edition, which was first issued alongside the original David Company volume in 1987, represents itself both bibliographically and linguistically as a more comprehensive and authentic collection of Brooks's work, repositioning her early books in relation to the material of the 1970s and '80s, rather than as the defining texts of her career. The copyright page makes this point subtly but powerfully, with the following note: "Some of the material in this compilation has been previously published by Harper and Row, New York, under the following titles: *Maud Martha, The Bean Eaters, In the Mecca, Annie Allen, A Street in Bronzeville* and *The World of Gwendolyn Brooks.*" By (unnecessarily) including Harper and Row's location, this seemingly routine copyright notice both emphasizes the Chicago production of *Blacks*, both in its David Company and Third World Press editions, and figures *Blacks* itself as the defining volume of Brooks's career, subsuming her Harper and Row publications within its field of bibliographic and linguistic blackness.

The cover, a solid blue field with only the title and author in gold type, presents *Blacks* as a collection which brings together not just the disparate elements of Brooks's career, but also the historical and cultural connections among African, American, and diasporic black experiences. As Brooks tells Hawkins, "I don't like the term *African American*. It is very excluding, I like to think of Blacks as *Family*. Parts of that family living in Brazil or Haiti or France or England are not going to allow you to call them African American because they are not" (quoted in Hawkins 279, original emphasis). The title *Blacks*, which derives its power from its direct simplicity, is echoed in the basic but expressive cover design, particularly in the dark blue background's suggestion of multiple colors merging into a single field.

The back cover, in contrast to *Selected Poems*, features no blurbs from scholars or reviewers, instead devoting the entire three paragraphs to highlights of Brooks's career. From her birth in Topeka, childhood and junior college education in Chicago, to her many awards and honors, this biographical sketch figures Brooks as both highly accomplished and locally oriented. Following two paragraphs of career accomplishments, the back cover continues:

She is the daughter of the late David and Keziah (Wims) Brooks. She is married to Henry Blakely, author of *Windy Palace*, and is the mother of Nora Blakely, director of "Chocolate Chips" theater group, and Henry Blakely, Athena Group.

Ms. Brooks holds the Gwendolyn Brooks Chair in Black Literature and Creative Writing at Chicago State University.

This close identification between Brooks's Chicago family and her endowed chair at Chicago State again portrays Brooks's intimate engagement with local artistic production, through her daughter's theater group and her teaching. At the same time that *Blacks* linguistically summarizes Brooks's career up to that point, it also paratextually summarizes her life, implying a close overlap between the personal and the professional. This kind of interaction would not have been possible had Brooks stayed with Harper and Row (much less HarperCollins), as this New York–based firm would have continued positioning Brooks's poetry for implicitly white audiences and figuring her by extension outside of the black Chicago community to which she devoted the last decades of her career and life.

In addition to this paratextual refashioning, *Blacks* affords Brooks the opportunity to shape her collected works by choosing which texts to include and in which order. At 512 pages, in contrast to *Selected Poems'* 127, *Blacks* features several early poems which do not appear in the 1963 volume, including the following: from *A Street in Bronzeville*, nine poems from the sequence "A Street in Bronzeville," the entire sequence "Hattie Scott," and the individual poems "Queen of the Blues" and "Ballad of Pearl May Lee"; from *Annie Allen*, "Memorial to Ed Bland," five poems from the sequence "Notes from the Childhood and the Girlhood," and three poems from the sequence "The Womanhood"; *Maud Martha* in its entirety; and fifteen poems from *The Bean Eaters*, primarily those which depict individual characters. In general, *Blacks* restores Brooks's character studies and fleshes out the extended descriptions *in Annie Allen*. Along with *Maud Martha*, which in Hortense Spillers's estimation "punctuates a significant period of work in the poet's career" (270 n21), these poems expand Brooks's focus to a wider range of perspectives, experiences, and characters, creating a detailed and varied description, which, by its absence, renders *Selected Poems* both a narrower portrait and a more abstract response to Brooks's cultural and social environments. Such a shift is, of course, in keeping with the book's paratextual emphasis on Brooks as a poet who renders her "special" community in "universal" terms.

Brooks also uses *Blacks* as an opportunity to rearrange the sequence of some of her later poems, creating what Bornstein terms a "contextual code" through the new order's intertextual relationship with earlier published versions. Brooks is surprisingly parsimonious with her later work in *Blacks*, a decision that interestingly re-emphasizes her earlier works in a new bibliographic context, at a time when most of her books from the 1970s and '80s were still in print. The last book excerpted in *Blacks* is *The Near-Johannesburg Boy*, first published in 1986 by Third World Press. Brooks cuts half of the fourteen poems for *Blacks* and moves the title poem from first to third in the volume's order, so that it now appears after "Whitney Young" and "Tornado at Talladega" and before "The Good Man" and "Infirm." This new sequence juxtaposes "Whitney Young" with "To Black Women," which closes the selections from the preceding volume, *To the Diaspora*, and so makes adjacent two powerful expressions of united black voices.

"To Black Women" calls this voice into being, closing its address with these lines:

> *But there remain large countries in your eyes.*
> *Shrewd sun.*
> *The civil balance.*
> *The listening secrets.*
>
> *And you create and train your flowers still. (502)*

Similarly, "Whitney Young" expresses a unified black voice, this time expressed in the first person:

> *We*
> *Remark your bright survival over death.*
> *We share your long*
> *comprehension that there is exhilaration*
> *in watching something caught*
> *break free. (505)*

This rearrangement thus emphasizes Brooks's call for and expression of such insistent responses to the ongoing struggle against discrimination, and thus heightens the effects of Brooks's pronominal shifts in "The Near-Johannesburg Boy," which begins in the child's voice but shifts at the end to a plural, in the four lines beginning "we shall" (509). Finally, by ordering the poems in this way and cutting others—both those with a more personal focus, such as "Telephone Conversations" and "Shorthand Possible," as well as those addressing more general segments of the black population, such as "To a Proper Black Man" and the pair of poems in "Early Death"—Brooks emphasizes a closing call in *Blacks* for new, joint expressions. Thus "Infirm," and *Blacks* as a whole, ends:

> *Everybody here*
> *is infirm.*
> *Everybody here is infirm.*
> *Oh. Mend me. Mend me. Lord.*
>
> *Today I*
> *say to them*
> *say to them*
> *say to them, Lord:*
> *look! I am beautiful, beautiful with*
> *my wing that is wounded*
> *my eye that is bonded*
> *or my ear not funded*
> *or my walk all a-wobble.*
> *I'm enough to be beautiful.*
>
> *You are*
> *beautiful too. (512)*

This poem's artful inscription of a singular and, at the end, a potentially plural voice closes the volume by returning us to the title, Brooks's inclusive term for people around the world who have been identified as not "beautiful" because they are "black." By transferring agency from the poem's speaker to its audience, "Infirm," especially as the final poem in *Blacks*, enacts contextually and linguistically the mission of Brooks's career, especially in its post-*Mecca* years. The direct address hails into being an audience of beautiful readers, continuing Brooks's project of writing about the same communities in which her later work was produced and distributed, and of eventually widening that project to encompass new kinds of white readers as well. I focus on those revisionary efforts in my closing section, examining the production and contemporary reception of Brooks's last book of verse, *Children Coming Home.*

"BLACK IS AN OPEN UMBRELLA": TEXTUAL
BODIES IN *CHILDREN COMING HOME*

Children Coming Home ties together the thematic concerns stretching across Brooks's career, but also sends her work in a new direction, one echoed by the book's unique bibliographic format. Both linguistically and bibliographically, *Children Coming Home* is significantly different from the books Brooks published with Harper and Row, or from those she likely could have published with the New York firm. Just over 9 inches high and 7.5 inches wide, it exceeds most standard sizes. Its cover, with title and author embedded in the black-and-white marbling of an elementary school composition book, juxtaposes that bibliographic signifier with the book's twenty-one poems, all but one of which appear with a child's name in capital letters on the upper-right corner. By thus writing on behalf of and "as" the black Chicago children figured throughout, Brooks uses her third-period bibliographic blackness to give voice to a community that is often otherwise silent. Such envoicing is characteristic of Brooks's entire career, of course; the significant difference in this case derives from the production and distribution of this book within that community as well, rather than as a textual object to be exported to New York for production.[6]

The illustrations in Brooks's Broadside volume *Aloneness*, as I note earlier, respond directly to the *Bronzeville* drawings by insisting on portraits of "real" black children. The cover design for *Children Coming Home* takes this dynamic in a new direction: whereas the Bronzeville illustrations connect "universal" images to "special" content, and the *Aloneness* drawings mirror "local" content with "special" images, the *Children Coming Home* cover marries much more local and specific content with a universal design, for a child's composition notebook (see fig. 3). Adding the circumstances of textual production to the above analogy, we would see the external imposition of white illustrations onto Brooks's text by Harper with *Bronzeville*, a production consistent with both form and content in *Aloneness*, and a local production and content in *Children* that takes on a universal design. This is a subtle bibliographic indication, I will argue, of Brooks's attempt, as both author and publisher, to produce on both levels a book which grows out of its particular cultural context, but which can also lead broader audiences toward new ways of reading. The cover design is appropriate

Fig. 3. Front cover of Gwendolyn Brook's *Children Coming Home* (1991)

for both Brooks's local and universal audiences—and for her ultimate efforts to undo such divisions—as a composition notebook is the textual space in which children learn to fashion themselves as writers. For Brooks to take on this image in her final volume of verse, then, suggests the book's "educational" content, which revises accepted notions of home, blackness, and childhood, pointing toward a broader rewriting (or re-education) of both Brooks's local audience and readers outside of her Chicago community.

The cover design extends into the book's typesetting and organization, as each of the twenty-one poems appears in a typewritten font, with the last twenty poems organized by their child "authors," whose names appear neatly printed in the upper-right-hand corner, and an oversized page number at the bottom center of each page. Following a Mari Evans epigraph—"Speak the truth to the people"—is the poem "After School," then a list of the children's names followed by a table of contents organized by poem title. The usual problems with an anthology's falsely regularized field of print are especially evident here. To read "The Coora Flower" in Norton's American literature anthology (third edition, volume E), for example, is to read the poem in isolation not only from its original text, but also from its carefully constructed printed appearance. The Norton version does not connect "The Coora Flower" with Tinsel Marie, the name appearing with it in Brooks's book, shifts the underlined "coora" of the opening line to italics, and presents the poem within the same typographical field as the rest of the anthology, a visual dimension clearly resisted in the original book. While the Norton anthology does at least gesture toward Brooks's late career—its two post-1968 poems are "To the Diaspora," from the 1981 book of that title, and "The Coora Flower"—it presents these poems within a reading environment which obscures their bibliographic origins, and thus their full meanings. Reading "The Coora Flower" not as the first of twenty poetic portraits, not as identified with a particular child named Tinsel Marie, and not as a text which exhibits typographically the speaker's simple yet powerful expression of what "at least, is Real, and what I know," means reading the poem instead as an isolated example of Brooks's late work with the same linguistic and bibliographic features of the rest of her career.

Within *Children Coming Home*, "The Coora Flower" initiates the book's inscription, and then ultimate elision, of the geographical and cultural boundaries motivating the contrast between Tinsel Marie's "Real" home environment and the impossibly distant "mountains of Itty-go-luba Bésa." Several other poems present similar shifts between other worlds—of the blacks in Brazil, Nigeria, Ghana, Botswana, Tanzania, Kenya, Russia, Australia, Haiti, Soweto, Grenada, Cuba, Panama, Libya, England, Italy, and France in "I Am A Black" (Kojo); in the Middle East in "In the Persian Gulf" (Gladys); in the Supreme Court and Wall Street in "Our White Mother Says We Are Black But Not Very" (Fleur); and of Nigerian and Puerto Rican heritage in "Puzzlement" (Diego). These distant locales seem all the more so in comparison to the daily struggles—against drugs and domestic violence in "The Coora Flower" (Tinsel Marie); against white girls' "shameless eyes" in "White Girls Are Peculiar People" (Richardine); against an uncle's molestation in "Uncle Seagram" (Merle); and against drug dealers in "Song: White Powder" (Al).

At the same time, then, that *Children Coming Home* is a locally produced description of a local community, it also thematizes an audience beyond that community, transferring the geographical motifs of outside/inside to the book and its readers. This dynamic begins with "After School," the only poem not identified with a particular child speaker, but rather with Brooks herself. That poem begins:

> Not all of the children
> come home to cookies and cocoa.
> Some come to crack cocaine.
> Some come to be used in various manners.
> One will be shot on his way home to warmth, wit and wisdom. (n.p.)

These lines announce the stark differences between the home of Brooks's verse and those of privilege and security, where parents can easily imagine that "all of the children" enjoy the safety of cookies and cocoa, or at least allow themselves to forget about those returning home to crack and other dangers. *Children Coming Home* thus both gives voice to the unrepresented children of its title and compels its readers to rethink conventional, unquestioning notions of class, race, and home.

Rather than filtering this cultural lesson through a standard white-black divide, however, Brooks in this volume challenges as well accepted notions of blackness, especially in such poems as "I Am A Black" (Kojo), "Our White Mother Says We Are Black But Not Very" (Fleur), and "Puzzlement" (Diego). While Fleur struggles against an innate black identity which seems contradicted both by physical factors ("creamy skin" [13]) and socioeconomic distinctions (expensive lunchboxes, "the biggest house on our street" [13], and multilingual parents), Diego responds to Black Pride Day with his desire to be identified as a "TAN" (14) in response to his Nigerian and Puerto Rican heritage. Kojo, finally, reports that his teachers, by calling him an African American, "call me out of my name" (5). "BLACK is an open umbrella," this poem insists, opening to include people from all continents who are "other than Hyphenation." These ideas from "Kojo," of course, are in keeping with Brooks's own resistance to "African American" as a limiting cultural marker. By seeking to undo this racial economy in *Children Coming Home*–through subverting contradictory "white" and "black" identities, or expanding "black" to include "tan" and "African American" to include blacks from all countries— Brooks ultimately revises the text's sense of "home" at this broader level, just as the poems have already illustrated the false particularity of "home" as a space defined by cookies and cocoa.

Morrison similarly rewrites "standard" connections between race and home in her paper of that title, in which she asks "how to convert a racist house into a race-specific yet nonracist home. How to enunciate race while depriving it of its lethal cling?" ("Home" 5). Morrison delivered this lecture while at work on *Paradise*, a novel she describes as responding to the problem that "it is difficult to sign race while designing racelessness" (8), by evoking "contemporary searches and yearnings for social space that is psychically and physically safe" (10). Such a social (and textual) space develops in part in *Paradise* through Morrison's withholding of the single white identity among the nine principal characters, a device which prompts readers to acknowledge their conscious and unconscious tendencies to read for racial identity, while finally undoing and transcending those habits through the novel's refusal to engage in such systems of racial marking.

Brooks arrives at this conceptual destination from a different path in the last decades of her career, engaging "black" as a broad racial term, but one that still signs race rather than racelessness. By consistently adopting a broad notion of blackness, though, Brooks implies a similar expansion of whiteness and, indeed, of all racial categories, which she opens to include "tan" and any other mix of otherwise distinct racial categories and colors. Whereas Morrison, both in *Paradise* and in her earlier short story "Récitatif," maintains a racial binary in order to demonstrate the epistemological uncertainty that always confounds such strict racial categorization, Brooks, in much of her career and especially in *Children Coming Home*, opts out of a black-white system from within the sphere of blackness, transforming that previously singular and limiting designation into a marker of a range of racial backgrounds and identities. That *Children Coming Home* does not take the corresponding step of portraying "white" as a similarly expansive category is in part a function of the poems' focus on how the children see themselves. Unlike Morrison's inquiry into the reader's subjectivity—the effect of *Paradise* and "Récitatif" is to render whiteness and blackness as opaque, causing readers to reflect on the systems of racial marking that can no longer "see" race in these texts—Brooks's portraits of children compel her readers to inhabit those perspectives and, thus, to see through their eyes in a text that evinces linguistic and bibliographic blackness.[7]

This conceptual difference in Brooks and Morrison corresponds as well to their very different engagements with popular audiences. During the time that Brooks was opting out of the mainstream publishing industry, Morrison was working as an editor at Random House, serializing *Song of Solomon* in *Redbook*, providing her own narration for audiobook versions of her novels, and, most famously, participating in Oprah's Book Club. Morrison's first appearance on *Oprah* came five years after Brooks published *Children Coming Home* and represents the culmination of her opposite cultural strategy, to which I turn in chapter 4. Morrison's commercial alliance with Winfrey, I argue there, transforms both partners, bestowing a mantle of aesthetic complexity on a TV book club and enabling a serious dialogue between Winfrey's mass audience and Morrison's challenging narratives.

CHAPTER FOUR

TONI MORRISON, OPRAH WINFREY, AND POSTMODERN POPULAR AUDIENCES

In June 2003, Oprah Winfrey launched her television book club anew, with John Steinbeck's *East of Eden* as the first selection. Paperback copies of the fifty-one-year-old novel immediately appeared in bookstores nationwide (they had been held in sealed cartons until Winfrey's official announcement), with wrappers around the front cover declaring it "The Book That Brought Oprah's Book Club Back." The *Oprah Winfrey Show* also brought *East of Eden* back: by July it had risen to the second spot on *USA Today*'s best-seller list (above Hillary Rodham Clinton's memoir but below the latest installment in the Harry Potter series). Annual sales for *East of Eden* had been strong, at 40,000 to 50,000, for a lengthy and difficult novel, but 1.2 million copies were in print a month after Winfrey's selection ("Oprah Helps"). Following a fourteen-month book club hiatus, Winfrey had demonstrated once again her extraordinary success in literary marketing.

In this chapter I examine Oprah's Book Club as an antidote to the fundamental problem confronting Larsen, Brooks, Reed, Ellison, and all American minority writers before 1996, when Winfrey began her first book club. Over the next six years, every *Oprah* selection became a best-seller, with Winfrey's publishing power manifesting itself in reduced prices for *Oprah* books and numerous requests from editors and agents that Winfrey bestow her magic touch on their books. As a *New York Times* profile concluded, "Winfrey has taken considerable cultural authority away from publishers" (Max 40). I focus especially on the "Oprah effect" and Morrison, who after three appearances on Oprah's Book Club has become the most dramatic example of postmodernism's merger between canonicity and commercialism. I argue that the alliance between Morrison's canonical status and Winfrey's commercial power superseded the publishing industry's field of normative whiteness, enabling Morrison to reach a broad, popular audience while also being marketed as artistically important, in contrast to an established white male author like Thomas Pynchon, of whom Gates satirically observes, "Now there was someone you never saw on 'Oprah Winfrey'" (*Loose Canons* 15). By embracing Oprah's Book Club, Morrison replaces separate white and black readerships with a single, popular audience.

Before her first *Oprah* appearance in December 1996, Morrison was a Nobel and Pulitzer prize winner, held an endowed chair at Princeton University, and was one of the most respected voices in contemporary American literature. While Pierre Bourdieu's inverse equation between cultural and commercial capitals would make this aesthetic success dependent on a consequent lack of marketability, since aligning herself with Winfrey Morrison became the best-selling author of *Song of Solomon*, nineteen years after its first publication; of *Paradise*, probably the least accessible book she has yet written; of *The Bluest Eye*, Morrison's first novel; and, most recently, of *Sula* (2002).[1] In each case Morrison appeared on *Oprah* to discuss her novels with Winfrey and selected viewers, while stores sold the books with special Oprah's Book Club stickers and often in displays based more on Winfrey's appeal than Morrison's. While Morrison's books had long sold well, her *Oprah* connection propelled her into an altogether higher order of marketability. (Winfrey also devoted an episode to a discussion of the film version of *Beloved*, which she produced while playing Sethe.) Morrison's embrace of popular markets extends as well to the audiobook versions of her novels, which constitute another important merger of "high" art with "low" media.

In this chapter, I argue that for African American women writers in particular, the connection between high cultural forms and popular audiences is a crucial stage in their adaptation of authorship's public space. These writers, who have only very recently established themselves commercially, let alone canonically, engage in a complex interaction with the market and the canon. Television and audiobook audiences commodify Morrison's texts while also crediting her with a new kind of social authority. By constructing an audience built through popular, ostensibly low, culture for her serious novels, Morrison explodes the high-low divide that still holds for much of postmodern art. Morrison sells herself and her novels, like jazz, through popular media and thus constructs herself as a self-consciously commodified textual authority.

No doubt it is tempting to conclude that Morrison simply sells herself out by appearing on *Oprah*, reducing her sophisticated texts to the lowest common denominator of daytime TV discourse. To a certain extent, this expectation turns out to be true: Winfrey's discussion of *Song of Solomon*, for example, reads the characters within the rubric of previous *Oprah* programs. "It's about 10 OPRAH shows rolled into one book," Winfrey told her audience when announcing the selection ("Newborn" 23). In explaining one excerpt from the dinner with Morrison, Winfrey begins: "Many times, on this stage, we've talked to women on how low would you go for love, and what would you do to keep a man. Well, the character named Hagar needed to be on one of those shows" ("Behind the Scenes" 16). About the first fifth of the show focuses on Winfrey's dinner preparations; as she tells her TV audience, "If you're more into party planning than life lessons, you can get some great tips on planning a dinner party, too" (1–2). John Brenkman observes that the novel's political subtext develops through the narrative's conclusion in 1963, just before the national rise of black consciousness and the assassinations of Martin Luther King and Malcolm X. Despite Winfrey's efforts to promote African American writers and "to make even the most innocuous talk show programs racially conscious" (Masciarotte 109 n42), then, Milkman's extensive genealogical investigation does not enter the dinner discussion, and so the novel's analysis of black and white cultural heritages drops away.

Within this framework *Song of Solomon* loses its vital political subtext, as the book club's discussion ignores the critique of American racial history. But to read Morrison's novel *only* as a high-cultural text stained by a low-cultural medium risks identifying Winfrey's viewers *only* as the same kinds of women who have been traditionally figured as the target of popular culture. Citing the "positioning of women as avid consumer[s] of pulp" as a "paradigmatic" conception of the modernist high-low divide, Andreas Huyssen concludes that for postmodernism "it is primarily the visible and public presence of women artists in *high* art, as well as the emergence of new kinds of women performers and producers in mass culture, which makes the old gendering device obsolete" ("Mass Culture" 190, 205, original emphasis). Through her association with Winfrey, Morrison occupies both spheres, remaining visibly public as a producer of high art yet simultaneously discussing and marketing it through a mass cultural medium. Rather than writing off Winfrey's viewers as nothing more than dull housewives, Morrison builds her distinct form of textual authority precisely through this popular audience.

The controversy surrounding Winfrey's selection of Jonathan Franzen's *The Corrections* clearly arises from these same issues. Franzen initially explained his discomfort with the selection by saying, "I feel like I'm solidly in the high-art literary tradition. She's picked some good books, but she's picked enough schmaltzy, one-dimensional ones that I cringe" (quoted in "A Novelist"). I would certainly agree with Franzen that some books on the Oprah's Book Club list, including all three of Morrison's novels, display greater aesthetic complexity than her other selections, including *The Corrections*. But as Janice Radway notes, the cultural distinctions on which Franzen's comments rely constitute "a dismissal of women's engagement with literature, rather than recognizing that it's a particular and very vital way of making literature a part of daily life" ("A Novelist"). Elizabeth McHenry argues similarly that "those traditionalists who devalue popular culture and value canonical literature . . . are unwilling to realize that . . . Winfrey's use of the popular medium of television and her choice of reading selections, drawn from both popular literature and texts that are eligible for future canonization, complicates and challenges distinctions between elite and popular cultural forms and canonical and noncanonical literature in important ways" (314).[2]

Morrison's appearances on *Oprah* and her taped readings of her abridged novels constitute important changes in the textual horizon because they reconfigure the implied author-reader (or author-consumer) dynamic around a new construction of the popular audience's relation to textual authority. What Bornstein terms the "textual aura"—a text's material signifiers which "plac[e] the work in time and space" ("Yeats" 224)—changes significantly for Oprah's Book Club reprints, as these books' readers find the original textual auras written over by the new incarnations. The "Oprah" editions are thus less "authentic," in Benjamin's terms, than the first editions, but also more expressive of the postmodern turn toward reproductions or copies as the constitutive forms of popular culture. "Although Benjamin himself saw the aura as 'withering' in the age of mechanical reproduction," Bornstein explains, "we may revise Benjamin by emphasizing that, for literary works, original mechanical reproductions can create their own aura and that it is the earlier auras that wither under successive reproductions of the work, particularly if the 'work' is thought of as merely identical to the words" (224). The postmodern cultural market, Jameson contends, has centered on "consumption of the very process of consumption itself, above and beyond its content and the immediate commercial products" (*Postmodernism* 276). As I suggest below, a significant portion of the consumer response to Oprah's Book Club seems to be part of the larger phenomenon Jameson describes; that is, the experience of participating in this TV event accounts for the club's popularity at least as much as the books themselves. But it is also vital to recognize that Morrison's interaction with *Oprah* produces more than just another example of contemporary society's obsession with media events, as the actual experience of reading *Song of Solomon, Paradise,* or *The Bluest Eye* intersects with these texts' transformations into objects of TV discourse. In the end, Winfrey and Morrison both emphasize the experience of reading these books, not simply consuming them.

A senior editor at Random House when her own authorial career began, Morrison has always displayed a special awareness for her texts' material messages, beginning with the original dust jacket for *The Bluest Eye*, which consisted entirely of the novel's opening three paragraphs below a small line for title and author. (I refer to the paragraphs beginning "Quiet as it's kept" in *The Bluest Eye*, rather than the "Dick and Jane" section preceding them. Morrison also refers to these sentences as the book's beginning in her discussion of that sentence in "Unspeakable Things Unspoken" [20–23]). *The Black Book* (1974), which Morrison edited after publishing her second novel, *Sula*, enacts a striking disruption of the conventions of print and publishing, offering some excerpted material in fragments and cutting abruptly from one topic and one medium to another. While this project was "confined by a cover and limited to type," Morrison writes, it still became a "book with a difference" ("Rediscovering" 16). As Morrison explains in "Behind the Making of *The Black Book*," it "has no 'order,' no chapters, no major themes. But it does have coherence and sinew. It can be read or browsed through from the back forwards or from the middle out, either way" (88–89). Morrison also displayed an early interest in popular markets with the appearance of *Song of Solomon* as the "*Redbook* novel" in the magazine's September 1977 issue. Well known for its fiction offerings until being sold to Hearst Publications in 1982, *Redbook* presented a recognizably literate and feminist audience for Morrison's novel.[3] In charting the shifting relationships among Morrison, her publisher, and her readers, my primary bibliographic examples in this chapter will be the original cover for *The Bluest Eye*, the new cover design for the Oprah's Book Club edition of *Song of Solomon*, and *Song* and *Jazz* as audiobooks. These material texts chart Morrison's changing relationship with both the canon and the market.

WHAT WHITE PUBLISHERS HAVE PRINTED

While commentators on the "Oprah effect" tend to focus on Winfrey as a prime example of the immense power television celebrities wield in contemporary culture, I would contend, first, that it is equally important to understand her book club—and especially Morrison's appearances on it—within the historical spectrum of twentieth-century African American authorship and, second, that we can fully understand Morrison's contemporary situation only in contrast to that of her precursors. Hurston, reviewing her career in the 1950 essay "What White Publishers Won't Print," lamented that, as "the accredited representatives of the American people," publishers would only accept novels which perpetuate the unspoken premise that "all non Anglo-Saxons are uncomplicated stereotypes" (86). Viewed from the other side of the literary market, though, Oprah's Book Club joins a long line of African American literary societies, going back to the nineteenth century and to the Saturday Nighters in Washington, a group which included Jean Toomer and Georgia Douglas Johnson. As McHenry notes, the Saturday Nighters and similar groups worked against the waning (white) publishing interest in black literature during the 1930s (295).

While white modernists often figured themselves as uninterested in or opposed to market acceptance, there was no such choice to make on the other side of the racial divide. As Houston Baker explains, "any behavior that is designated 'modernist' for Afro-America is also, and by dint of adequate historical accounts, always, coextensively labeled popular, economic, and liberating" (*Modernism* 101). While this inverse connection between commercial appeal and aesthetic complexity remained in effect for African American literature well beyond the modernist period, the seeds of its undoing are apparent at the beginning of Morrison's career, with the relative popularity of Reed's first two experimental novels, for example. Throughout her career, and especially through Oprah's Book Club, Morrison continues to merge "popularity" and "difficulty" for a new brand of African American literature.

In addition to her responses to the historical problems of race and authorship, Morrison's public authorial status reflects and reacts against the twentieth-century history of women writers' relations to the market and the canon. While such male modernists as Joyce and Eliot could circulate stories of their disdain for consumers, masking their true desires for commercial success, such female modernists as Woolf more openly courted the economic power of sales. Woolf wrote articles for *Vogue* editor Dorothy Todd in the 1920s, but worried that this work would mark her as commercially corrupt, asking Vita Sackville-West, "Whats [*sic*] the objection to whoring after Todd? Better whore, I think, than honestly and timidly and coolly and respectably copulate with the Times Lit. Sup." (*Letters* 200). For Morrison, there is not the same question of "whoring after" Winfrey, because African American women writers have been historically excluded from both the market and the canon. But just as Woolf helped produce commercial success for such popular women writers as Vita Sackville-West through the Hogarth Press, Morrison at Random House ushered into print a new generation of African American women, including Gayl Jones and Toni Cade Bambara.[4]

This relationship among canon, market, and gender in the modernist period generally holds true, but there are significant counterexamples, such as H. D. As Lawrence Rainey points out, the financial backing H. D. received from Bryher (Winifred Ellerman) positioned her differently in relation to the coterie literary market in which Eliot, Joyce, and Pound engaged. Whereas the small-press edition represented in part, at least in the pre-Depression era, a way for authors to "exploit the limited demand for modernist literature, turning each book into an objet d'art that acquired potential investment value for collectors" (Rainey 154), for H. D. the private press was that and nothing more: the tiny print runs of her novels were aimed only at the individual coterie defined by Bryher, and so needed no investment value from a broader collector's market. While the extent to which H. D. could disconnect herself from the mechanics of the literary marketplace is certainly not typical, there are varying levels of economic freedom to consider. Gertrude Stein and Alice B. Toklas could afford to sell a Picasso painting in order to finance the self-published Plain Editions of selected Stein works in the 1930s, for example, and while the Hogarth Press was a key source of income for Virginia Woolf beginning in the late 1920s, she and Leonard could afford to launch a hand-press in the first place, more as an avocation than a profession. Such levels of economic freedom were largely unavailable to minority writers, however; witness Hughes's and Hurston's complex relationships with the white patron Charlotte Osgood Mason, for example.[5]

When *The Bluest Eye* appeared in 1970, the Second Black Renaissance was well under way. This period of marketability was beginning to wane in the mid-'70s, but, Gates observes, "the burgeoning sales of books by black women, for many of whom Morrison served as editor, began to reverse the trends that by 1975 had jeopardized the survival of black studies. Morrison's own novels, especially *Tar Baby* (1981), which led to a cover story in *Newsweek*, were pivotal in redefining the market for books in black studies" (*Canons*, 92–93). *Tar Baby* capitalized on the success of *Song of Solomon* (1977), which, after serialization in *Redbook*, won the National Book Critics Circle award and was the first black novel since *Native Son* in 1940 to become a Book-of-the-Month Club main selection.

Morrison's gradual entry into the public sphere of authorship occurred in part through her career as an editor, which, she says, "lessened my awe of the publishing industry" (quoted in Schappell 91). But during her eighteen years at Random House, Morrison never called herself an author, even though she published her first three novels during that time. "I think, at bottom, I simply was not prepared to do the adult thing, which in those days would be associated with the male thing, which was to say 'I'm a writer,'" Morrison explains. "I said, 'I'm a mother who writes' or 'I am an editor who writes.' The word 'writer' was hard for me to say because that's what you put on your income-tax form" (quoted in Dreifus 73). This equation of professionalization with male authorship signifies an important continuity between the modern and postmodern periods for female authors: publishing, even as more women have been employed within its ranks, remains a male cultural field, assigning authorship's economic and cultural status as a "male thing." While African

American men made some inroads into the authorial and canonical fields during the 1950s and '60s, women of color remained on the outside. At the start of her career, authorship was for Morrison "an intervention into terrain that you are not familiar with—where you have no provenance. At the time I certainly didn't personally know any other women writers who were successful; it looked very much like a male preserve" (quoted in Schappell 96–97). By the time Morrison left Random House in 1983, little had changed; she had become the first black woman to rise to senior editor in company history, but three years later there were no black women holding that position in any major house (Taylor-Guthrie 223; Berry 44). Morrison was also essentially alone among African American women writers in terms of market success at the time. As she noted in a 1981 interview: "When I publish Toni Cade Bambara, when I publish Gayl Jones, if they would do what my own books have done [in sales], then I would feel really fantastic about it. But the market can only receive one or two [black women writers]. Dealing with five Toni Morrisons would be problematic" (quoted in Taylor-Guthrie 133).

Finally, Morrison's decisions to change the closing word of *Beloved* (in the sentence "Certainly no clamor for a kiss") and to alter the title of *War* to *Paradise* speak to the continuing questions of power circulating between her and her editor and publisher. While Morrison clarifies in "Home" that the editor's objection "was simply that—not a command" (6), she adds that after agreeing to the revision, she is "now sorry that [she] made the change" (7). Morrison does not specify the original word which "kiss" replaced, except to explain, "I gave up a word that was racially charged and figuratively coherent for one that was only the latter, because my original last word was so clearly disjunctive, a sore thumb, a jarring note combining as it did two linguistically incompatible functions—except when signaling racial exoticism" (8). Leaving aside speculation on Morrison's original last word, it is important to note here that this editorial decision is inevitably racially inflected, as the word "kiss" can only be "figuratively coherent" *because* it is not "racially charged."

MORRISON ON *OPRAH*

It is against this historical background that we should consider Morrison's appearances on Oprah's Book Club as a register for the new cultural avenues

Winfrey has created for Morrison and other women writers of color. While the publishing industry has maintained a normative whiteness, Winfrey's book club created an enormous market for the kinds of books Winfrey wants to read, just as Morrison wrote *The Bluest Eye* because she could not find books like it to read. (In one version of this often-cited remark, Morrison explains, "I am not being facetious when I say I wrote *The Bluest Eye* in order to read it" [quoted in Taylor-Guthrie 89]). More than anything else, the original instantiation of Oprah's Book Club coalesced around a national audience of women readers, highlighting the often hidden gender and racial dynamics of popular literary culture. Noting the book club's preponderance of women writers and female protagonists, D. T. Max concludes, "The implication is this: we are women, and we are going to read about women" (37). Gates's satiric point (in my earlier quote) is that Pynchon, because of his famous reclusiveness and his established canonical status, would never betray his side in the culture wars by appearing on a daytime talk show. Indeed, when Winfrey launched her television book club, *Time* assured "purists, that dying literary breed," "Don't expect *Ulysses* or *Gravity's Rainbow* to show up anytime soon" (Gray, "Winfrey's Winners" 84). This remark reflects the extent to which high culture remains a white male preserve in the popular press, with Joyce and Pynchon too "pure" to be marketable on TV. Pynchon's refusal to wear the trappings of literary celebrity creates a Romantic aura for him: by distancing himself from all public discourse about himself or his work, Pynchon becomes an even greater, albeit more mysterious, celebrity than most authors manage in all their interviews and memoirs.[6] The result, as a literary agent noted in a *New York* profile, is "very big business" (Sales 63). Indeed, the very idea of Pynchon making any media appearances would negate his commercial image as a recluse. Farrar, Straus and Giroux's publicity director told *New York*: "I'm not interested in his high-school photo or if he shops at Zabar's. . . . It doesn't matter whether he's sexy or gives good sound bites, or can tell Oprah about his pain. There's such integrity to him and his work" (quoted in Sales 64).

This opposition between "integrity" and *Oprah* holds especially, I contend, for white male canonical authors. First, *Oprah*, like all daytime programs, is designed and marketed for a predominantly female audience. Second, the tradition of identifying authorship with isolated genius reflects a history of male authorship. The anonymity nineteenth-century women writers often found in pseudonyms, usually male, marks their anxiety about entering this public space. There is no sense of physical presence to connect with Pynchon, while for women writers the question of body remains a significant one. For African American women writers in particular, cultural anonymity is the default position; rather than choosing Pynchon's seclusion they must attain public identities in order to be recognized as authors. Interviews with Morrison frequently begin with a physical description, and her television appearances and audiobook readings further embody her as an author. A 1994 *New York Times Sunday Magazine* profile, for example, begins: "The woman breezing into a Princeton, N.J., restaurant in a brilliant silk caftan and with salt-and-pepper dreadlocks is Toni Morrison, 63, the Robert F. Goheen Professor in the Council of the Humanities at Princeton University and the 1993 Nobel Prize winner for literature. Heads turn as she moves to a table. Princetonians in khaki stare" (Dreifus 73). Morrison's consistent representations as an embodied author depict her in more direct, social contact with her readers, trading on her celebrity in a fashion that would be deemed unseemly for Pynchon's audience. The paperback cover for *Playing in the Dark* consists primarily of a photograph of Morrison holding a straw hat and gazing into the horizon to the left of the cover, a striking embodiment for a work of literary criticism. *New York*'s 1996 profile of Pynchon, which established that he was living in a fashionable New York City neighborhood with his wife and son, included only a photograph of Pynchon and child shot from behind; even this rupture of Pynchon's seclusion could not produce a frontal view of the author as isolated genius.[7]

In contrast, as I note below, the new Plume editions of Morrison's novels feature a back-cover photograph in which she looks directly at the reader/consumer. Morrison's visibility and accessibility extend also, of course, to her appearances on *Oprah*, first at Winfrey's Chicago apartment for a dinner party held to discuss *Song of Solomon* with a few selected viewers, then in her Princeton office to examine *Paradise* with Winfrey and a larger audience, and finally in a different office to talk about *The Bluest Eye* with Winfrey and four viewers. Morrison's physical presence changes accordingly in each program; for *Song* she sits at Winfrey's dinner table with the guests, while for *Paradise* she stands near her desk, in front of Winfrey and the rest of the audience, fielding questions and directing discussion as in a seminar. The *Bluest Eye* episode takes a middle approach, locating Morrison and Winfrey on their own chairs, while two pairs of viewers each share a couch.

The *Paradise* discussion in particular performs a striking reversal of the "death of the Author," which, as Nancy Miller argues, maintains a critical indifference to the differences of female authorship even as it should work in concert with feminist aims of decentering cultural traditions. "It is, after all, the Author anthologized and institutionalized who by his (canonical) presence excludes the less-known works of women and minority writers and who by his authority justifies the exclusion," Miller writes (104). While Barthes and Foucault declare the "Author" dead, this move "prematurely forecloses the question of agency for [women]" (Miller 106). A similar disjunction operates for male authors and the market: with access to the canon assumed, dismissals of the market as a site for cultural authority are easier to make. Morrison's efforts to construct herself as an author who participates equally in both high and popular cultures—"I would like my work to do two things," she has remarked, "be as demanding and sophisticated as I want it to be, and at the same time be accessible in a sort of emotional way to lots of people, like jazz" (quoted in Dreifus 75)—develops from a tradition of mutual exclusion out of which a commercial *and* canonical text appears a double dream deferred.

Morrison's open desire for the market—for there to be "such a thing as popular black women's literature ... Popular!" (Schappell 74)—directly opposes Pynchon's carefully guarded seclusion. By circulating her authorial image and her texts via Winfrey's book club, and by reading her abridged novels on tape, Morrison aims for the most popular audience for serious works of fiction. Through these kinds of promotional activities, Morrison does not so much reify the high-low cultural gap while seeking to bridge both sides of it as she denies the terms on which the dichotomy is grounded, finding no principled incongruence among *Oprah* viewers, audiobook consumers and readers of "demanding and sophisticated" fiction. Previewing her book-club dinner, Winfrey recalls: "I called up Toni Morrison and I said, 'Do people tell you they have to keep going over the words sometimes?' and she said, 'That, my dear, is called reading' " ("Newborn" 24). Morrison's response encourages a serious readerly reaction to her writing within a popular discourse. Since Winfrey plays the role of Morrison's reader for the *Oprah* viewer, Morrison speaks by extension to Winfrey's audience, embracing them as readers beyond a television format that does not allow time "to keep going over the words." This level of discourse is much more prominent for the *Oprah* discussion of *Paradise*. By teaching Winfrey's viewers her most difficult novel, Morrison continues her emphasis on reading as a sustained engagement with the text. "If it's worth writing, it's worth going back to," Morrison responds to the audience's pleas of confusion (quoted in Max 39). *Paradise* is Morrison's least accessible novel, a fact which several of Winfrey's viewers bemoaned on the show, but with Winfrey's help it became a number-one best-seller. (And this despite the fact that the *Paradise* discussion drew some of the lowest ratings for any book-club show [Max 39].) Winfrey thus commercializes Morrison's most "serious" novel, but does so within a rubric of reading, rather than simply buying, the text.

The level of Winfrey's commercial success has been, of course, the most astonishing feature of her book club. Winfrey's first selection, Jacquelyn Mitchard's *The Deep End of the Ocean*, went from a modest initial run of 68,000 copies to 750,000 copies in print by the time of the *Oprah* broadcast, with another 100,000 copies rushed to stores after *Deep End* rose to the top of the best-seller list (Feldman 31). Within a week of Winfrey's announcement that *Song of Solomon* would be the club's next selection, Morrison's nineteen-year-old novel had reached the top spot on *Publishers Weekly's* trade paperback best-seller list. Even in hardcover, *Song* sold more than 40,000 copies in less than a week, ten times the sales it had accumulated during the previous year (Maryles 22), and sales for Morrison's other books increased as well (Gray, "Paradise Found" 68). As Gayle Feldman commented in the *New York Times Book Review*: "The club has also made manifest that Ms. Winfrey is the most powerful book marketer in the United States. On a really good day, she sends more people to bookstores than the morning news programs, the other daytime shows, the evening magazines, radio shows, print reviews and feature articles rolled into one" (31).

Morrison's commercial alliance with Winfrey complicates what might otherwise be a straightforward commodification, for here Morrison sells herself through a television medium that is already inscribed with Winfrey's ownership of her own cultural product. Oprah's Book Club sells and controls the images of Winfrey herself, and of her club's authors, for both black and white consumers. Her surprising influence on book buyers, including consumers outside the established literary market, produced what *Publishers*

Weekly called the "Oprah Effect." The massive sales generated by Winfrey's selections have led publishers to court her as never before, and even to reprice their books following complaints from Winfrey's viewers. The hardcover *Song*, for example, went from $26 to $18.95 (Feldman 31), and the hardcover *Bluest Eye* from $25 to $15, with additional discounts available at many chain bookstores. "I go, 'This book should be $15, I be—do believe,' Winfrey said in announcing the selection. 'So it's $15 if you want the hardback—really cute, fits in the hand—just to make it more affordable for everybody'" ("Ashley Judd" 26). Winfrey also asked publishers to donate 500 copies of each book for the show's studio audience, as well as 10,000 to libraries (Max 40). As McHenry notes, Winfrey's "regular promotion of book drives has been instrumental to getting books into the hands of people who otherwise would not have easy access to them" (312). Morrison, through her connection with Winfrey, was thus able to remake her audiences for *Song*'s and *Bluest Eye*'s revivals, transmitting through the price reductions a bibliographical message of financial and social accessibility. Winfrey enjoys an indirect power over publishers' prices that Morrison could never hold. This level of influence changes the terms of the cultural exchange for the books selected for Winfrey's club; rather than selling black texts through white publishers, Morrison on *Oprah* benefits from Winfrey's market power and thus they both redraw the lines among art, commodity, publisher, and reader.

"In our brand-name culture, 'Oprah' *is* a brand name, something that publishing houses in America no longer are—if they ever were," Feldman writes: "Random House, Doubleday or Viking on a book's spine doesn't signify much. But Oprah signifies a lot" (31). Aside from the obvious distinction here between roughly similar publishing houses and a television entertainer's seal of approval, what exactly does "Oprah" signify? In Gloria-Jean Masciarotte's analysis, Winfrey crosses multiple cultural boundaries, including race, class, and body image (109 n42). Since Masciarotte's 1991 essay, Winfrey has increasingly constructed herself as a media celebrity, frequently devoting programs to new Hollywood films and popular television sitcoms, and in the process moving out of the conventional talk-show format emphasizing an equalizing conversation among guests, audience members, and callers.[8] Jameson's contention that postmodern "'culture' has become a product in its own right; [that] the market has become a substitute for itself and fully as much a commodity as any of the items it includes

within itself" (*Postmodernism* x), applies usefully to Winfrey's current status (and to my reading of it). As Feldman wryly notes of the "Oprah Effect"
on book sales, "perhaps the phenomenon is more about Ms. Winfrey than
about books" (31). But whereas in Jameson's account the textualization of
the market erases the work of art that would ordinarily lie beneath its commodity form, for Morrison's novels in Oprah's Book Club the conflation of
culture and commerce marks a necessary step in claiming both public spaces
of authorship for African American women.

The question remains, however, whether we should read Morrison's novels in this context as more about Winfrey than about Morrison. "You have to
buy the book—not from me, on your own," Winfrey tells her audience when
announcing the *Song* selection: "Don't send me a check, please don't send
me your credit card numbers. The book is available in hardcover and as well
as in paperback. We called the bookstores early so they'd all be stocked up for
you" ("Newborn" 24). Winfrey's clarification that she is not selling the book
is true only in the narrowest sense; her announcement is structured to create
an immediate consumer desire for a book she figures as already in such
demand that Winfrey's staff has alerted the bookstores in advance. " 'Even
before the Book Club, people would come in and say Oprah had this author
or that author on her show," a bookseller told *Publishers Weekly*. "It is as if
they mean, 'My friend Oprah recommended this' " (Kinsella 278). The greatest desire in buying membership in Oprah's Book Club is thus to feel a personal connection to Winfrey. Winfrey has now reached the level of celebrity,
that is, at which she no longer needs to market herself specifically as a talk-
show host conscious of race and gender issues, as an interviewer of movie
and television stars, as a fitness spokesperson, as a new-age guru, or in any
other single capacity; she sells herself simply as Oprah, with the brand-name
recognition achieved by the most famous commodities and celebrities. For
such writers as Mitchard, appearing on *Oprah* confers celebrity status because
Winfrey has deemed her novel worthy of discussion on her show. The same
exchange is in effect for Morrison, but her appearance on *Oprah* adds her
own cultural capital to Winfrey's book club, elevating it to a more serious
level while also marketing *Song of Solomon*, *Paradise*, and *The Bluest Eye* to
previously untapped and unimaginable audiences. The terms of Winfrey's
marketing changed significantly for *Paradise*, which, unlike *Song of Solomon*,
was a new novel at the time of its selection for the show. While the Oprah

effect had previously boosted sales for novels already in circulation, Winfrey was now in the position of advertising a new literary product, attesting anew to her commercial influence within the publishing world and also, of course, continuing the indirect promotion of *Beloved*, the movie.

JUDGING A BOOK BY ITS COVER

As Oprah's Book Club returns its members to Morrison's early career through discussions of *Song of Solomon* and *The Bluest Eye*, it also highlights the significant differences between contemporary African American writers and their precursors from the late 1960s and early '70s. In this section I compare the bibliographic codes for *Song of Solomon* and *Bluest Eye* in their earlier and *Oprah* editions, drawing on this material evidence to illustrate the different configurations of author and audience in each period.

For *Song of Solomon*, the most significant bibliographic differences develop between two nearly simultaneous editions: *Song* in Plume's paperback reprint series and in its *Oprah* edition (both are listed as the thirtieth printing of Plume's 1987 edition). The *Song* cover already had been redesigned before its selection for *Oprah*. According to Melissa Jacoby, Plume's art director and the cover designer for both editions of *Song*, Plume had planned new covers for all the Morrison titles on its backlist "so that they would look sort of like a series" and "to reassure the author that her contribution to the imprint is considered valuable and worth the extra attention of repackaging and reissuing."[9] Apart from its special significance as an *Oprah* book, then, this edition of *Song* also marks itself as part of a series of Morrison titles, commodifying *Song* in relation to Morrison's general popularity and reputation. By redesigning its Morrison backlist to appear as a set, Plume encourages its consumers to purchase the entire "Morrison collection."

The bibliographic codes emanating from the *Oprah* cover, in contrast to the earlier Plume reprint, emit an even stronger image of Morrison as a celebrity commodity, so I will analyze them here at some length.[10] On the earlier Plume paperback the cover art—a drawing of an African American man before a blazing sun—dominates. Morrison's name and the title appear in equal-sized gold type, above and below a small band reading "WINNER OF THE NOBEL PRIZE IN LITERATURE." The *Oprah* edition reduces the drawing to a small square in the center of the cover, again with Morrison's name above and the title below, but

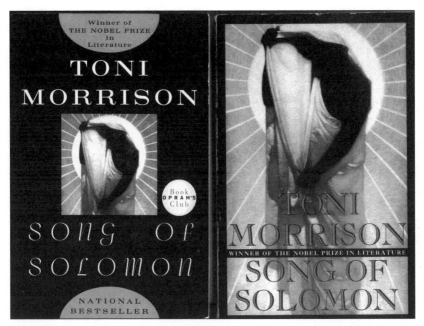

Fig. 4. Plume paperback front covers for Toni Morrison's *Song of Solomon* (Oprah's Book Club edition on left)

now with "TONI MORRISON" in plain type and the title italicized. Yellow semi-circles hang from the black cover at the top and bottom, reading "Winner of/ THE NOBEL PRIZE/in/Literature" and "NATIONAL/BEST-SELLER." To the right of the illustration is the book club stamp, superimposed over the symbol for Winfrey's show, an "O" bordering the inside of a circle (see fig. 4). This cover is designed to draw the eye's attention immediately to the center: both semi-circles point toward the illustration in the middle of the cover, with the author's name and title also in balancing positions. There, in a highly accessible position as the only object not in symmetry with the rest of the design, is the book club seal, guaranteeing this text's commodity status. *Song of Solomon* already exists as a book by the Nobel prize winner and as a best-seller (although in this incarnation the tag may refer to the sales of the reprint itself); this edition's most significant textual message is Morrison's alignment with Winfrey. By reducing the size of the original cover art, the *Oprah* cover sends the message that the book itself is less important (or marketable) than its selection for the book club. Rather than reflecting the narrative inside the book, the *Oprah* cover advertises the success of the book itself—again, a shift

Fig. 5. Plume paperback rear covers for Toni Morrison's *Song of Solomon* (Oprah's Book Club edition on left)

from a commodity *in* the market to the market *as* commodity. The title's new font further reflects this dynamic: the author's name and title in gold type blend into the yellow background and receive equal weight on the earlier Plume cover, while the title's serif type on the *Oprah* edition makes "TONI MORRISON" a more heavily grounded element and the white lettering pushes the words out from the black background. When you are buying Toni Morrison, Nobel prize winner and *Oprah* guest, the reprint cover suggests, which particular book you select is less important than your purchase of Morrison's new cultural status, as the *Oprah* logo acts as a kind of seal of approval.

The Plume back covers for *Song of Solomon* continue the shift from Morrison as writer to Morrison as commodity. Both are black fields, with blurbs, Morrison's name, and a colored band bearing the legend "Winner of the Nobel Prize in Literature," along with the usual publishing and ISBN information (see fig. 5). The earlier Plume cover prints this band in lavender and Morrison's name in outlined capital type, allowing this text to blend easily into the black background. A small black-and-white photograph of

Morrison adorns the center left, situated so that Morrison looks away from the rest of the cover. The *Oprah* edition includes a color photograph of Morrison at the top and center, with Morrison looking straight ahead. This angle circumscribes the consumer in her gaze, in contrast to the profile shot. Yellow bands run across the top and bottom of the second photo, reading "Winner of THE NOBEL PRIZE in Literature" and "TONI MORRISON." The capitalization reduces the top inscription to its barest signification, equating Morrison's name directly with her prize. With Morrison's name beneath her face and the black background, this photo looks strikingly like a television image. As Alexander Nehamas notes, television's frequent use of close-ups, coupled with the small size of the screen, creates an important feeling of physical closeness between television viewer and object (173). By recalling this physical connection, the *Oprah* author photo engages the consumer/reader in another purchase of Morrison herself as commodity, repeating the experience of individual familiarity on which Winfrey's talk-show empire depends.

While *Song of Solomon* in its *Oprah* edition thus comments on Morrison's multi-layered commodification, the *Oprah* cover for *Bluest Eye* demonstrates how far removed Morrison was from such cultural centrality when the novel first appeared in 1970. The first edition's front jacket simply lists title and author in type the same size as the rest of the jacket copy (see fig. 6). As an unknown author in 1970, Morrison was not marketable herself. So her first novel transfers its strongest selling point, a haunting story, onto the front jacket, where it advertises the novel's narrative power by quoting the book itself. There is no difference between the book's inside and outside, in other words, because Morrison in this edition exists as an author only through this book's words.

But this conflation of textual inside and outside also carries a political significance, which Morrison describes in "Unspeakable Things Unspoken," her Tanner Lecture on Human Values, as an attempt to produce a novel that "would not theatricalize itself, would not erect a proscenium" between book and reader (20). As the opening sentence's gossipy tone suggests, this story represents "the public exposure of a private confidence" (20), and making the story public becomes a political as well as literary act. This tension between private and public slides easily into James Weldon Johnson's tension between black and white audiences, especially in the back jacket's description: "This is a love story—except there isn't much love in

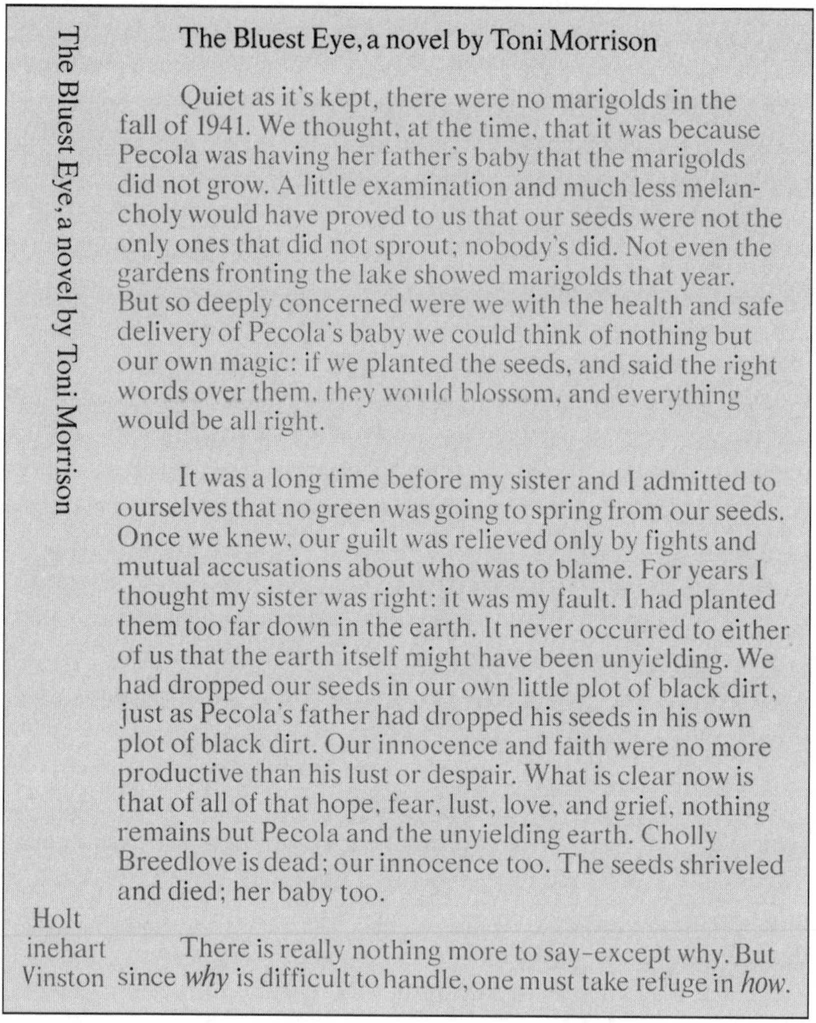

The Bluest Eye, a novel by Toni Morrison

Quiet as it's kept, there were no marigolds in the fall of 1941. We thought, at the time, that it was because Pecola was having her father's baby that the marigolds did not grow. A little examination and much less melancholy would have proved to us that our seeds were not the only ones that did not sprout; nobody's did. Not even the gardens fronting the lake showed marigolds that year. But so deeply concerned were we with the health and safe delivery of Pecola's baby we could think of nothing but our own magic: if we planted the seeds, and said the right words over them, they would blossom, and everything would be all right.

It was a long time before my sister and I admitted to ourselves that no green was going to spring from our seeds. Once we knew, our guilt was relieved only by fights and mutual accusations about who was to blame. For years I thought my sister was right: it was my fault. I had planted them too far down in the earth. It never occurred to either of us that the earth itself might have been unyielding. We had dropped our seeds in our own little plot of black dirt, just as Pecola's father had dropped his seeds in his own plot of black dirt. Our innocence and faith were no more productive than his lust or despair. What is clear now is that of all of that hope, fear, lust, love, and grief, nothing remains but Pecola and the unyielding earth. Cholly Breedlove is dead; our innocence too. The seeds shriveled and died; her baby too.

Holt inehart Vinston

There is really nothing more to say—except why. But since *why* is difficult to handle, one must take refuge in *how*.

Fig. 6. Front jacket cover for Toni Morrison's *The Bluest Eye*, first edition (1970)

it.... It's also a fairy tale—except only the fondest nightmares come true.... It's a murder story—except the victim lives.... It's not only a black story, it's a very very dark one." This self-conscious play between a "black story" and a "dark one," within the jacket copy's broader subversion of expected narrative categories, implicitly addresses the question of what it means to read a "black story" in 1970. During the New Negro Renaissance, a "black story" was by definition a "dark one," bearing in mind Hurston's analysis of the white publishing industry, but for the Second Renaissance a "black story" was no longer necessarily "dark." Morrison explains: "One needs to think of the immediate political climate in which the writing took place, 1965–1969, during great social upheaval in the life of black people. The publication (as opposed to the writing) involved the exposure; the writing was the disclosure of secrets, secrets 'we' shared and those withheld from us by ourselves and by the world outside the community" ("Unspeakable" 20–21). Just as the civil rights movement made possible the disclosure of such secrets, *The Bluest Eye*'s jacket remarks on the double audience for this first novel, those readers who are either inside or outside Morrison's community. Inside the novel, the "Dick and Jane" sentences, run together as one long, nearly unreadable string, remind Morrison's audience (especially her white readers) of the unspoken but universalizing assumptions attached to this elementary school image.

As an Oprah's Book Club selection by a now world-famous author, *The Bluest Eye* transmits an entirely different set of bibliographic messages. The front jacket for Knopf's hardcover *Oprah* edition features Consuelo Kanaga's black-and-white photograph of a black Caribbean girl alongside the Oprah's Book Club logo,[11] while the back jacket carries a photograph of Morrison above a *New York Times* blurb (see fig. 7). The Oprah's Book Club logo adds one more reason to buy this novel by a Nobel prize winner. In contrast to the original edition, where only the story's power motivates its consumers and readers, this edition capitalizes on Morrison's celebrity and achievement to remarket her first novel to the millions of readers who have discovered her, through *Oprah* or independently, since 1970.

Similarly, the politics of reading *Bluest Eye* shift dramatically from the jacket description in the original and *Oprah* editions. What was a "black" and "dark" story in the first edition becomes, in the *Times* blurb, "an inquiry into the reasons why beauty gets wasted in this country. The beauty in this case is black." Here the same descriptive structure shifts from the original description of *Bluest Eye* as a "black" story that is also "dark" to a mainstream review focusing on "beauty" which "in this case is black." Johnson's double audience still pertains to the 1970 *Bluest Eye*, as black and white readers approach differently the matter of reading a black story, but the Knopf and *Oprah* readers are figured in the *Times* blurb as a single audience

Fig. 7. Front jacket cover for Toni Morrison's *The Bluest Eye,*
Oprah's Book Club edition

interested in beauty, no matter its color. What the inside jacket calls a "new"
afterword (though dated 1993) also speaks to the significant bibliographic
changes, as Morrison concludes: "With very few exceptions, the initial publication of *The Bluest Eye* was like Pecola's life: dismissed, trivialized, misread.
And it has taken twenty-five years to gain for her the respectful publication
this is" (216). Transferred from one hardcover reprint to another, Morrison's reference to "the respectful publication this is" speaks implicitly to the
difficulty of such publication for African American authors in 1970 or,
indeed, for much of Morrison's career. Similarly, Winfrey tells her studio
audience that when she stopped in an airport bookstore and saw bookshelf
rows full of *The Bluest Eye,* "my eyes started to water, because I thought,
'Pecola has her day.'" Interestingly, Winfrey here figures perhaps the most
commercial of popular audiences, airport travelers, as part of Morrison's
new audience. While the original *Bluest Eye* cover represents Morrison's

entry into the public space of authorship as both an exposure of secret knowledge and as an expression of the progress made since Hurston's career, when such exposure would have been impossible, the Oprah's Book Club jacket design and afterword remark on Morrison's self-conscious journey to a mainstream presence within both the market and the canon.

Similarly, the use of Kanaga's photograph "School Girl" on the cover reconfigures that image for *Bluest Eye*'s new audience. A white photographer whose nearly seventy-year career was largely forgotten until a 1992 Brooklyn Museum retrospective, Kanaga "painted with light to portray African Americans as people of beauty, inner strength, and unassailable dignity" (Millstein and Lowe 35). By appropriating Kanaga's photograph, the new *Bluest Eye* cover comments on Morrison's ascendancy to a position of cultural power, as she uses her greater fame and marketability to recover an obscure photographer for her broad audience.

In announcing her selection of *The Bluest Eye* for the book club, Winfrey also aims at a single audience—only now a singularly white audience. "I'm telling you, I took this book on vacation with me just a—about a month ago," Winfrey recalls. "I had all of my girlfriends—who happen to be white because Gayle couldn't make it—sitting around the pool—sitting around the pool. I had all these white girls crying over 'The Bluest Eye,' asking me if this is what life was really like as a colored child" ("Ashley Judd" 25). Without Gayle King, Winfrey's best friend and a frequent guest for *Oprah* discussions (including the *Paradise* program), Winfrey becomes the point of entry for white readers into the experiences of a "colored child."[12] Promoting *Bluest Eye* in these terms represents a striking departure from the effect of *Paradise*, Winfrey's previous Morrison selection. *Paradise*'s now famous opening line, "They shoot the white girl first," launches a textual mystery that, never resolved in any identification of the single white character, reverses the tradition of establishing a character's whiteness by not remarking on it at all. Published by Knopf and made a number-one best-seller by Oprah's Book Club, *Paradise* compels all its readers to reconsider the social dynamics that have defined how we read whiteness and blackness. Not knowing which of the main characters is white, readers cannot approach *Paradise* with the usual, though often unconscious, racial associations.

While the epitome of a "single audience," in these terms, *Paradise* generated some of the lowest ratings for any *Oprah* book, and for *Bluest Eye*

Winfrey makes sure to emphasize the text's accessibility. Recognizing that "a lot of people" found *Paradise* "difficult," Winfrey reassures her audience that *Bluest Eye* is the "shortest" and "the simplest of [Morrison's] books" ("Ashley Judd" 25, 26). This description sounds exactly like what one would expect of a televised book promotion, but it still leaves room to reconfigure audience expectations once *Oprah* viewers become Morrison readers. Winfrey's rhetoric plays into the novel's own subversion of "easy" and "difficult" narratives, what Morrison has called a "simplicity [that] was not simple-minded, but devious, even loaded" ("Unspeakable" 20). The experience of reading *Bluest Eye* rests on reacting against its *seeming* simplicity, as in the text's opening jumble of the "Dick and Jane" sentence. In promoting Morrison's first novel as her "simplest," then, Winfrey uses a marketing rhetoric that transfers the novel's internal guise of accessibility onto a television audience who will presumably find the book emotionally and intellectually powerful despite their initial expectations. (Winfrey exults after announcing the selection, "If you don't like this book, then I don't have nothing else to say to you. You will like this book. OK? I love this book" ["Ashley Judd" 25].) Winfrey previews a more thoughtful reaction as well, noting that *Bluest Eye* frequently appears on literature curricula and seeking responses from English classes. "You cannot read 'The Bluest Eye' without having it touch your soul," Winfrey concludes. "If it doesn't, then I don't know who you are" (26). The balance between audience accessibility and cultural significance, or between selling and reading, is never easy to maintain for Morrison on Oprah's Book Club. If the book club *Bluest Eye* risks sacrificing the intellectual engagement required by *Paradise* for the sales promised by Morrison's shortest and simplest novel, it also still encourages Winfrey's vast audience to continue reading Morrison, for and beyond *Oprah*.[13]

HOW TO READ (?) A BOOK ON TAPE

"If you ever want to hear something powerful," Winfrey tells her viewers during the *Song of Solomon* dinner, "it's [Morrison] reading the book. She had us crying for mercy" ("Behind" 11). Shifting from *Oprah* editions to books on tape, we find related but distinct ways of merging high and popular cultural audiences. Morrison's audiobooks, I will argue, complete her response to the problem of the double audience by commodifying an African American authorial voice within texts which themselves place a black oral tradition alongside their narrative representations of race in America.

Hearing Morrison read her work aloud activates the same commodified desire that operates for Winfrey's book club: consumers buy a sense of connection to Winfrey just as they purchase Morrison's voice, a much more direct representation of the author, it would seem, than the printed novel. Sarah Kozloff finds that " 'envoicing' the narrator creates a sense of connection stronger than reading impersonal printed pages: the communicative paradigm—storyteller to listener—that underlies printed texts has again become flesh" (92).[14] Not quite flesh, of course, and, in fact, it seems more accurate to consider the book on tape's mechanical reproduction of the voice as recalling an oral culture while also displacing that culture's aura, in Benjamin's terms. While in Kozloff's analysis audiobooks function as part of what Walter J. Ong calls secondary orality, in which oral texts derive from written origins or forms (as with television and radio programs), I would argue that Morrison's audiobooks, at least, are not just derivative versions but are, in fact, importantly *new* textual forms. Morrison "authors" these texts by reading them aloud, rather than letting someone else perform this task for her, and in so doing she constitutes *Song of Solomon* or *Jazz* on tape as a new version of the existing work. The textual aura, in Bornstein's terms, withers here, as the audiobook displaces the original edition's historical context, but this loss becomes less important than the textual auras created by the books on tape as "new" authorial productions. In this section I focus on the audiobook versions of *Song of Solomon* and *Jazz*, for in these novels we see Morrison's most powerful incorporation of the African American oral tradition. The popular audience engaged by these audiobooks includes consumers who might not ordinarily read or purchase Morrison's novels, as well as those listeners already familiar with the print versions but interested in hearing Morrison reading.

Before turning to specific examples, I will first address the general question of how to locate the book on tape within the field of textual interpretation. Ong's prediction in 1977 that "in the foreseeable future there will be more books than ever before but . . . books will no longer be what books used to be" (*Interfaces* 83) certainly did not foresee the audiobook specifically, but it does anticipate the kinds of radical changes the book has undergone in the last decade. Audiobooks are now an established part of the contemporary publishing industry, alongside movie novelizations, corporately owned publishing houses, hypertext fiction, and, most recently, books "published" electronically by such successful writers as Stephen King and Tom Wolfe, and thus represent a distinct medium that changes the public nature and reception of the text.

Books on tape look like books, not tapes. Most packages contain two tapes within a box about the size of a book,[15] arranged on bookstore shelves with the spine displaying the author and title. Priced on average at $17, Morrison's audiobooks cost as much as, if not more than, their print cousins.[16] These products thus imagine a consumer desire for a product of technological convenience packaged to recall its high cultural sources, yielding the image of a customer who is not too *lazy* to read important literature but too *busy* to read print texts.

The audiobook's reconfiguration of author/reader to reader (aloud)/listener creates a complex series of revisions for the ways we normally understand authors. The voice of the author shifts from an internalized, imagined voice in the reader's mind to an actual, or at least recorded, presence delivering an oral text. Read by the author, a Morrison audiobook presents a disembodied author: Toni Morrison, Nobel prize winner, reads her novel to you as you drive to work or sweep around the house. Paradoxically, the audiobook establishes a greater sense of intimacy between audience and author, even while the experience of the text is in some ways less immediate. Authors like Morrison who read their own works on tape are relatively rare; more often actors, both famous and unknown, deliver these performances. Morrison's audiobooks thus literalize the African American trope of the "talking book," enlivening a narrative metaphor through direct contact with the author, or at least with the author's recorded voice.[17] This tradition began, Gates speculates in *The Signifying Monkey*, because "[b]lack people . . . had to represent themselves as 'speaking subjects' before they could even begin to destroy their status as objects, as commodities, within Western culture" (129). In the postmodern era, African American literature has now developed enough of a heritage for authors to adapt their commodified status as speaking and selling subjects. While an initial response might judge audiobooks to be a diluted, popular version of the novels on which they are based, for African American books on tape the terms of commodification work differently. In representing and selling herself as a "speaking subject," Morrison avoids the usual cultural positions of authorship: neither a genius recluse nor a producer of stereotypical black stories, Morrison adapts the African American oral tradition in her narratives and extrapolates that heritage onto her audiobooks.

Morrison's audiobooks commodify her voice in a way that recalls yet departs from the complete commodification of the slave's body, while also invoking a storyteller figure, in accordance with Morrison's desire for her reader "to respond on the same plane as an illiterate or preliterate" audience (quoted in Middleton 24). The power to sell oneself, either through books, television, or on tape, represents a unique opportunity in the history of African American women's writing. In her analysis of the "female authorial voice" in cinema, Kaja Silverman insists, "Once the author-as-individual-person has given way to the author-as-body-of-the-text, the crucial project with respect to the female voice is to find a place from which it can speak and be heard, not to strip it of discursive rights" (192). Morrison's voice on tape becomes an even more literal body of the text than many of Silverman's examples: in this medium, Morrison no longer disseminates just her words but also her performance of her writing, representing herself directly to the audience as a physical (if recorded) presence. The book on tape thus addresses the feminist problem of what to do with real writers and readers in the wake of poststructuralism's dissipation of author and subject: hearing Morrison read her novels returns us to a version of immediate presence in the author-reader exchange.

Song of Solomon is an especially appropriate text through which to consider the relationship between commerce and culture, as Milkman Dead similarly shifts the object of his quest from buried gold to the suppressed histories of his family and culture. As a book on tape, *Song of Solomon* also activates the oral nature of Milkman's family narrative as a dismantling of written traditions.[18] Toward the end of his journey, Milkman reflects on such hidden American histories: "He read the road signs with interest now, wondering what lay beneath the names. The Algonquins had named the territory he lived in Great Water, *michi ganni*. How many dead lives and fading memories were buried in and beneath the names of the places in this country. Under the recorded names were other names, just as 'Macon Dead,' recorded for all time in some dusty file, hid from view the real names of people, places, and things.

Names that had meaning" (329). By the end of the novel, the white erasure of names and meaning from Indian and African history supersedes Milkman's naive search for Pilate's mysterious cache of gold. In its secondary textual forms as talk-show topic and audiobook, *Song of Solomon* becomes a more "postmodern" text by expressing the narrative's debates between profit and purity within media that are themselves designed to create auxiliary profits for the publishing industry.[19] Even as the novel's linguistic text supplants gold with history, that is, its new bibliographical codes mark its commercial existence as a new and significant meaning.

Oral history organizes the narrative quest, as the family and cultural history Milkman traces consists of remembered stories, children's songs, and misheard names. The original *Song of Solomon* itself consists of alternating male and female poetic voices, a device recalled in the tape's use of a male narrator's voice to signal an abridgment (the male voice delivers the first sentence or two of the next passage before Morrison resumes reading). Performed orally, *Song* asks its listeners to pursue narrative memories as in an oral culture. The different versions of the word "Solomon," for instance— first it appears in a song as "Sugarman," then as a Virginia town named "Shalimar," and finally again in a children's song as "Solomon," the most common surname in Shalimar—form a developing memory in the print version that a reader can check by returning to an earlier page. But as Ong notes of primary oral cultures, "In the total absence of any writing, there is nothing outside the thinker, no text, to enable him or her to produce the same line of thought again or even to verify whether he or she has done so or not" (*Orality* 34). A listener to the *Song* audiobook is not exactly in this position; the listener could rewind the tape if necessary or even check an oral memory against the printed text. But Milkman's gradual realization of his nominal heritage activates a powerfully similar oral awareness in the listener who has not rewound the tape or referenced the original novel. While the traditional view of history equates progress with the shift from an oral to a written culture, Morrison's novels, especially as audiobooks, complicate this picture by emphasizing an oral heritage.

Jazz takes the talking book a step further through an unnamed first-person narrator. In the foreword to the 2004 Vintage paperback, Morrison explains that while drafting the novel she was "playing, just playing with the voice, not even considering who the 'I' was until it seemed natural, inevitable, that the narrator could—would—parallel and launch the process of invention, of improvisation, of change" (xix). In the closing paragraphs, this anonymous speaker finally becomes the book itself:[20]

I envy them their public love. I myself have only known it in secret, shared it in secret and longed, aw longed to show it—to be able to say out loud what they have no need to say at all. *That I have loved only you, surrendered my whole self reckless to you and nobody else. That I want you to love me back and show it to me. That I love the way you hold me, how close you let me be to you. I like your fingers on and on, lifting, turning. I have watched your face for a long time now, and missed your eyes when you went away from me. Talking to you and hearing you answer—that's the kick.*

But I can't say that aloud; I can't tell anyone that I have been waiting for this all my life and that being chosen to wait is the reason I can. If I were able I'd say it. Say make me, remake me. You are free to do it and I am free to let you because look, look. Look where your hands are. Now. (229, original emphasis)

Where "your hands are. Now" is holding the book that ends with these words, at least in the printed text. As a book on tape, *Jazz* recalls its original scene of writing but also revises the impact of this conclusion. Whereas the tactile interaction of reader and book dominates this passage in print— especially through the descriptions of the reader's hand and fingers holding and turning the pages—as a spoken text *Jazz* re-emphasizes such sentences as "Talking to you and hearing you answer—that's the kick." What the book cannot say aloud the book on tape can: while "where your hands are" is no longer in direct contact with the material text, that text now allows for a spoken delivery from author to reader, or at least the simulation of one. In this sense the audiobook narrator is less clearly the book itself; with Morrison reading these passages the lines between book and author are re-blurred. Morrison as the voice of the audiobook narrator *can* "say that aloud," compelling the listener—not the reader—to "remake" the text in new ways. This audiobook's textual aura thus recalls its original context while also creating its own aura, in which Morrison's audience hears the author/narrator/book self-consciously speaking aloud to them in ways that original versions of the "talking book" never could.

This new form of the talking book also has significant feminist implications for Morrison as an author. In keeping with the American feminist goal of retaining some form of the authorial self, Morrison re-emphasizes her presence in the text while constructing an essential element of her authority through audiences that would ordinarily be dismissed as too low on the cultural scale to make an interpretive difference. The difference they do make for Morrison is in her image of cultural authority, which grounds itself, like jazz, as a sophisticated discourse aimed at both a specialized and popular audience. In contrast, it is almost impossible to imagine Pynchon reading his books on tape because he has so deliberately set himself apart from the mechanics of the market—and could afford to do so, I have been arguing, due in no small part to differences of gender and race. The book on tape is packaged to recall its print antecedent, but its new author-audience structure sells the audiobook as a direct representation of authorship which is inaccessible to the print experience. The audiobook's commodity status complicates this theoretical shift, especially when we note that Morrison usually reads abridged versions of her novels, in response to the marketing assumption that not enough consumers would buy a longer, more expensive, but complete edition. Morrison may seem again to sacrifice artistic integrity for commercial success, but even in an abridged form the audiobook performs the arguably more important function of actualizing the oral backgrounds of Morrison's novels, which most critics agree are vital to any interpretation of *Song of Solomon*, for example. Additionally, as the appearance of a much more abridged *Song of Solomon* in *Redbook* indicates, Morrison has long privileged access to a broader audience over textual "integrity." In these ways, the commodification of Morrison's novels as audiobooks is a commercialization of the African American oral tradition and cultural history they recall.

Madhu Dubey presents a similar reading of the *Jazz* narrator in terms of the tension between urban and folk African American traditions, observing that "the novel ironically thematizes its own seduction by urban modes of vision" (138). While Dubey finds that the "concluding paragraphs of *Jazz* are remarkable for the intensity of their desire to draw sensuous use values from the conditions of commodity consumption that determine the act of reading," she concludes that the book's "visual format as well as its commodity status prohibit an unmediated oral connection" (141, 142). Dubey considers *Jazz* only in its print form, and so does not "read" the more directly oral version of the audiobook. There the text operates even more overtly as an object of commodity consumption, as effectively an oral "copy" of the original printed book. Yet because the book's "incapacity to speak" (Dubey 142) is figured in the audiobook *as* speech, that version's relationship to commodity culture does more complexly negotiate between a "lost" oral tradition and the consumerism that has contributed to its erasure, as I have been arguing in this section.

Morrison's immersion in popular culture, coupled with her insistence that her books be *read*—by her on tape, by *Oprah* viewers, and in all the usual sites of reading as well—creates, finally, an importantly different version of textual authority from that available to her thirty years ago. Whereas the original edition of *The Bluest Eye* bespeaks bibliographically a conflicted presence within the mainstream, white publishing structure, Morrison's *Oprah* editions and audiobooks present a voice of authentically black experience that demands attention, for its words and through its sales, from black and white readers.

My final chapter turns to a different attempt to merge black and white readerships, Ralph Ellison's *Juneteenth*, in this case through the portrayal of a white racist senator who has been raised in an African American community. The editorial question in this case is how best to represent a text for which no clear authorial intention can be determined, as Ellison's second novel was unfinished at the time of his death—and had persisted in that state for more than two decades. Just as I have argued that contemporary editions of *Passing* should incorporate its material—and thus cultural—history, so I conclude that Ellison's editor's efforts to portray his final narrative as textually whole misrepresent its material history, and thus the cultural history the inherently fragmented narrative represents.

CHAPTER FIVE

JUNETEENTH AS A TEXTUAL AND RACIAL FRAGMENT

Juneteenth is a fragment that passes for a novel. Its first edition includes 380 pages of text, with introduction, notes, and an afterword, all elegantly printed on thick, ragged-edge paper. The front jacket presents Ellison's name in large brown capitals, above the title in smaller white letters, and, in smaller white letters still, the legends "A Novel" below the title and "BY THE AUTHOR OF INVISIBLE MAN" beneath a photo of an African American band performing on a sidewalk. The back jacket consists entirely of a black-and-white photo of Ellison, the back of his head and neck fading into dark shadow, along with a white square for the ISBN number and bar code. The book's surface appearance—its "skin"—creates the aura of a complete, coherent, continuous work of fiction. But *Juneteenth* is actually a small section of the more than 2,000 pages of the forty-year work-in-progress that Ellison left behind at his death in 1994. In this chapter I examine the rhetorical strategies employed by Ellison's editor and literary executor, John F. Callahan, sometimes to acknowledge, but more often to gloss over *Juneteenth*'s fragmentary state. More importantly, I argue that reading *Juneteenth* faithfully, as a fragment and nothing more, in fact produces a more accurate sense of both the text and of Ellison's representations of race in America at the end of the twentieth century.

Editing, as various textual scholars have maintained, is a form of interpretation. Responding to the presumed distinction between the "physical" documents on which the "immaterial" reading of a text is based, Steven

Mailloux writes: "Whether based on replicating a communally published artifact or on reconstructing the author's final authorial intentions, the concrete text produced in editing exemplifies the materiality of all interpretation. To interpret is to translate materially one text into another" (586). In the argument that follows, I take up this broad point both to demonstrate the particular interpretive decisions made by Callahan in *Juneteenth*, and to offer my own editorial interpretation of this text in relation to the unpublished materials it represents metonymically. To edit—and thus interpret—Ellison's manuscripts into *Juneteenth*, I will conclude, reveals a desire for a coherent, stable text, rather than a "disorderly" representation of Ellison's unfinished work.

The history of what would have been Ellison's other novel(s) is well-known by now, so I will recount it only briefly here. (See Callahan's introduction for a more detailed discussion.) After beginning work in 1954, Ellison was near completion by 1967, with an original contract calling for the delivery of a complete draft by September 1 of that year (*Juneteenth* xii). In November, however, a nearly legendary fire at the Ellisons' Berkshires home destroyed a substantial portion of the manuscript. As Callahan's introduction notes, Ellison's last public comment on this event, in 1994, estimated the loss at 360 pages, "a good part of the novel" (xiii). Beginning with the inclusion of "And Hickman Arrives" in Saul Bellow's 1960 collection *The Noble Savage*, Ellison published several sections of the manuscript that would become *Juneteenth* and made various revisions to these printed stories that are included in the posthumous edition (366).

Callahan does not include other manuscript sections published separately, such as "Cadillac Flambé," which appeared in a 1973 issue of *American Review*. In a 1974 interview with John Hersey, Ellison refers to "Cadillac Flambé" as part of "this book" at which he was then at work (*Essays* 792), but Callahan includes only one paragraph in *Juneteenth*, presumably because the story would not "fit" with that book's central focus on Hickman and Sunraider. As Callahan makes clear in the introduction and afterword, the published text of *Juneteenth* does not exactly correspond to any single manuscript, but is rather the result of various combinations and splicings. These include "And Hickman Arrives"; a set of manuscripts labeled "Book II" by Ellison, which "was retyped in 1972 and contains subsequent revisions and corrections made in Ellison's hand up until at least 1986; a thirty-eight page manuscript referred to as 'Bliss's Birth,' now Chapter 15; one paragraph from 'Cadillac Flambé' (*American Review*, 1973), inserted to give the Senator's speech in Chapter 2 greater continuity with the novel's final scene; and several words and brief passages from later versions of the Lincoln Memorial scene in Chapter 14 inserted to clarify and intensify the action" (*Juneteenth* 366).

While Ellison was apparently near completion in late 1967, over the next twenty-seven years the manuscript expanded to thousands of pages and notes, and probably would have become a series of interlocked narratives, similar to Faulkner's Yoknapatawpha saga or Balzac's *Comédie Humaine*. The section of this saga that Callahan selects for *Juneteenth*, apparently the middle section of a projected three-part work, focuses on Adam Sunraider, a racist New England senator who has been raised by Reverend Alonzo Hickman in an African American Oklahoma community. After being shot during a speech on the Senate floor, Sunraider moves in and out of consciousness, discussing his past (when he was known as Bliss) with Hickman when awake. The remainder of the narrative shifts between Sunraider's and Hickman's unspoken memories, positioning Sunraider as a white man who has violently rejected his black roots.[1]

Louis Menand points out a potentially fundamental problem in Callahan's selection of the middle sections of the manuscripts for inclusion as Ellison's more "finished" material: "That Ellison hung onto the entire manuscript until his death seems a pretty clear indication that he did not imagine the sections of his novel to be freestanding" (4). Against Robert Butler's contention that "a close reading of *Juneteenth* reveals that the novel is anything but the 'Frankenstein monster' which Menand described" (294), I would argue that Butler misreads Menand's criticism as contentful rather than conceptual. Menand's claim in his review—and mine in this chapter—is not so much that the narrative presented in *Juneteenth* is in itself incoherent, but that the production of this section of Ellison's manuscripts as if it were a novel runs counter to the state of the text at Ellison's death. Butler similarly remarks that Ellison "artfully structur[es] *Juneteenth* in terms of scenes which draw heavily from national myth and ritual" (309), when, in fact, such structuring must be attributed to Callahan, given the inherent incompleteness of the manuscript's narrative structure at Ellison's death. This is a broader critical problem, also applying, for example, to Barry Shank's reading of the scene in which Hickman cuts baby Bliss's umbilical cord: "Placed at the end of the novel, whether through the work of Callahan, the literary executor, or Ellison's own explicit designs, this is another of those scenes where Ellison wants to make sure you don't miss his meaning" (49). First, there is no "novel" without Callahan's shaping of the manuscripts; second, there is ultimately no way to understand Ellison's "explicit designs" for this text beyond the *lack* of design with which he left the manuscripts. Certainly, individual sections of the manuscripts hold together on their own and can be positioned together to form a larger whole, as Butler (and Shank, by implication) see happening in *Juneteenth*: the point, rather, is that to do so is to map a narrative structure onto a disordered text. Because it is possible to impose such an order does not mean that we should.

No doubt a number of factors contributed to Ellison's inability to complete one or more of the novels related to this story, but, as Ellison's editor and literary executor, Callahan was faced with the choice of leaving the vast collection of documents as they stood on Ellison's death or cutting and stitching pieces together into an ostensible whole. In an interview with Christopher C. De Santis, Callahan recounts his attempts to organize the jumble of documents into a unified work: "I set them out according to when Ellison wrote them and the development he was trying to achieve, and then I read them straight through over several days, and there were moments of elation. But although I dearly wanted all the hundreds and hundreds of pages to make a book, when I finished, I realized they didn't. Taken all together, the manuscripts before me were an anthology, a succession of fragments, an archive more than a book" (609). Callahan's distinction between the coherent whole of a book and the component parts making up an anthology, a succession of fragments, or an archive is precisely the underlying aesthetic ideology against which I will argue in this chapter. (Interestingly, Callahan's attitude toward the anthology here diverges from Reed's in *Mumbo Jumbo*, where the Book of Thoth is originally an anthology, and Hinckle Von Vampton plans to control Jes Grew's power by eventually reassembling its disparate parts into an anthology.) *Juneteenth*, of course, is a "book" in Callahan's terms, a narrative that offers the kind of linear progression and stability Callahan "dearly wanted" to achieve. But as we shall see, appearances can be deceiving.

I should emphasize at the outset that my aim is not to discount Callahan's prodigious work in editing this material into a single volume.

Alan Nadel notes similarly that "the more-or-less complete section of Ellison's more-or-less incomplete second novel remains, nevertheless, an important work" ("Integrated" 167). The publication of *Juneteenth* constitutes a major addition to contemporary American fiction. But its intricate textual history raises important questions about how to represent editorially an unpublished manuscript whose textual condition is clearly unfinished. At present there is no way to assess the particular editorial selections Callahan has made, as the *Juneteenth* papers at the Library of Congress will remain sealed until after the publication of a scholarly edition, also edited by Callahan. This chapter focuses rather on the experience of reading *Juneteenth* in its current form, without the scholarly edition or the Library of Congress archive as background evidence, in order to examine Callahan's construction of the text as novel. Even in the future, though, when researchers can compare *Juneteenth* to its scholarly edition and to the archive, no doubt the most common experience will be to read the text without reference to these other documents. Consider the case of Hans Walter Gabler's intricately edited synoptic edition of *Ulysses*, which appeared in 1984 in both a reader's edition and a three-volume scholarly work, complete with a complex system of color coding to distinguish various levels of Joyce's revisions. With the notable exception of editorially minded Joyceans,[2] the single-volume reader's edition remains the focus of discussion, both inside and outside the academy. Most readers are content with the results of Gabler's research and remain uninterested in the dense web of evidence that explains how he arrived at this particular version, which, incidentally, corresponds to no edition published in Joyce's lifetime. I would imagine the same fate awaits the scholarly edition of *Juneteenth*, and certainly the library archive. As Menand suggests, *Juneteenth* "will go into the world and become 'Ralph Ellison's second novel.' People will teach it and write about it as though the story it tells is a story Ellison wanted to tell" (4). So while this chapter presents a necessarily provisional reading, absent the oceans of evidence that will become navigable in the years ahead, it also looks forward to a future which will probably resemble, for most readers, the present.

In keeping with that eye to Ellison's "common readers," my discussion examines the narrative "proper" with and against *Juneteenth*'s paratexts: the dust jacket, copyright page, epigraph, introduction, Ellison's notes, and Callahan's afterword.[3] Many Ellison critics, I imagine, will follow the path of Trudier Harris-Lopez, who opts not to enter the "sea of troubled waters" represented by the text's many editorial questions, choosing "instead to focus on what Ellison has done with his characters. After all, no matter the editorial selections and placements, the words and creations are finally Ellison's" (176). Harris-Lopez presents a worthwhile discussion of those characters, but her reading is conceptually flawed from the outset: the "words and creations" may be "finally Ellison's" on their face, but to read those characters as part of a distinct, stable narrative requires fundamentally misunderstanding the nature of Ellison's manuscripts, what Elizabeth Yukins terms a "work in process" (1260). Thus the only final authorial intention we could accurately ascribe to Ellison in the *Juneteenth* manuscripts is the intention to remain in the process of composition and revision. The idea of these characters as "*finally Ellison's*" rests on a teleological fiction, for it requires the assumption—shared by Callahan—that Ellison was moving toward *Juneteenth* as a fixed point in his prolonged period of drafting, when the archival evidence would suggest that Ellison's second novel rather remained forever becoming.[4]

PARATEXTUAL IMAGES

The usual first step in reading books, through what Gerald Graff terms the "unofficial interpretive culture," is to orient the enclosed text by the cultural markers contained on its front, back, and inside jacket copy (for hardcovers). "Dust jackets provide a clue not just to the meanings of a single work," Graff writes, "but, much more important, to the *type* of thing that a meaning can be (its intrinsic genre) and the type of talk it is possible to construct about it" (7, original emphasis). While Graff focuses primarily on dust jackets' linguistic codes, their visual markers certainly offer similar clues, as part of the book's broader bibliographical environment. In the case of *Juneteenth*, the front and back jackets present a striking study in contrast. Even though the author's name appears in much larger type than any other words on the front jacket, the brown letters fade slightly into the dark background, drawing the eye to the image by jazz photographer Duncan Schiedt just below the cover's center (see fig. 8). This space is occupied, naturally, by the title itself. The photograph's eloquent staging balances the three middle figures, whose own central figure is himself balanced by the oboist and singer, both pointing to the left

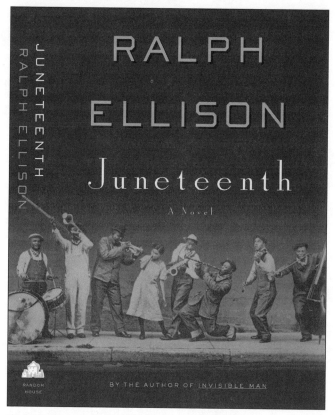

Fig. 8. Front jacket cover of Ralph Ellison's *Juneteenth* (1999), published by Random House, Inc.

with their knees. The trombone to the left of the woman directs the eye back toward the image's center, while the violinist and bassist on the image's right side look up, respectively, toward the title and out to the reader. This effect, coupled with the overall jacket design, locates the title and legend, "A Novel," at the center of the viewer's attention, and thus places a special emphasis on those words and their white type. *Juneteenth* is, as we learn from the inside jacket copy, the story of an ostensibly white senator who has been raised within a black community. The narrative implicitly positions this individual story as a larger American condition, as we see on the back flap: "For even as Senator Sunraider was bathed from birth in the deep and nourishing waters of African-American folkways, so too are all Americans."

Fig. 9. Back jacket cover of Ralph Ellison's *Juneteenth* (1999),
published by Random House, Inc.

The combination of brown lettering for Ellison's name and white lettering
for the title and subtitle expresses this same confluence of outwardly white
identity and black, or brown, "deep and nourishing waters." A similar effect
emerges from the back jacket, through the juxtaposition of Ellison's dark face
emerging from deep shadow with the white square for the ISBN number and
bar code (see fig. 9). Ellison appears here as a distinctly black figure, whose
visible blackness is contrasted both to the even darker shadow and to the
lighter shirt and then to the bright box for publishing information. Just as the
black copyright page in *Mumbo Jumbo*'s first edition signifies on the white
ownership of a black text, here the back jacket illustration strikingly contrasts
the dark image of the writer with the white border surrounding the coded

expression of the book as commodity. The ISBN number and bar code—what Ron Silliman calls the "lingering traces of a would-be invisible language" of commodity capitalism (8)—strikingly, if perhaps inadvertently, signify both the book and Ellison himself (or at least this image of Ellison) as marketable commodities. *Juneteenth*'s status as a coherent whole is relevant here as well, as the book must be a clearly identifiable object in order to be marketed. While Silliman's example is an ISBN number (for Noam Chomsky's *Reflections on Language*) which "the producer does not wish the customer to read," as evidenced by its being "printed in a different direction and in a lighter color than the rest of the page's text" (8), the ISBN and bar code for *Juneteenth* are anything but invisible.

In this sense *Juneteenth*'s back dust jacket (and by extension the book itself, of course) exhibits the different kinds of reification that Jameson outlines for postmodern consumerist objects and "culture." Whereas "you don't want to have to think about Third World women every time you pull yourself up to your word processor, or all the other lower-class people with their lower-class lives when you decide to use or consume your other luxury products," Jameson writes, when consuming cultural products "we [do not] particularly want, let alone need, to forget the human producer T. S. Eliot, or Margaret Mitchell or Toscanini or Jack Benny, or even Sam Goldwyn or Cecil B. deMille" (*Postmodernism* 315). Yet, Jameson continues, reification at this second level still distances consumers from the objects of their consumption, as "a product somehow shuts us out even from a sympathetic participation, by imagination, in its production. It comes before us, no questions asked, as something we could not begin to imagine doing for ourselves" (317). This postmodern commodity exchange represents a marked change from Marx's sense of alienation, as in the later stage of capitalism both the physical producers of objects and the consumers' relationship to the objects result in a new and greater distancing between consumers and their ability to imagine themselves as artists.

Because the back-jacket portrait focuses so closely on Ellison's face, with his eyes pointing away from the photograph toward some unknown horizon, I read this image that lies, literally, behind the book, as that of an isolated genius, whose work "we could not begin to imagine doing for ourselves." Like so many marketing designs, this one relies on a willful illusion regarding the actual circumstances of production. While all books are the result of various and complex social exchanges among writer, editor, author's friends and family, publisher, printer, etc., this is especially true of *Juneteenth*, with its posthumous collaboration between Ellison and Callahan only the most prominent of several social interactions required to produce the book. Yet because *Juneteenth* is reified, in Jameson's terms, as a cultural object that lies beyond its ordinary consumers' capabilities, this image of Ellison as sole genius taps into the marketing strategies employed for "genius" authors (usually male), from Eliot and Joyce to Pynchon and DeLillo. Again, the juxtaposition of this image with the highly visible ISBN and bar code re-marks on the book's commodity status and on the transformation of this image itself into a related commodity. You are buying an image of Ellison when you buy *Juneteenth*, an image which is itself the kind of unified, coherent whole that we normally associate with genius authors and their texts. But you are also buying an object that has been produced and distributed by Random House, and then sold by your local bookstore (or Web site). While we might ordinarily think of such texts as *Juneteenth* as "beyond" or "above" these mundane transactions, the highlighted ISBN number and bar code oddly emphasize the book as commodity, even if most consumers will be unable to "read" these signifiers of commodification.

This point returns me to the front jacket's subtle indication that *Juneteenth* is indeed "A Novel," that is, a stable entity which we would expect to find in a particular section of the bookstore. This status is reflected as well in the back flap copy: "At the time of his death, he was still *expanding his novel in other directions*, envisioning a grand, perhaps multivolume, story cycle. Always, in Ellison's mind, the character Hickman and the story of Sunraider's life from birth to death were *the dramatic heart of the narrative*. And so, with the aid of Ellison's widow, Fanny, his literary executor, John Callahan, has edited *this magnificent novel at the center* of Ralph Ellison's forty-year work-in-progress—*Juneteenth*, its author's *abiding testament* to the country he so loved and to its many unfinished tasks" (emphasis added).[5] This rhetoric depends on the presence of a unified textual center, the novel *Juneteenth*, around which Ellison's forty years of work revolves. For Ellison to be "expanding his novel in other directions" at the time of his death implies a stable embarkation point from which to investigate new horizons. The story of Hickman and Sunraider, as "the dramatic heart of the narrative," again becomes the center around which the unfinished text's more tangential sections revolve, making this posthumously published book America's lasting inheritance from Ellison, an aid in the completion of the country's "many unfinished tasks."

This sense of *Juneteenth* as a basically finished work continues on the copyright page, with its note that "portions of *Juneteenth* were previously published in different form in *The New Yorker*, *The Noble Savage*, and *The Quarterly Review of Literature*." Coupled with the jacket statement that *Juneteenth* was always the "dramatic heart of the narrative," this notice of earlier publication suggests the revisionary movement toward a clearly marked ending, a teleology which Callahan's discussion of the text does not always support. But as a revised work, *Juneteenth* is presumably a more finished, more polished "novel," a stable text which can be read clearly as an independent narrative.

Interestingly, Ellison's dedication—"To That Vanished Tribe into Which I Was Born: The American Negroes"—and epigraph from Eliot's "Little Gidding" both precede Callahan's introduction, implicitly positioning the introduction as of a piece with the narrative. Rather than locating the scholar's preface as a separate item, detachable from Ellison's work, this placement of the dedication and epigraph, in fact, conveys a more accurate impression of *Juneteenth* as a collaborative project, produced by the interaction of Ellison himself, his widow, and his editor, along with the various Random House employees involved in the book's production. These multiple collaborations could have resulted in any number of other versions, so claims for the published book's centrality must address its inherently contingent status.[6]

"ELLISON'S GREAT, UNFINISHED HOUSE OF FICTION": CALLAHAN'S CONSTRUCTION OF *JUNETEENTH* AS A NOVEL

In this section I will examine Callahan's paratextual claims for *Juneteenth* as a novel, focusing on the book's introduction and afterword, as well as on his remarks in the De Santis interview. Callahan's extended argument for *Juneteenth*'s aesthetic unity contrasts with the facts of its composition and editing, producing a disjunction between appearance and reality. The introduction and afterword frame the "body" of the narrative (a metaphor

Callahan employs in his own discussion of the text), surrounding the narrative "proper" with a doubled indication of its status as both scholarly document and contingent text. In both places Callahan explains the story of Ellison's composition and of his own editing, set against a discussion of how these different processes manifest themselves in the text at hand. While the front and back matter aim to reinforce the readers' impression of the text's wholeness, I will argue that they, in fact, emphasize its contingent nature, expressing against their will (so to speak) the suppressed reality of the fragment.

Throughout his published comments, Callahan voices a desire for textual completeness, beginning with the introduction's account of his initial meeting with Ellison's widow, Fanny. Having traced Ellison's complex compositional journey, Callahan describes his first encounter with the piles of documents awaiting him.

Ellison left no instructions about his work except the wish, expressed to Mrs. Ellison and me, that his books and papers be housed at the national library, the Library of Congress. A few days after his death, Mrs. Ellison walked me into his study, a room adjoining the living room and still wreathed in a slight haze of cigar and pipe smoke. As if to protest his absence, the teeming bookshelves had erupted in chaos over his desk, chair, computer table, and copying machine, finally covering the floor like a blizzard of ash. Anyone else might have given up, but Fanny Ellison persevered in her effort to do the right thing by what her husband had left behind. . . . At her direction I removed several thick black binders of typescript going back to the early 1970s from the first of two long, rectangular black steel filing cabinets next to his desk. The other cabinet, I was to discover, contained folder after folder of earlier drafts painstakingly labeled according to character or episode.

"Beginning, middle, and end," Mrs. Ellison mused. "Does it have a beginning, middle, and end?"

The question can't be put any better than that, I thought. (xiv)

This scene artfully contrasts the space of Ellison's writing, rendered even more chaotic after his death, with the desire for narrative order expressed by both Fanny Ellison and Callahan.[7] The search for beginning, middle, and end is common to almost all fiction editors, of course, whether dealing with authors live or dead, but my point is that from the start of his editorial quest, Callahan attempts to discover order within the chaos of Ellison's papers, or, failing that, to impose order upon them (or upon those portions that will fall into place). Ellison's editor and widow both rely on a traditional narrative structure, while, in fact, *Juneteenth* itself proceeds outside of chronological order, subverting conventional ideas of beginning, middle, and end.

Callahan's is not an unusual editorial attitude, but it leaves unexamined the premises behind his editorial principles. The question of how to handle an unfinished manuscript is the bread and butter of editorial theory. In his influential *Principles of Textual Criticism*, James Thorpe distinguishes between a work's "actual" and "potential" versions, with potential versions comprising "those which are not communicated to the public—like drafts or working versions" (187). Acknowledging that potential versions are sometimes the only ones available to an editor, Thorpe cautions: "The natural inclination of editors to rejoice when they reveal an unfinished work to an unsuspecting world should be tempered by the realization that what they are dealing with is not quite in the status of an 'actual' work of art" (188). While more recent textual scholarship has not always privileged the published version of a literary work to the extent that Thorpe recommends, the problem of presenting potential versions, whether published or unpublished, has remained central. Thorpe insists, "When the literary work emerges as a public version it then has the integrity of its unique authorial form" (42), a conclusion which extends his earlier claim that "the work can only have such integrity, or completeness, as the author chooses to give it, and our only reasonable test of when the work has achieved integrity is his willingness to release it to his usual public" (38). For many contemporary editorial theorists, this approach would place the author in too central a position in relation to a work's "integrity," at the neglect of the others involved in textual production.

Over the last twenty years or so, textual scholars have framed this debate, basically, into three competing camps. One approach weighs most heavily the author's final intentions (however those might be determined); another privileges the first edition published in an author's lifetime, as the version most representative of the initial social exchange enabling publication; and the third seeks to produce a "genetic" text which combines published and "intended" versions. (Gabler's *Ulysses* is probably the best-known example of the genetic approach.) Each of these editorial systems derives from a differently weighted relationship between authorial intention and historical context. Historical circumstances are obviously multiple and complex, but, as editorial theorists have increasingly emphasized in recent years, the same is true of authorial intention. As Greetham asks, "What if this intention, when discoverable, turns out to be manifold rather than single? What if it is dynamic rather than static?" (*Scholarship* 353). Clearly this is the case for Ellison's sprawl of manuscripts; Callahan certainly would not claim a "single" or "static" intention for the sections he delimits as *Juneteenth*, much less for the two-thousand-plus pages of narrative and notes from which the "novel" is culled. Yet, as I have discussed throughout this chapter so far, the paratextual claims made by Callahan in the introduction and afterword, and by Random House in the jacket copy, presume a single and essentially static authorial intention, at least for those portions of the manuscripts that become *Juneteenth*.

Part of Callahan's underlying reliance on the fiction of a "fixed" text may well derive from the impossibility of editing *Juneteenth* according to final authorial intention or to its publication history, strictly speaking. As I note in this chapter's conclusion, however, publishing the scholarly edition without the earlier *Juneteenth* could have most accurately expressed the text's non-publication at the time of Ellison's death as well as, arguably, his final authorial intentions. As Callahan notes in the passage above, Ellison "left no instructions" about how his work should be published, or even that it should be published at all; technically, Ellison's final authorial intention was to leave unpublished the manuscripts that had already occupied forty years of his career. Nevertheless, Callahan often infers an authorial intention, for example, in his decision of where to end the narrative. After explaining in the afterword his reasons for adding chapter divisions and arranging three of the middle chapters in their published order, Callahan continues, "Ellison also provided an important clue, this one silent, about how to end *Juneteenth*. In this instance he added a key passage in different, larger typeface to page 284 of the most recent manuscript of Book II. In a few words he brings the episode in question to climax and closure" (367–68). Callahan's earlier decision to use Book II as the basis for *Juneteenth* derives primarily from a best-text approach, as Callahan explains that Book II "is not Ellison's most recent effort, but it is the most ambitious and latest, freestanding, compelling extended fiction in the saga" (366).[8] That is, Callahan makes an essentially aesthetic rather than historical judgment in his selection of copy text, replacing authorial intention with editorial preference. Callahan then uses Ellison's emphatic typeface to justify his decision of how to end the narrative. Here again, this decision ultimately relies on a best-text approach, as Callahan goes on to explain: "The passage projects what Ellison called 'that aura of a summing up, that pause for contemplation of the moral significance of the history we've been through,' and, therefore, it strengthened my impression of this scene as the most logical and emotional place to end the novel that I think Ellison might have called *Juneteenth*" (368).

I should emphasize here that my argument is not so much with Callahan's specific editorial decisions—if there will be a *Juneteenth*, after all, it must end somewhere, and editors almost invariably rely on a range of principles in making various local decisions. What I do want to stress is Callahan's rhetorical construction of his own and Ellison's intentions, for instance, when Callahan explains in the afterword, "As I tried to discern one coherent, inclusive sequence, I realized slowly, *somewhat against my will*, that although Ellison had hoped to write one big book, his saga, like William Faulkner's, could not be contained within the pages of a single volume" (365, emphasis added).

Callahan's realization against his will further manifests itself in two fantasy scenarios he describes in the De Santis interview. In response to the question, "Was there ever a time when you seriously questioned whether or not there was indeed a novel emerging from the thousands of pages of manuscripts and notes," Callahan explains:

I hoped I would find a last complete manuscript; or, almost as good, that I'd find the manuscript complete up to the last scene, and then a draft, perhaps unrevised, of a last scene, and all but finished conclusion to the book. I dearly wished for that to be the case; I *hoped* that would be the case. For a long time, I kept thinking, there must be more. I dreamed about hidden manuscript pages. I went back several times and looked in the apartment. . . . So I thought, let's go to Random House and the archives. Again, a dead end. Finally I told myself, "Look, John, what you have is what he left." I had to say, "Well, it isn't finished, it isn't even almost finished," and then I had the notes, and I went through them. It was a jolt realizing that what he left was not nearly finished. There was not one coherent, continuous narrative. I suspect there never was; at least I couldn't find it. And so I went on from there. (608–9, original emphasis)

Before analyzing these remarks, let me pair them with related comments from the end of the interview.

I can't help but wonder what would have happened had I said, "Well, by God, yes, Ellison had all these pages; yes, he published eight excerpts; and yes, folks, here, in this handwriting, in his papers, is a note saying, 'I was writing a huge, sprawling narrative, and it was going to be an epic novel along the lines of *War and Peace*, or three novels, or six novels along the lines of Faulkner, but now I, Ralph Ellison, age eighty, in sound mind, as my last will and testament, give you my second novel. It's called *Juneteenth*.'" I wonder what people would have said? Would they have said, "Ahhh, at the end of his life Ellison said, 'By God, within all that I've done, here's the book that I want to go out with?'" . . . But we have *Juneteenth*, and then we have all the outtakes which will be included in the 2000 or more pages of the scholarly edition. (619)

In both cases Callahan imagines a document—a completed manuscript or a last will and testament—that would authorize his decision to isolate Book II as the published text *Juneteenth*. Callahan's dreams of the "hidden manuscript pages" posit a lost key that, though not directly marked as such (at least in contrast to Ellison's imaginary will), declares the narrative to be complete, or at least "all but finished." The will and testament, in contrast, grants the impossibility of the manuscripts completing themselves, as in Callahan's dreams, and instead absorbs from Callahan the authority for announcing that textual condition to the public. Yet, his closing comment, "But we have *Juneteenth*," implies that *Juneteenth* is all we *could* have, not that it is one version out of countless possible iterations of the manuscripts into a single narrative.

The conceptual difficulties that arise from this textual attitude emerge as well in the analogies through which Callahan describes the editorial process, in which *Juneteenth* and the surrounding manuscripts become either a body and its limbs or a house and its wings. Both these examples demonstrate the underlying assumptions in Callahan's editorial approach, as the body and house metaphors express a desire for a complete structure, for even as a disfigured body or unfinished house, the *Juneteenth* manuscripts only appear disfigured or unfinished when perceived in relation to the ideal of completeness they cannot reach. In Callahan's remarks to De Santis, the text figures as a body requiring editorial plastic surgery. "All the fragments could have been arranged one after another," Callahan explains, "but that would have made an anthology, and one that wasn't continuous or coherent. The *whole thing* would have been a novel only if I had stretched and elongated certain limbs and lopped off others. Those were things I was not going to do" (612, original emphasis). (Callahan clarifies that by "stretched" and "elongated" he does not mean that he would have added words to the text, but rather that he would have "tried to arrange" the various sections into a whole [612].) What is striking about this corporeal analogy is the peculiar emphasis on symmetry in the metaphorical body: only by elongating some limbs and eliminating others does the textual body become "continuous or coherent." Otherwise, to pursue the terms of Callahan's analogy, the published text would appear too disorderly, even too monstrous, to be anything but an anthology, and an incoherent one at that.

This bodily metaphor contrasts interestingly with the depiction of *Juneteenth* as a house in Callahan's introduction. "To use an architectural metaphor," Callahan explains, "this [the Hickman/Sunraider story] was the true center of Ellison's great, unfinished house of fiction. And although he did not complete the wings of the edifice, their absence does not significantly mar the organic unity of the novel we do have, *Juneteenth*" (xv). From elongated or truncated limbs to the unfinished wings of an edifice, the extra pieces of the text become superfluous elements of an essentially complete structure, rather than disfiguring body parts. But again, the text only manifests itself in this metaphorical form because of the unspoken need to see the text as potentially complete, as a book or novel. By marking his desire for coherence and meaning through these metaphors of structure and containment, Callahan treats Ellison's notes and manuscripts as a "text presumed to know," in Lacanian terms. As Žižek notes, the idea of the analyst as a subject presumed to know is a necessary illusion, for "in the end only through this supposition of knowledge can some real knowledge be produced" (185). Callahan engages in a similar illusion with the Ellison manuscripts, which against his will he recognizes do not contain a single, coherent narrative; only by imagining that they do can he arrive at the "real knowledge" of *Juneteenth* as the "great, unfinished house of fiction." Yet the real knowledge about *this* illusion, in a kind of editorial counter-transference, lies in the recognition of Callahan's textual fantasy and the Lacanian "kernel of the real" which lies behind it: the truly fragmentary nature of the manuscripts and their subject, race in America.

"A JUNKYARD CONSTRUCTION AND YET IT RUNS": TEXTUAL AND NARRATIVE FRAGMENTATION

Before turning to that final connection, I first consider *Juneteenth* on its "own" terms, as the stable narrative it appears to be. Read as a novel, *Juneteenth* comments artfully on the novelistic form itself. As Callahan remarks, *Juneteenth* works along a jazz structure: "its form is neither linear nor circular—it flows out and back and around in a spiral" (quoted in De Santis 611). As I note in this chapter's conclusion, however, publishing the scholarly edition without the earlier *Juneteenth* could have most accurately expressed the text's non-publication at the time of Ellison's death, as well as, arguably, his final authorial intentions. The narrative returns periodically to the scene of its present, Hickman talking to Sunraider in his hospital bed, while departing from that main narrative line into long riffs of remembered and imagined scenes from each character's past. In this section I examine the narrative's loose form alongside the tighter surface structure of Callahan's construction.

The narrative begins with several straightforward, naturalistic scenes, in which Hickman and his followers seek Sunraider in order to warn him of the impending assassination attempt, but are always rebuffed by his staff. But the opening sentence—"Two days before the shooting, a chartered planeload of Southern Negroes swooped down upon the District of Columbia and attempted to see the Senator" (3)—previews the event which will set the rest of the narrative in motion, and so shifts the opening scenes out of a naturalistic mode, as the reader knows already how the plot will develop. In this way *Juneteenth*—like Morrison's *Paradise*, which begins, "They shoot the white girl first" without ever identifying which one of the women shot is white—renders plot a secondary concern, focusing primarily on the reasons behind and consequences of a seemingly inevitable story of racial violence.

Juneteenth ends in the midst of Sunraider's semi-conscious reverie, in which he imagines a magical car built by three black men, "*a junkyard sculpture mechanized!*" (347). Throughout the text, Sunraider's memories appear in plain type, with dream sequences in italics. The text's last sentence, then— "*And as a dark hand reached down, he seemed to hear* the sound of Hickman's consoling voice, calling from somewhere above" (348)—typographically combines Sunraider's dreaming and waking states, a fantasy occurring out of time and within the almost endless present against which the long narratives of memory and dream are set. This last sentence also reinforces the narrative's defining narrative dynamic, in which Sunraider, who is identified as black during his days as the boy preacher Bliss but who performs whiteness in his new roles as Mr. Movie Man and Senator, seeks consolation from the African American presence he has rejected in order to refashion himself as white.[9] In what is presumably his dying moment, Sunraider desires the comforting presence of the black surrogate father he has abandoned, figuring as well America's need to acknowledge the black roots it has historically denied, since before the Jefferson(-Hemings) era through today.

The foregoing discussion takes for granted that *Juneteenth* develops its own narrative patterns and structures, but, of course, the experience of reading this text also encompasses the effects of Callahan's editorial decisions. The three most significant of these are the title, the chapter divisions, and the many ellipses, which represent either Callahan's cuts or Ellison's omissions. A title has perhaps the greatest effect of any paratextual element, as it marks a text's public identity and influences its interpretation. As Genette notes, "if the text is an object to be read, the title (like, moreover, the name of the author) is an object to be circulated—or, if you prefer, a subject of conversation" (*Paratexts* 75). In terms of interpretation, a title sets the initial terms in which readers approach a text—imagine, again, reading Morrison's *Paradise* if it were called *War*, or, as Genette asks, "limited to the text alone and without a guiding set of directions, how would we read Joyce's *Ulysses* if it were not entitled *Ulysses*?" (*Paratexts* 2).

Ulysses is a unique case, but we might also ask how we would read *Juneteenth* if it were not entitled *Juneteenth*, for while Ellison's narrative might still lend itself to the same general angles of interpretation, this title does shape the direction of reading. *Juneteenth* locates the text within a particular historical framework, of course, and broadens the interpretive frame of reference from the two principal characters to the American racial dynamics they represent. Another of Callahan's working titles was "God's Own Straight Man" (a phrase from the text), which would clearly shift the interpretive frame in different directions, toward a more sustained focus on the narrative's many scenes of formal and informal preaching, toward humor as a defining style, and toward the question of whether to understand Hickman or Sunraider as the "straight man" (or both, as each experiences different kinds of cosmic jokes).

The question of the title is also appropriate because Ellison never applied it to his work-in-progress (though he did select the Eliot epigraph). As Callahan notes, "In all of Ellison's papers—and there are literally thousands of notes—he didn't leave a title for the book. It was commonly referred to, though not by Ellison, as 'the Hickman novel,' 'the second novel,' or simply 'untitled' " (quoted in De Santis 611). (Interestingly, the designation "the Hickman novel" shifts the narrative emphasis away from Sunraider, as also happens, for example, to Stephen Dedalus in references to the events in *Ulysses* as Bloomsday). While working on the manuscript, Callahan tells De Santis, he kept a list of "about a dozen phrases" that could serve as a title: "One morning I was walking up the stairs to my study and 'Juneteenth' came full force into my head like an unforgettable melody, and that was it. Later on I said rationally, 'Hell, it's the pivotal chapter; Juneteenth—the day, the night, the metaphor of liberation—is pivotal in the book.' But the first inkling was intuitive, sudden, direct. And Juneteenth had a special magic for Ellison. In 1965, when he published the excerpt which comprises most—not all, but most—of the turning-point episode in Book II, now much of Chapter 7 in *Juneteenth*, he called it 'Juneteenth' " (612). In chapter 7, Sunraider remembers the Juneteenth celebration in which he participated as a child preacher, waiting inside a white coffin for Hickman's call of resurrection. Labeling Juneteenth the *"celebration of a gaudy illusion"* (115, original emphasis), Sunraider reluctantly returns his memory to that day, when he was still Hickman's surrogate son, Bliss. "Like a great, kindly bear along the streets, my hand lost in his huge paw," Sunraider remembers. "The true father, but black, black. Was he a charlatan? Am I—or simply as resourceful in my fashion? Did he know himself, or care? Back to the problem of all that. Must I go back to the beginning when only he knows the start? . . ." (117, original ellipsis). This chapter is literally pivotal, then, because it tilts Sunraider's memories back to the beginning, and metaphorically so because it evokes the defining event of his childhood and the rejection of Hickman that will eventually follow from it. But other possible versions of the text, even if readers of *Juneteenth* can only imagine them as distant abstractions, might well not pivot at this point, might not evoke "Juneteenth" as an "unforgettable melody." Keeping that sense of possibility alive within the text is my principal goal here, but in order to do so I will first consider Callahan's more local editorial decisions, the chapter breaks and the ellipses.

Callahan explains in the afterword that "Ellison's entire manuscript has numerous space breaks, but within Book II he did not designate chapters as such. As editor, I have respected Ellison's breaks; in addition, keeping the reader in mind, I have divided *Juneteenth* into chapters at appropriate points in the manuscript and the action" (367). Interestingly, Callahan follows Ellison's apparent wishes for textual breaks, but assumes that Ellison would have also "kept the reader in mind" by eventually adding chapter divisions "at appropriate points." To publish a novel without distinct chapters would not, of course, be unprecedented; *Mrs. Dalloway*, for example, includes only extra spaces between selected paragraphs, but no chapters as such. (Indeed, the Woolfs had to remind their printer to add extra spaces where she had designated them.) So we cannot necessarily assume that Ellison would have divided a published novel—granting momentarily that he would have chosen this particular manuscript for publication on its own, and even that he would have called it *Juneteenth*—much less intuit at what "appropriate points" these divisions would have occurred. Again, I am not arguing that Callahan as editor should have produced the text precisely as Ellison left it, but the imposition of chapter breaks, beyond its local effects on the narrative, serves primarily as a cosmetic enhancement, making the text look more like a novel, with markers for the beginnings and endings of discrete narrative units and the consequent privileging of the moments that become these chapters' opening or closing scenes.

Of particular interest to me are the ends of Callahan's chapters that close with ellipses, comprising nearly half of the text (seven of sixteen chapters: 2, 7, 9, 10, 11, 14, and 15). Callahan does not address the text's many ellipses in the introduction, afterword, or De Santis interview, except to note that, "for clarity's sake and to avoid a redundancy I believe Ellison would have addressed before publication, I have slightly pruned several passages in Chapter 2. In Chapter 3 I deleted two brief passages referring to a different speech than the one the Senator gives in Chapter 2" (368). From this evidence we would have to infer that these ellipses and others sprinkled throughout the text (about thirty by my rough count) appear in *Juneteenth* because they reflect Ellison's manuscript(s); in addition there are many ellipses which signify a break in a character's speech or thoughts, and so seem more clearly original to the manuscripts. But the evidence is not always clear; for example, chapter 2 divides what had been two consecutive paragraphs in "And Hickman Arrives," and the new middle chapter begins and ends with ellipses. The publication of the scholarly edition and the opening of the Library of Congress archive will settle this kind of question; until then *Juneteenth*'s readers can only speculate on the precise extent of the text's fragmentation. In *Juneteenth*'s current textual form, an ellipsis at chapter's end suggests either Callahan's truncation, an instance of "lopping off a limb," or a gap in Ellison's manuscript which perhaps contributed to Callahan's sense of the most appropriate places for chapter divisions.

To extend the question of the title's interpretive effects, how could we read *Juneteenth* without chapters? First, readers might well find a more organic development to the narrative—as happens with *Mrs. Dalloway*, another story focusing on two principal characters within the course of a single day, alternating between present events and memories of pivotal experiences. Just as the deliberate omission of chapter divisions in *Mrs. Dalloway* connotes a deep connection between present and past, and between Clarissa Dalloway and Septimus Smith, such an omission in *Juneteenth* might suggest a similar overlay between Sunraider and Bliss as present and past versions of this character, as well as between white and black versions of American history. As Ellison told John Hersey of his work-in-progress in 1982, "It's just a matter of the past being active in the present—or of the characters becoming aware of the manner in which the past operates on their present lives" (*Essays* 816). Callahan's desire to "keep the reader in mind" may actually direct the reader away from an alternative narrative flow the chapter designations interrupt.

In fact, *Juneteenth* points in various places toward precisely this more fluid narrative dynamic. During Sunraider's opening Senate speech, for example, he departs from his intended message to call for a new approach to

American history. "'Thus we must forget the past,'" Sunraider declares. "'Indeed, our history records an undying, unyielding quest for youthful sages, for a newfound wisdom fired by a vibrant physicality. Thus again we must forget the past by way of freeing ourselves so that we can reassemble its untidy remnants in the interest of a more human order'" (18). The forgetting and reassembling of the past as a route to freedom, I would argue, conveys an approach to history consonant with a chapterless text; we might imagine this stylistic decision as the forgetting of a usual narrative structure as a way to facilitate the reader's reassembly of the textual remnants into a freer sense of the narrative's implications for racial understanding. If Ellison, as James Allan McPherson suggests, "was trying to *Negro-Americanize* the novel form, at the same time he was attempting to move beyond it" (quoted in *Juneteenth*, xxi, original emphasis), we might well consider a chapterless narrative the structural manifestation of a "Negro-Americanized" novel, one that no longer seeks to divide and categorize its component parts, but instead presents them as part of a more organic, fluid whole. Ellison describes the text in similar terms in an earlier interview with Hersey: "As a product of the imagination it's like a big sponge, maybe, or a waterbed, with a lot of needles sticking in it at various points. You don't know what is being touched, where the needles are going to end up once you get them threaded and penetrated, but somehow I keep trying to tie those threads together and the needle points pressing home without letting whatever lies in the center leak out" (*Essays* 791). Ellison is speaking here as much about the process of composition as about the narrative itself, but in thinking about the parts of the manuscripts that become *Juneteenth* as a "big sponge," we might also consider Callahan's imposition of chapter divisions as "needle points" which potentially interfere with the narrative's fluid development.

The absence of chapter divisions, that is, might lead readers to "discover" thematic resonances for this stylistic decision, just as Callahan's selection of *Juneteenth* as title leads him to understand Ellison's long years of work in ways that had not coalesced previously. "As I tried it out on the manuscript," Callahan tells De Santis, "I began to remember references I'd heard Ellison make to Juneteenth, and I came upon references in his papers, in his letters to Albert Murray, where Juneteenth was a reality and a reference point in his life. I remembered him talking about Juneteenth movingly and eloquently at Harvard in 1973, the second time I had ever seen him" (612). Having selected *Juneteenth* as a title, Callahan begins to take on a Whiggish view of its compositional history, as those moments when Ellison privileges *Juneteenth* as a textual and historical reference take on added significance, pointing toward the newly discovered end of the text's progression. A more strictly evolutionary textual outlook—in which evolution implies not teleology, but a full history of the circumstances surrounding textual production— would be satisfied to leave Ellison's unfinished work-in-progress without a title and, thus, to view the various moments of its composition all in equal relation to each other, rather than as pointing toward a retrospectively imposed end.[10]

The editorial point here is again that *Juneteenth* is a version, one version among an almost countless number, and therefore not a defining or delimiting instantiation of this textual sprawl into an orderly system. The end of the narrative published as *Juneteenth*, from this non-Whiggish editorial perspective, remarks on precisely this kind of textual contingency. In the midst of Sunraider's dying fantasy, he imagines himself among three black men who have constructed a magically flying car.

And it came to the Senator that he was watching no ordinary automobile. This was no Cadillac, no Lincoln, Oldsmobile or Buick—nor any other known make of machine; it was an arbitrary assemblage of chassis, wheels, engine, hood, horns, none of which had ever been part of a single car! It was a junkyard sculpture mechanized! An improvisation, a bastard creation of black bastards—and yet, it was no ordinary hot rod. It was an improvisation of vast arrogance and subversive and malicious defiance which they had designed to outrage and destroy everything in its path, a rolling time bomb launched in the streets . . . [. . .] And they've made the damn thing run! No single major part goes normally with the rest, yet even in their violation of the rigidities of mechanical tolerances and in their defiance of the laws of physics, property rights, patents—everything—they've forced part after part to mesh and made it run! It's a mammy-made, junkyard construction and yet those clowns have made it work, it runs! . . . (347–48, original ellipses except in brackets)

Sunraider obviously fears this "junkyard construction" because it does function, and because as an improvisation it threatens to "destroy" all icons of order "in its path." This fantasy image of a "bastard creation" which violates all applicable laws, combining disparate parts into a working whole, reflects as well on the narrative itself, and on its broader implications for contemporary views of race in America. In the essay "Change the Joke and Slip the Yoke," Ellison writes, "The white American has charged the Negro American with being without past or tradition (something which strikes the white man with a nameless horror), just as he himself has been so charged by European and American critics with a nostalgia for the stability once typical of European cultures, and the Negro knows that both were 'mammy-made' right here at home" (*Essays* 108). The "mammy-made junk-yard construction" similarly seems to strike the white Senator Sunraider with a "nameless horror," even while his use of the term "mammy-made" belies his own African American cultural heritage, a repressed influence that emerges at the moment of his greatest fear.[11]

Similarly, in a letter to Albert Murray just after reviewing the page proofs for *Invisible Man*, Ellison writes, "Things are rolling, alright and I guess I'm now a slightly mammy-made novelist" (Callahan 32). Ellison also refers here to the publication of the novel's prologue in *Partisan Review*, a deci-sion that was a "reversal of policy" given Ellison's feeling that the journal had abandoned Soviet Russia too quickly (Jackson 433, 349). Yet as Lawrence Jackson notes, Ellison's appearance in *Partisan Review* just before *Invisible Man*'s release provided "publicity and the imprimatur of high art. . . . A glossy setup in *Partisan* would ensure that the New York intellec-tual and artistic crowd would take notice of his work, the group that increasingly mattered to Ellison" (434). As a "mammy-made" novelist, then, Ellison acknowledges the impure roots of his novel's public appearance, just as the "junkyard construction" in *Juneteenth* stands in for a similar transgression and mixture of ostensibly "pure" racial categories.

As the closing scene in the novel *Juneteenth*, this scene artfully ties together the narrative arc and strikingly demonstrates the impossibility of the cultural rejection on which Sunraider has tried to base his adult life. Considered alternatively, as one version of a narrative ending among many, and thus as representative of the textual disorder from which it springs, this scene reflects the "mammy-made junkyard construction" back onto the text itself, as constructed by Callahan. The fear here is not of an isolation from history, but of an alienation from literary tradition and its privileging of recognizable, interpretable, coherent narratives over fragments, variants, and versions. Yet that contingent textual condition, in fact, more faithfully expresses the American racial condition and, therefore, works against the coherent sense of an ending produced by Callahan's editorial decisions.

To be sure, both Ellison and Callahan have followed an improvisatory style in assembling the disparate parts of the working text, Ellison in the mixture of various narrative voices, styles, and modes and Callahan in the assembly of selected manuscript pieces into a single novel. It would be easy to conclude that Callahan's editorial methods appropriately and artfully mirror Ellison's compositional habits; by making choices that Ellison would or could not make, this argument would proceed, Callahan does not so much finish *Juneteenth* as arrest it at a particular point, allowing readers to approach this orderly system within a surrounding disorder (and, eventually, to widen their interpretive lenses to include the scholarly edition's materials). Indeed, Callahan concludes in his introduction, "Always in progress, Ellison's work may now find pause, not cessation but pause, in the gift of *Juneteenth* to his readers" (xxiii).

No doubt the publication of the scholarly edition will end this pause (at least for those readers who pursue the textual evidence there), enabling readers to appreciate *Juneteenth* in something closer to its fluid state. Even within the readerly edition, though, *Juneteenth* subverts Callahan's distinction between pause and cessation through the interplay between the successive endings he presents for the text: the junkyard passage above, followed by Ellison's notes, and then Callahan's afterword. Callahan, of course, has selected for publication here only a very small number of the "literally thousands of notes pertaining to all facets of [Ellison's] novel-in-progress" (351). (The scholarly edition will include "a large selection of Ralph's notes" [quoted in De Santis 619].) The last note Callahan selects—in this edition there is no way to locate it chronologically within the archive—ends: "Incompletion of form allows the reader to impose his own imagination upon the material with too little control from the author. Thus I don't like to show my work until it is near completion" (363). There is a wonderful irony to this note as Ellison's last word in this book, and effectively in his career, as the posthumous publication of his unfinished work puts the reader—guided by Callahan—precisely in this too controlling position. But these words are, ultimately, Ellison as ventriloquized by Callahan, who selects this note as the closing one and thus imposes a certain narrative progression even on the least orderly texts within the *Juneteenth* archive. By Ellison's own standards, the manuscripts, and certainly the notes, were not "near completion," or at least not near enough for public consumption, and yet here they are, improvised into a junkyard narrative that runs, even if by doing so it threatens to leave the remaining manuscripts in its wake.

And, of course, *Juneteenth* proceeds from there to Callahan's last words, followed by biographical sketches of author and editor and, finally, the colophon. This publisher's last word begins, "This book was set in Perpetua, a typeface designed by the English artist Eric Gill, and cut by the Monotype Corporation between 1928 and 1930. Perpetua is a contemporary face of original design, without any direct historical antecedents." This fifth textual pause (not cessation) within *Juneteenth*'s closing pages ironically presents Perpetua as an ahistorical typeface, even while its use in 1999 recalls the historical moment of its design seventy years before. For a text whose narrative has focused so insistently on the denial of racial history and its consequences for the present, and whose editing has sought to contain sections of an enormous archive into a readable whole, this colophon strikingly repeats the same desire for a pastless present that, the narrative demonstrates, can only function as a denial of contemporary culture's shaping influences. While this denial has been the perpetual American attitude, *Juneteenth* suggests, importantly, both in its narrative form and in its relation to the remainder of the archive, that the forgetting of history can only succeed when it entails an assembly of the past's remnants and junk into a new, and necessarily fluid, system.

"THERE HAS TO BE A PATTERN AND WE ONLY HAVE BLACK AND WHITE": A FRAGMENTARY AESTHETIC

In a 1992 address to the Whiting Foundation, Ellison tells the story of his grandfather, "Big" Alfred Ellison, who became a freed slave in Abbeville, South Carolina, and then served as town marshal for most of the 1870s. Despite being elected to this position even after white Democrats had returned to political power, the marshal endured Jim Crow delays and harassment whenever he registered to vote. From this history Ellison draws the conclusion that, "deny it or not, we live simultaneously in the past *and* the present, but all too often while looking to the future to correct our fail-ures, we pretend that the past is no longer with us" (*Essays* 852). Ellison thus argues that one of the American writer's "implicit functions" is "to trans-form the misses of history into hits of imaginative symbolic action that aid their readers in reclaiming details of the past that find meaning in the expe-rience of individuals" (852, 853). This theme resounds in a number of Ellison's essays, such as "The Novel as a Function of American Democracy," and certainly in his fiction. In the thirtieth-anniversary edition of *Invisible Man*, Ellison calls his great novel "a raft of hope, perception and entertain-ment that might help keep us afloat as we tried to negotiate the snags and whirlpools that mark our nation's vacillating course toward and away from the democratic ideal" (*Essays* 483).

The same political aesthetic appears throughout *Juneteenth*, for instance, in the picnic scene with Mr. Movie Man and the Native American woman he calls Miss Teasing Brown. Bliss, in his second incarnation, is raising money to make a movie in a small Oklahoma town, while planning all the while to use the donations to fund a trip to California. The two characters engage in an implicit discussion of aesthetic representations of race.

What will the story be about? she said.

I haven't decided yet, I said, but I'm working on it.

Well, I'm sure glad to hear that.

Why?

Because I saw your friends taking pictures all over the place. What were they doing that for?

Oh that, I said, they're just chasing shadows, shooting scenes for background. Later on when we're working we'll use them, splice them in. Pictures aren't made in a straight line. We take a little bit of this and a little of that and then it's all looked at and selected and made into a whole. . . .

You mean you piece it together?

That's the idea, I said.

Well tell me something! she said. Isn't that just marvelous? Just like making a scrap quilt, I guess; one of those with all the colors of the rainbow in it—only more complicated. Is that it?

Just about, I said. There has to be a pattern though and we only have black and white.

Well, she said, there's Indians and some of the black is almost white and brown like me. (83, original ellipsis)

This ironic exchange, in Miss Brown's mistaking of film's black and white for the broader racial spectrum that is itself usually conflated into a simple dichotomy, reflects as well on the process of artistic creation. Mr. Movie Man, formerly "the little boy of indefinite race who looks white" (*Essays* 814) and later the race-baiting New England senator, voices a film aesthetic grounded in a jumbled artistic process, in which pictures of shadows are spliced together to make a background. The filming process, operating outside of a "straight line," reflects both the jazz structure of Ellison's narrative and his nonlinear sense of history, in which "the past still lives within each of us and repeats itself with variations" (*Essays* 855). While that past has insisted on rigid racial categories, imposing a pattern on blacks and whites in which they can never intersect despite their hidden, shared origins, Miss Teasing Brown artfully redirects this need for a pattern onto both Indians as an ignored identity and, further, onto the "almost white and brown" blacks who expose the fictions of racial history through their very appearance.

In closing, I will connect this merger of art and history to another need for patterns, in the imposition of form onto resistant textual fragments. Stephen Jay Gould writes, in a different context, "We see pattern, for pattern surely exists, even in a purely random world. . . . Our error lies not in the perception of pattern but in automatically imbuing pattern with meaning, especially with meaning that can bring comfort, or dispel confusion" (181–182). Written narratives are not quite the same as the natural world (at least from most perspectives on the philosophy of fiction), but the same desire for meaningful pattern affects our approach to texts, especially those that appear before us in an unfinished, "disorderly" documentary state. Similarly, Christine Froula reads the quest for textual stability as an instance of Lacanian transference, in which we see revealed "the inevitable implication of the reader/interpreter/editor's search for certainty, authority, truth in the textual 'certainty' that interpretive and editorial labors produce" (299).

Froula's examples are several modernist works that both exist in fluid textual states and announce their own shifts away from monumental textuality (*The Waste Land, The Cantos, Ulysses, Nightwood,* Woolf's novels, Yeats's poems). These works' drafts and manuscripts only highlight the contingent nature of the published texts. "Insofar as modernist texts change or signal that they might change or at least should change—insofar as they actively resist representing themselves as finished, autonomous, bounded objects—they actively unsettle our conceptions of textual authority," Froula writes. "As the textual 'object' dissolves into unfinishable becoming, the text ceases to be authoritative in the traditional sense. It resists the 'locus-of-truth' status that we readers/editors/subjects in search of our certainty project upon it" (302). In the case of *Juneteenth*, we see a similar "unfinishable becoming" in the genetic texts (or rather, we will be able to observe that textual effect once the scholar's edition and archive become available) as well as a published document which "actively unsettle[s] our conceptions of textual authority," despite Callahan's rhetorical efforts to resist this unsettling. That is, the contemporary editors working with Eliot, Pound, Joyce, Barnes, Woolf, and Yeats no longer presume the published work will "know" itself as a coherent object, while Callahan continues to operate from a more traditional editorial perspective.

To be sure, Callahan does not posit *Juneteenth* as a "definitive" text of Ellison's manuscripts, but he does propose to edit them "into a single, coherent, continuous work" (365). As Alan Nadel points out, this goal is at odds with Ellison's own "impossible" artistic task of exposing the fundamental fiction and truth of American racial relations.

Perhaps, given the impossibility of the task, it is apt, even fortunate, that the novel is an unfinished portion of a larger unfinished work, a larger work moreover that admits infinite possible versions. Only Ellison himself—and perhaps not even he—could know definitively which passages in the material he left behind were alternative versions of the same section, and which were additional sections. While in jazz, alternative versions are always additions, in fiction, we generally rely, albeit imprecisely, on the principle of unity that delimits a work by separating what it is from what it is not. In an irony that Ellison might have appreciated, his unpublished works bring us to an impossible impasse guaranteeing that the limits of Ellison's second novel will be no more clearly defined and finalized than the subject of that novel: America.

In giving us his version of *Juneteenth*, editor Callahan has no doubt deprived us of another version. That is the problem endemic to *versions*, a problem that cannot be solved by Callahan's promise to produce a scholar's edition or to make all the Ellison papers available at the Library of Congress. Of course I regret that the book entering the public consciousness and the American canon as Ellison's last novel does not contain more of the material he wrote over the last 45 years of his life. ("Canon" 400, original emphasis)

I agree with Nadel's critique but would extend its local attention to *Juneteenth*'s versions and their implications for representations of race to an even broader claim for a fragmentary aesthetic that relates both to *Juneteenth* and to other ostensibly complete narratives, including Ellison's first novel.[12] *Invisible Man,* read as a new version with Ellison's 1982 introduction to the "30th Anniversary Edition," features what Stephen Marx terms a "crucial sequel" to the original edition (705), in which the voice of the author shares textual space with the voice of the protagonist. While the 1982 *Invisible Man* is a "finished" text in a way that the *Juneteenth* manuscripts are not, the addition of the foreword does create a new version, compelling Ellison's (re)readers to approach the novel in terms of the foreword, and thus unsettling the textual fixity of Ellison's first novel.

Just as Callahan's edition of *Juneteenth* replaces unfinished manuscripts with a fragmentary "whole," reading a particular edition of *Passing* requires choosing a fragment of the larger work, with its two possible endings. Rampersad's edition of *Native Son* is effectively a fragment of another, larger textual whole, as the *Oprah* editions of Morrison's novels and the first edition of *Mumbo Jumbo* signify bibliographically their retrospective and prospective fragmentation. *Juneteenth* is only a more dramatic example at the far end of this textual spectrum, but containing one version of Ellison's manuscripts within a material text ultimately carries the same effect as reducing the multiple versions of the above novels into a single edition. Such a project also stands in contrast to Ellison's critique of presumed orderly systems in *Invisible Man.* That novel "suggests that what order exists is best seen as an ongoing process that begins with the discovery that the patterns imposed on chaos are merely imposed and do not derive their authority from accurately representing things as they are," Kenneth Warren writes (170). Bryant terms such collections of versions "fluid texts," explaining that "the very nature of writing, the creative process, and shifting intentionality, as well as the powerful social forces that occasion translation, adaptation, and censorship among readers—in short, the facts of revision, publication, and reception—urge us to recognize that the only 'definitive text' is a multiplicity of texts, or rather, the fluid text" (2).

Bryant thus encourages editors to produce their own fluid editions, which acknowledge the contingency of any single version. "We cannot edit the fluidity away," he insists; "in fact, we are obliged to edit it into existence, to showcase it for readers, and to help readers pleasurably read it so that they are better equipped to comprehend its reality and to make of it what they will. This editorial and readerly enterprise inherent in fluid-text editing is a professional concern, but it is finally a moral one, too" (174). In this way Bryant connects editing American literature to the representation of America itself: "Our culture is a fluid text, but we want to read it as a fixed thing, never seeking to find the dynamics of its changing but always to discover the authority of its imagined fixity, its nonexistent past purity" (200).

Returning to the interpretive and ideological—in Žižek's sense—implications of editing, we can understand this "imagined fixity" finally in terms of the related fantasies of stability that apply both to *Juneteenth* and to notions of race in America. While Callahan no doubt seeks to represent Ellison's critique of contemporary images of whiteness as falsely premised on the rejection of a shared cultural heritage with blackness, he does so by editing—that is, interpreting—the material documents behind *Juneteenth* into a seemingly coherent form. Callahan thus misrecognizes the true condition of Ellison's text(s), seeing there a lack of completeness, which he acknowledges against his will and then responds to with the discovery of *Juneteenth* as organizing principle.[13] To read *Juneteenth* as representing metonymically the manuscripts from which it is drawn would then be a misreading, but of the sort that Žižek posits as necessary. "If we want to spare ourselves the painful roundabout route through the misrecognition," Žižek explains, "we miss the Truth itself: only the 'working-through' of the misrecognition allows us to accede to the true nature of the other and at the same time to overcome our own deficiency" (63). Along these lines I would view Callahan's version of Ellison's manuscripts as a necessary misreading of a textual other, deriving from the perception of a lack in the other which "gives the subject—so to speak—a breathing space[;] it enables him to avoid the total alienation in the signifier not by filling out his own lack but by allowing him to identify himself, his own lack, with the lack in the Other" (Žižek 122). Connecting this idea back to Bryant's and Nadel's claims for the fundamental instability of both textuality and culture, we might understand *Juneteenth* as a working-through of the real impossibility of editing Ellison's manuscripts and, furthermore, of their necessary failure to represent race itself as a stable narrative. If the Sunraider/Hickman story presents whiteness as a "mammy-made" construction which is ultimately inseparable from blackness—and if we further view this racial identity as a Lacanian kernel of the real which finally cannot be disguised by fantasy—we would also read *Juneteenth* as ultimately indistinguishable from its manuscripts, and thus also as a kernel of the textual real. Rather than acceding to *Juneteenth*'s "passing" as a stable narrative, then, we could read it more faithfully as an unfinished and unfinishable representation of racial narratives which similarly resist classification and teleology. In the conclusion, I expand on the ethical implications produced by such editorial representations of material—and, by extension, social—history.

CONCLUSION

Race, History, and Editorial Ethics

In the December 1945 issue of *Negro Digest*, Zora Neale Hurston published a bitingly satirical article entitled "Crazy for This Democracy," in which she wonders if she has misunderstood Franklin D. Roosevelt referring to the "arse-and-all" of American democracy "when I thought he said plain arsenal?" (*I Love Myself* 165–66). With the war over and without the editorial constraints imposed by Lippincott, Hurston included in this piece much of the social criticism she had allowed to be deleted or softened in *Dust Tracks on a Road* three years earlier. Within the African American community, the end of the war served as a bitter reminder of continuing racial injustice domestically, even as black soldiers returned from service overseas, often in segregated units. In 1941, a black private was lynched in Fort Benning, and other episodes of racial violence erupted across the country's military bases, in a pattern that would continue over the next four years (Potter 68–70).[1]

In keeping with this tension between domestic discrimination and the international presence of hundreds of thousands of black soldiers, Hurston identifies Jim Crow as "common in all colonial Africa, Asia and the Netherlands East Indies," calling for "complete repeal of All Jim Crow Laws in the United States once and for all, and right now. For the benefit of this nation and as a precedent to the world" (*I Love Myself* 167, 168). Like most of Hurston's work from this period, "Crazy for This Democracy" was not reprinted during her lifetime and fell into obscurity until its inclusion in the 1979 Feminist Press collection *I Love Myself When I Am Laughing . . . And Then Again When I Am Looking Mean and Impressive*, edited by Alice

Walker. There the essay appears in a volume that promotes itself in the frontispiece as "an essential part of a recent reevaluation of Hurston, an attempt to grant her her rightful place among the major American writers of the 1930s and 1940s." Following "How It Feels to Be Colored Me" (first published in *World Tomorrow* in 1928), the collection's second section features "Crazy for This Democracy," two other wartime essays—"The 'Pet' Negro System" (*American Mercury*, 1943) and "My Most Humiliating Jim Crow Experience" (*Negro Digest*, 1944)—and "What White Publishers Won't Print" (*Negro Digest*, 1950). For the three selections from the 1940s, the headnote offers the year of original publication, but no other textual or contextual history.[2]

The publication of *I Love Myself* responds indirectly to the earlier muting of Hurston's political commentary in *Dust Tracks*, granting Hurston's more ephemeral periodical publications the stability of a book. The changed cultural circumstances surrounding this collected edition also recall the political tensions Hurston had confronted with her autobiography. Valerie Boyd notes that Bertram Lippincott was particularly sensitive to perceived attacks on the American government in the wake of Pearl Harbor. After Lippincott had cut "whole chunks" of Hurston's manuscript (V. Boyd 357), the resulting text drew praise from white critics in large part because "Hurston eliminated—or allowed her editor to eliminate—all overt statements in *Dust Tracks* that might have been viewed as inflammatory" (360). Trudier Harris-Lopez, however, reads Hurston's acquiescence to such changes as part of a "duping" strategy in which "Hurston's readers concluded that they were getting what her editors intended" (66) when, in fact, the autobiography carefully "executes physical or psychological violence upon substitutes for authorial coercion" (53). While Harris-Lopez presents a compelling argument for Hurston's subtle subversion of Lippincott's circumscription of her raced authorial image, the fact of that power imbalance is most important for the historical background I am tracing here.

Thus, to read "Crazy for This Democracy" in 1945 in *Negro Digest*, a magazine launched three years previously, is a different kind of textual event than to read this essay in *I Love Myself*, a collection which contributed importantly both to Hurston's return to college curricula and the canon and to the revaluation of New Negro Renaissance writers, especially women, that has extended from the 1970s to the present. With its direct engagement of Roosevelt's reluctance to reform military racial practices, "Crazy for This

Democracy" in its original publishing context contributes interestingly to postwar black protests, through a new magazine seeking a national African American audience. Reprinted in a collection of Hurston's rediscovered work, the essay and its companion pieces appear as reactions to the earlier "How It Feels to Be Colored Me," which Walker terms "an excellent example of Zora Neale Hurston at her most exasperating" in her introductory notes to the essay section (151). Walker's general editorial approach, though, is at odds with the collection's larger project, as the lack of textual apparatus removes Hurston's publishing history from the otherwise detailed record through which the collection seeks to recover her career. In a marked departure from Walker's well-known efforts at recovering Hurston's lost biographical record, in this collection and elsewhere, the wartime essays appear as if published outside of their historical context, and so figure Hurston more in relation to her career than her cultural environment.

I cite this example here to begin a concluding discussion of cultural, social, and textual histories as reflected and represented through editorial theory and practice. As a host of postmodern novels—including *Flight to Canada, Beloved, Jazz,* David Bradley's *The Chaneysville Incident* (1981), and Octavia Butler's *Kindred* (1979)—make clear, America's racial past informs its present to such an extent that one is not explicable except in terms of the other. Such texts will eventually require editions that juxtapose this approach to history and culture alongside their own histories of textual production. That is, textual history should be as important an object of inquiry as its social and cultural cousins: we should examine Morrison's commercial alliance with Oprah Winfrey alongside the contemporaneous accounts of Margaret Garner's trial, just as we should recover the circumstances of *Passing*'s production as well as the details of the Rhinelander case.[3] For future editions to ignore or gloss over their texts' production histories, and the traces of surrounding cultural and social contexts generated therein, will mean creating new editions which are ahistorical at their core because they are ahistorical about themselves. This issue ultimately speaks to the ethics of editing, for to represent the present outside of the past is to perpetuate what Ellison calls, in "The Novel as a Function of American Democracy," America's "tradition of forgetfulness" (*Essays* 764).[4]

History's role in the present is always fluid, of course, and so the study of textual production should adapt itself to multiple lines of criticism. Indeed, another version of this book could have focused on race and ethnicity within international post- and neo-colonial contexts, rather than on race within a purely American atmosphere. The same authors could even have appeared at least as brief examples: Larsen's *Quicksand* (1928) follows its heroine from the United States to Denmark and back, as does a veiled portrait of Larsen's own unreliable autobiographical claim, for Knopf's publicity department (repeated on *Passing*'s dust jacket), that "her mother was Danish, her father a Negro from the Virgin Islands" (quoted in Larson 185); through the Before Columbus Foundation, Reed has worked to define multiculturalism so it will "include all the ethnics" (Dick and Singh 374); Brooks's late poems, especially, seek to dislodge "Black" from a restrictive (African) American meaning; Morrison examines multicultural Caribbean conflicts in *Tar Baby* (1981); and Ellison's typescript of *Invisible Man* triggers the protagonist's development through his reading of journals emphasizing "global color prejudice and the European domination of nonwhites" (Jackson 427).[5] Such a book would have other texts and authors as its primary focus, though, for instance, Claude McKay's *Banana Bottom* (1933), in which the glossary works as part of the novel's complex cross-cultural expression of McKay's "imaginative return" to a Jamaica "irremediably marked by European culture" (North 122), or *Divina Trace* (1991), a postmodern, postcolonial novel by Trinidadian Robert Antoni that represents the problem of the postcolonial audience through a mirror page inserted in the middle of the narrative. From this unique bibliographical environment, the Hindu monkey-god Hanuman compels Antoni's readers to question the politics of postcolonial literary consumption: "Seeing in de page you own monkeyface ee-eeing, quick out you dreamsleep walcott!" (205).[6] A third version of this book could have examined material productions of whiteness in opposition to racial and ethnic identity, as, for example, in E. M. Forster's revision of the Marabar Caves scene in *A Passage to India*, which transforms a definite description of an assault into a thoroughly modernist ambiguity, and so remakes a draft version of colonial disorder into what Homi Bhabha terms "the enunciatory disorder of the colonial present" (*Location* 126).[7] I have limited the scope of this book, in part, as a more effective means of opening a critical space within both editorial theory and African American studies, and with the hope that such a space, once opened, will lead in various directions. I point to these alternate versions, then, to suggest a few of the many topics that ideas of socialized authorship might pursue. Just as material textuality demonstrates the otherwise hidden significance of the book as a physical object on the way to destabilizing broader notions of textuality, so too do studies of ethnic identity as constructed from ultimately fictional physical markers lead to understandings of race and ethnicity as unmoored from an ostensibly stable materiality—yet just as one cannot approach textuality except through the physical book, one cannot avoid the ineluctable reminders of a social insistence on race as an ultimately material category. I explore this conceptual connection here through one last extended example, Colson Whitehead's *The Intuitionist* (1999), and the broader implications it carries for a racially aware editorial theory.

Whitehead's debut novel is still making its way into the canon of contemporary African American fiction, but I focus on it here, first, because the narrative presents a compelling fictional version of the real issues confronted by editors and, second, because contemporary texts are still, so to speak, "outside" of textual history (or rather still so far within that history as to yield only speculative conclusions about the kinds of editorial issues that will eventually arise). To imagine editing a contemporary text thus enables examination of what Paul Riceour calls in a different context "the *future of the past*, the unfulfilled potential of the past" (14, original emphasis). Such a perspective on the past, Riceour concludes, motivates a more ethical use of memory and history, as a way "of bringing memory and imagination together" (16). Editing also inevitably requires a similar combination of faithfulness to the historical archive—as well as the need to expand the scope and content of the archive—and an awareness of historical contingency. As Riceour asks, "How do we make the past visible, as if it were present, while acknowledging our *debt* to the past as it actually happened?" (16, original emphasis). Just as these kinds of historical and ethical questions are particularly significant for cultural groups that have not had access to power, and thus may not be represented adequately within a present archive, so too are such editorial questions especially important for authors and texts whose very presence within editorial history and practice requires that narrative to be revised.

As I mentioned above, these questions circulate through the fictional world of *The Intuitionist*, generating a narrative exploration of editorial ethics.[8] Whitehead's novel is a particularly apt exploration of textual and racial epistemologies, as the story revolves around conflicting ways of knowing the world—in this case, the world of elevators. The protagonist, Lila Mae Watson, is the first black woman to become an elevator inspector in the unnamed city's history, thus conferring a racial dimension on the novel's elaborate metaphor of Empiricism and Intuitionism, the rival theoretical branches of elevator inspection. When an elevator crashes in a building Lila Mae has inspected, she launches her own far-reaching inquiry, at first to explain the collapse before she can be blamed by the largely white Empirical department. As Lila Mae's investigation broadens to uncover the suppressed histories behind the theory and practice of elevator inspection, it culminates with the discovery that James Fulton, the founder of the Intuitionist approach, has passed for white because "no one would have worshipped him, his books probably never would have been published at all, or would exist under a different name, the name of the plagiarizing white man Fulton had been fool enough to share his theories with" (151). And because Lila Mae experiences her discovery of Intuitionism's racial secret through distinctly physical responses to manuscripts and printed books, the novel is well suited to my own investigations of textual and racial material fictions.

Strikingly, once Lila Mae identifies Fulton as black, she perceives his masterpiece, *Theoretical Elevators*, in new, racially inflected ways. In the Intuitionist House library, she finds that "Fulton's nigrescence whispered from the bindings of the House's signed first editions, tinting the disciples' words, reconnoting them. Only she could see it, this shadow. She had learned how to read, and there was no one she could tell" (151). What has changed for Lila Mae is not the text, whether linguistic or bibliographic, but rather the paratext of the author's racial identity, and yet this change leads her to perceive a physical reconstitution of the book itself. The personification of the bindings transfers a subtle, subversive whisper onto the book's frame and ligatures, metaphorizing the author's passing as the book's seemingly white yet really black bindings. The signed first editions are commodities, both cultural and capital, because of the signature's authenticity: the handwriting signifies that the author has truly signed them and, further, as Lila Mae learns, that the author is white. As Derrida might suggest, this hidden prohibition against blackness as a guarantor of authorial value already imagines its own violation, what he calls "the singularity of an imminence whose 'cutting point' spurs desire at its birth" ("Aphorism" 420). The secret blackness that Lila Mae begins to see on the very body of the books demonstrates a fundamental connection between passing and versioning: both practices rely on, and thus call into question, the stability of an inner, "true" self or text, which can appear in various superficial manifestations.

This conceptual confluence emerges in Whitehead's novel as inflected by racial history, one of several analogs to the elevator metaphor in its concern for "verticality" and the glass ceilings of race. As Lila Mae concludes her investigations, she gains access to a lost manuscript of Fulton's, a third volume of *Theoretical Elevators*. Approaching this secret draft, Lila Mae finds that "she has learned how to read, like a slave does, one forbidden word at a time" (230). Here Lila Mae interprets the recent past of Fulton's drafts and the present of her textual and elevator inspections in terms of slavery's past, before shifting forward historically in her reading methods, into passing as both historical background and interpretive practice. In this respect the novel ultimately portrays both schools of elevator inspection as premised on falsity: the fiction that Empirical knowledge can produce a definitive truth and the lie that Fulton has told by living as white in a society that "should" mark him as black, with all the implications Lila Mae initially feels for the theory Fulton crafts in response to his passing.

In the future beyond the narrative, then, Lila Mae will be an Intuitionist editor. The guardian of Fulton's estate, an African American maid who may have been his lover, entrusts the hidden manuscript to Fulton's intellectual heir because the line *Lila Mae is the one* appears in a notebook margin (253, original emphasis). Similarly, Lila Mae thinks of Fulton's wishes for the dissemination of his final work, "Fulton left instructions, but she knows she is permitted to alter them according to circumstances. There was no way Fulton could foresee how the world would change" (255). By editing Fulton's manuscript according to her "intuition," as Lila Mae thinks in the novel's closing line, she is approaching that text on a "nonmaterial" basis, as she has done with elevators, privileging her intuition about the proper form of the text over the material documents themselves (as an Empiricist editor would do). Further, as the black editor of an author whose work changes significantly when racial identity is put into play, Lila Mae adopts a different ethical stance than has historically been true of white editors. Rather than marking Fulton's blackness as a symptom of cultural particularity, and thus reducing his theoretical work to an expression of a "special" culture to a universal, implicitly white audience, Lila Mae seeks rather to maintain

Fulton's passing in order to reveal his elevator theories' racial implications without the veil of race acting as a marker of difference alone.

Before relating Lila Mae's treatment of the Fulton manuscript to the questions of editorial ethics it raises, I first outline the related theoretical issues conveyed by her (fictional) editing, as they relate to issues of versions and versioning. Strictly speaking, the first two volumes of *Theoretical Elevators* are not "new" versions for Lila Mae, once she discovers Fulton's passing, because there have been no linguistic or bibliographic changes to the texts themselves. Yet if we take Hans Zeller's still influential statement that "a new version implies a new intention" (241) at a broader level, a new intention clearly does appear (at least to Lila Mae) in rereading Fulton's published works with knowledge of his racial secret. We might understand these new versions as apparent only to those readers who know their full textual, or in this case paratextual, history. Lila Mae's future editing of Fulton's third volume therefore operates within different theoretical parameters, in this case touching on questions of how to represent unfinished or unpublished works in published form, and thus on corollary questions of how to position multiple versions of a work in relation to each other, or how to conceptualize the text in relation to the work (where "work" refers to a collection of variant documents, and "text" to a particular documentary instantiation of the work).

When a work has no specific tangible condition, we arrive at the question of whether a particular text refers to an "essential" work, or whether a work is no more and no less than a collection of documents. Peter Shillingsburg distinguishes between an "essayed version," which he describes as "a conceptual entity, not a physical entity" (70), and a "material text," by which he means "any union of a linguistic text with a physical medium that 'fixes' it, whether it is a manuscript or a printed book" (71 n28). This sense of fixity is key for Shillingsburg, who insists on the immaterial, potential text as necessarily transcending any particular material instantiation. "The material text—whether it is the author's or the publisher's, whether it represents version 1 or *n*, whether it is accurate or corrupt—is a necessary representation without which the work cannot be experienced," Shillingsburg writes, "but it is not identical with the work, for no *particular* copy of the work is needed for the work to be experienced" (92, original emphasis). For Shillingsburg, then, the work resides on an immaterial plane, even if the only route to the work takes us through a particular material path.

In response to Shillingsburg, Robin Schulze adopts a Darwinian metaphor to account for textual variants introduced at each stage of production, whether by authors or other figures. Schulze's emphasis is not so much on a larger sense of the work as an entity, but rather on the evolutionary shifts in texts; she concludes that "both an author's pre-production manuscript and his or her post-production first edition stand as equally valid versions of a text in that each version reflects a different, but historically important, notion of textual fitness in relation to its particular social, cultural, or textual conditions" (300). Schulze's sense of textuality is subtly but significantly distinct from Shillingsburg's because Schulze relocates authors and other agents as part of a broader evolutionary system, in which textual adaptation is ultimately its own force, beyond the control of either authorial intention or social pressure.[9] In applying these (actual) editorial theories and practices to the (fictional) case of Fulton's manuscript, we see Lila Mae following one of two paths: basing her eventual edition of *Theoretical Elevators*, volume 3, on the essayed version that Fulton could not produce during his lifetime, and so seeing its "fixed" state when published as an offshoot of an unpublished draft; or understanding the unpublished and published states of the manuscript in response to the original and eventual social and cultural conditions of its production, and so privileging neither "edition" within this evolutionary structure. The conceptual difference here lies in a choice between figuring the new edition as one manifestation of an ideal version, which corresponds to no single material document, or conceiving of the new edition as one point in a nexus, in which the process of textual production itself tells the textual story. For Lila Mae's editing of the Fulton manuscript—and for racially aware editing in general—this theoretical decision speaks as well to representations of race in terms of an ideal or essential origin, or as an expression of a particular historical condition. In her editorial interpretations of Fulton's manuscripts and Fulton himself in terms of racial identity and knowledge, Lila Mae could figure an "essayed version" of Fulton as black, which has been submerged beneath his passing, or understand Fulton's shifting racial identities as points along a social spectrum, none of which necessarily express an "essential" self.

The implicit authorial representations that derive from editorial theories and practices are especially evident in responses to unfinished drafts, for there the editor must fill in the final space(s) between manuscript and print, imposing at least a temporary textual fixity on a fundamentally fragmentary work. Just as Callahan supplements Ellison's compositional role in selecting which portions of the manuscripts to include, and in what order, as *Juneteenth*, Lila Mae will intuitively revise Fulton's volume. My arguments concerning the actual case of Ellison's unfinished second novel apply as well to the fictional case of Fulton's unfinished third volume; indeed, both projects are necessarily incomplete, for to impose a printed order onto either set of drafts would belie the unfinished condition of race in America, an incompleteness that compels Lila Mae to wait until Fulton's readers are prepared for a "second elevation." The difficulty for Lila Mae, as for any editor in this situation, lies in intuiting intention from a textual condition in which the primary intention has been, after all, not to publish. As John Whittier-Ferguson observes (in relation to Virginia Woolf's wish to leave her final novel, *Between the Acts*, unpublished), "manuscript study often appears to promise evidence of intention even as it undercuts any straightforward model of cause and effect, of design and execution" (301). Indeed, Whitehead's readers know that Lila Mae's presence as "the one" in Fulton's notebook is not necessarily an indication that he considers her his intellectual heir; watching Lila Mae through his window, Fulton observes merely that she is the only other one who is at work on campus late at night, then "dismiss[es] her from his mind. He's always writing things in the margin" (253). The empirical connection between these Intuitionists appears coincidental here, but this knowledge relies on an omniscient narrative perspective that is by definition fictional. That is, Whitehead's reader occupies a position of total knowledge that is unavailable to any character, so that even as the narrative reveals the contingency of Lila Mae's legacy, it also demonstrates the perspectival nature of (textual) knowledge, a condition that gives rise to the Empiricist/Intuitionist split to begin with, with each theory's ultimately false dream of "true" elevator (or textual) understanding.

The fictionality of the fiction here returns me to the usefulness of this example for my larger discussion of editorial ethics, race, and history, subjects that, after all, lie beyond the boundaries of fiction. Yet it is the imaginative space of fiction, the ability to point out the limits of the historical real while imagining a surpassing of those limits, that endows the genre with its cultural power—and positions the novel as the textual space through which to negotiate the inescapable play between material reality and fictional freedom that characterizes American racial identity, what Alain Locke calls, hopefully, in a 1928 essay "a situation of profitable exchange and real cultural recriprocity" (*Critical* 448). Thus Morrison seeks in *Paradise* "first to enunciate and then eclipse the racial gaze altogether" ("Home" 9), and Sunraider/Bliss pronounces from the Senate floor in *Juneteenth* that "again we must forget the past by way of freeing ourselves so that we can reassemble its untidy remnants in the interests of a more human order" (18). That process of articulating a racial gaze and a racial past in order to eclipse and reassemble these structures of epistemological and social oppression inheres as well in the ineluctable materiality of fiction: the world beyond the page is only accessible first through the page, the book itself, as Morrison brilliantly demonstrates through *Jazz's* book-as-narrator and the closing admonition to "look where your hands are. Now."

Race itself operates through this tension between fictionality and materiality. "Biologically fictitious," Charles Mills writes, "race becomes socially real, so that people learn to see themselves as black and white, are treated as black and white, and are motivated by considerations arising out of this group identity" (*Blackness* 134). As Mills demonstrates through the hypothetical example of "quace," our seemingly natural notions of race are neither foundational nor essentialist. "Race is not 'metaphysical' in the deep sense of being eternal, unchanging, necessary, part of the basic furniture of the universe," Mills maintains. "But race is a *contingently* deep reality that structures our particular social universe, having a social objectivity and causal significance that arise out of *our* particular history" (48, original emphasis). As I have argued throughout this book, editorial theory and practice have tended to neglect that particular racial history, both through the editions not produced and through the kind of theory generated for an implicitly social universe. The ethical editorial burden lies, then, in the kind of historical problem imagined in *Kindred*: like the time-traveling Dana, editors must look always to the past and the future simultaneously in order to operate within the present, in order to keep textual and racial pasts alive within present editions, so that those particular histories will remain legible to future readers. While editors sometimes occupy the space of textual authority from which they "have another look" through the windows of the cultural and textual past, they should remember the ramifications of representing those histories, and thus of interpreting the doubled racial and textual senses in which everything may be "dark."

NOTES

INTRODUCTION:
REAL FICTIONS OF RACE AND TEXTUALITY

1. Over the last fifteen years or so, of course, there has been a great deal of important critical work seeking to reverse this historical and cultural trend, inspired by such insightful readings as Shelley Fisher Fishkins's *Was Huck Black?* and Morrison's *Playing in
the Dark*. This branch of scholarship is certainly important to my study, but as I make
clear in the introduction, I am primarily concerned with the historical circumstances
of textual production and the extent to which they are visible to contemporary readers. For an insightful discussion of this field, see Stephen Knadler's introduction to *The
Fugitive Race*.

2. Charles Scruggs and Lee Vandemarr note that the phrase "black vaudeville" may have
been suggested to Boni and Liveright by Waldo Frank or Toomer himself, and that it
was "picked up frequently by early reviewers" (286 n35). The origin of the phrase is
less important to my argument than its role in the paratextual construction of *Cane*
as performing blackness for its white readers.

3. As Peter Flora demonstrates, Blanche Knopf was more directly involved than Alfred
with the firm's African American authors, and she employed Carl Van Vechten as an
unofficial adviser in this regard. "Blanche habitually followed Van Vechten's advice
blindly," Flora concludes. "She was loath to make any decisions on a manuscript by an
African American on her own, but she rarely sounded out anyone else at the firm
either. For black writers at Knopf, the buck clearly stopped at Van Vechten" (77–78).
In my estimation Flora overstates the degree of Van Vechten's influence somewhat;
James Weldon Johnson also read manuscripts for Knopf, for instance (Lewis 69). But
the Van Vechten–Blanche Knopf relationship is clearly an important element of this
history.

4. I have drawn the historical details in this paragraph from the thorough entries in
Donald Franklin Joyce's *Black Book Publishers in the United States*.

5. Samira Kawash notes that in these editions of the *Autobiography* "the reader is implicitly positioned as white; it is a white reader who is offered the 'glimpse behind the
veil,' and it is the white reader to whom the narrator confesses his crime and his guilt

because it is primarily in relation to whiteness's claim to purity that the narrator's passing for white might be taken as a crime" (146).

6. Interestingly, Ellison's revisions to the typescript of *Invisible Man* also removed a central white woman, Louise, who served originally as "the Invisible Man's impetus for going underground" (Jackson 427). The other major change at this stage was the deletion of journals, written by an activist named Leroy, which the Invisible Man reads at several crucial points. This text provided a more international emphasis on race and colonialism (426–27).

7. Consider here the counterexample of George Orwell's refusal to make the cuts to *1984* requested by the book club and the club's eventual acquiescence. Orwell, of course, was already an established journalist and novelist at this point in his career, and so could afford to risk losing the profits and status the club's selection would yield. Faced with the potential loss of £40,000 or more from the book club selection, and already near death, Orwell nevertheless assured his literary and personal executors that "he had already salted away enough money in insurance policies to cover a good education" for his son (Crick 386).

8. These imprints include Strivers Row, One World, and Harlem Moon, all part of the Random House conglomerate, HarperCollins's Amistad, and Kensington's Dafina Books. For a more extensive discussion of these labels, see Ween 100–1.

9. McGann's approach is hardly a universal one within the field, however; for useful counter-arguments and overviews of this larger debate, see Tanselle, *A Rationale of Textual Criticism*; Shillingsburg, *Resisting Texts*, chapters 2–3; Bryant, *The Fluid Text*, chapters 1–3; and Greetham, *Theories of the Text*, especially chapters 3 and 4.

 Strictly speaking, drafts, manuscripts, and advertisements would comprise a paratextual bibliographic code, within McGann's framework, as these documents are not part of the published text proper. I have included such materials within this study, however, as part of a broader focus on the various public and private states of texts' material histories.

10. Similarly, D. C. Greetham maintains that bibliographic codes "are the formalist 'envelope' without which the book does not even have existence let alone meaning. . . . [T]herefore these codes must be confronted and subsumed into our cognition of the bookishness of text, no matter what the medium may be or the demonstrable role of the author in controlling that medium. In fact, the only demonstration possible is the materiality of text, for it is the only remaniement we are left with" (*Scholarship* 457). Greetham and McGann disagree on this point with Tanselle, who insists, "We sometimes confuse the statement or work with its physical embodiment, forgetting that manuscripts and printed books are utilitarian objects designed to perform a function. Messages may be inextricable from their media, but the medium of literature and other pieces of verbal communication is language, not paper and ink" (*Rationale* 39–40). For effective responses by Greetham, see "Stepping Outside Ourselves: Tanselle's Universal Text," *Review* 12 (1990): 69–79; and his *Theories of the Text*, chapter 8.

11. For important exceptions, see especially Andrews, "Editing 'Minority' Texts"; Carson, "Editing Martin Luther King"; and Bornstein, *Material Modernism*, chapter 7. Other

noteworthy recent scholarship on African American literature and publishing history, while not necessarily concerned with editorial theory, includes Karen Jackson Ford, "Making Poetry Pay: The Commodification of Langston Hughes," in *Marketing Modernisms: Self-Promotion, Canonization, and Rereading*, ed. Kevin J. H. Dettmar and Stephen Watt (Ann Arbor: University of Michigan Press, 1996); Christopher Metress, "Langston Hughes's 'Mississippi—1955': A Note on Revisions and an Appeal for Reconsideration," *African American Review* 37 (2003): 139–48; and Christopher Mulvey, "Creating an Online Scholarly Edition: The Problems Posed by *Clotel*, the First African-American Novel," in *Histoire(s) de livres: Le Livre et l'édition dans le monde anglophone*, ed. Marie-Françoise Cachin and Claire Parfait (Paris: Institut d'Etudes Anglophones, 2002).

12. Bhabha maintains that "those elements of social 'consciousness' imperative for agency—deliberative, individuated action and specificity in analysis—can now be thought outside that epistemology that insists on the subject as always prior to the social or on the knowledge of the social as necessarily subsuming or sublating the particular 'difference' in the transcendent homogeneity of the general" (451).

CHAPTER ONE. PASSING (ON) TEXTUAL HISTORY: THE ENDS OF NELLA LARSEN'S *PASSING*

1. For such readings see McDowell's introduction to the Rutgers edition of *Quicksand* and *Passing*; David L. Blackmore, " 'That Unreasonable Restless Feeling': The Homosexual Subtexts of Nella Larsen's *Passing*," *African American Review* 26 (1992): 475–84; and Jacquelyn Y. McLendon, *The Politics of Color in the Fiction of Jessie Fauset and Nella Larsen* (Charlottesville: University Press of Virginia, 1995), Chapter 6. Lauren Berlant (111–13), J. Butler (173–85), and Kawash (159–61) consider lesbian interpretations while arguing ultimately for racial passing as the novel's dominant theme.

2. In his introduction to Larsen's *Complete Fiction*, Larson interprets Larsen's use of her maiden name as an indication that her marriage with Elmer Imes was failing. But after their divorce she referred to herself as Mrs. Imes, which Larson reads as her later wish to recover the marital identity (xiii, xvii).

3. For fuller discussions of Larsen's life and career, see especially Davis's biography, Haviland, "Passing," and Hutchinson, "Veil."

4. Harrison-Kahan argues insightfully that "Irene and Clare never 'are' black or white, and their desire cannot be defined solely in terms of heterosexuality or homoeroticism. . . . Their identity is a continual, rather than finished process. Instead of passing as white or as straight, they pass *between* binary positions" (117).

5. Greenberg Publishers reprinted *Passing* in 1935, but Larsen did not renew the novel's copyright when it expired in the 1950s (Larson 88) and the novel remained out of print until the Arno reprint in 1969 (Henderson 204).

6. I am grateful to Russell Maylone of the Northwestern University Library's Special Collections department for clarifying this point.

7. On publisher's intentions, see James L. W. West III, "Editorial Theory and the Act of Submission," *PBSA* 83 (1989): 169–85, and "Fair Copy, Authorial Intention, and 'Versioning'" *Text* 6 (1994): 81–89. On writers, editors, and publishers as "multiple" authors, see Jack Stillinger, *Multiple Authorship and the Myth of Solitary Genius* (New York: Oxford University Press, 1991), especially chapters 1 and 9.

8. Tate insists, "*Passing's* conclusion defies simple solution. I cannot resolve this problem by accepting a single explanation, since Larsen, on one hand, deliberately withheld crucial information that would enable me to arrive at a definite conclusion, and on the other, she counter-balanced each possible interpretation with another of equal credibility" (146).

9. The Norton critical edition of *Souls*, edited by Gates and Terri Hume Oliver, offers an interesting approach to related questions of editorial ethics, as the "Note on the Text" includes a chart listing nine anti-Semitic references from the original 1903 publication that Du Bois let stand until the 1953 Jubilee edition. Even Du Bois's changes are illuminating in this regard, however, as he typically revises "Jew" to "immigrant." By including the chart, rather than opting for one version or the other, Gates and Oliver enable readers to uncover the history of Du Bois's rhetoric, as well as the effects of the Holocaust on his eventual decision to make the changes outlined there. See also the edition of *Souls* edited by David W. Blight and Robert Gooding-Williams (Boston: Bedford, 1997), 209–10 n20.

10. On the teaching of textual scholarship, see George Bornstein, "Teaching Editorial Theory to Non-Editors: What? Why? How?" *Text* 9 (1996): 144–60; and Philip Cohen, "Textual Scholarship in the Classroom" *Text* 9 (1996): 135–43.

CHAPTER TWO. BLACK PAGE, WHITE COPYRIGHT: THE POLITICS OF PRINT IN ISHMAEL REED'S *MUMBO JUMBO*

1. Greetham notes of the relationship between manuscripts and printed books: "But manuscripts themselves, particularly those with multiple layers (or *couches*, in Derridean terms) of glossing, may paradoxically contain levels of trace that the printed and reformatted critical edition may subvert" (*Theories* 341). This claim is part of Greetham's larger argument that Derridean deconstruction typically neglects levels of textual instability at the material level that are common knowledge to textual scholars. See *Theories of the Text*, chapter 8, and "[Textual] Criticism and Deconstruction," *Studies in Bibliography* 44 (1991): 1–30, which responds both to Derrida and to G. Thomas Tanselle, "Textual Criticism and Deconstruction," *Studies in Bibliography* 43 (1990): 1–43.

2. Similarly, John G. Parks views *Mumbo Jumbo* "as a comic 'anti-epic,' in that it is concerned with a plague which is really an 'anti-plague' (because it 'enlivened the host')

and because it depicts the world not so much enfeebled by absurdity or irrationality, but rather a world suffering from too much rationality" (164).

3. I first encountered this example in Howard Ramsby II's insightful presentation at the 2003 meeting of the Society for Textual Scholarship, "Understanding 'The New' African American Anthologies of the Sixties," New York City, March 2003.

4. Interestingly, Walter Mosley has shifted back and forth between his mainstream publisher, W. W. Norton, and the independent Black Classic Press, which has issued *What Next: A Memoir Toward World Peace* (2003) and *Gone Fishin'* (1997), the sixth installment in the Easy Rawlins series. As *Gone Fishin'* actually returns to an earlier chronological period than the first novel in the series, *Devil in a Blue Dress* (1990), Mosley's choice of a black publisher perhaps signifies his interest in connecting the past to the present within the racial cultural contexts that provide the background for all his mystery novels.

5. Erzulie is the Haitian Vaudou goddess of love (Gates, *Signifying* 221).

6. Freedgood left Doubleday for Random House in 1970, and Reed followed her there beginning with *The Last Days of Louisiana Red*, in 1974. Weinberg has also been a cover designer for various rock albums.

7. A film version of Wallace's *The Man*, with James Earl Jones as the first African American president, premiered in 1972, gaining Hollywood release only after most television stations had shied away from its potential controversy.

8. In an interview with Reed and other *Yardbird* editors, Ellison interestingly quarrels with their insistence on a distinctly black cultural tradition. "Where on earth did the notion come from that the world and all its art has to be re-invented, recreated every time a Black individual seeks to express himself?" Ellison asks. "The world is here and art is here, and they've been here for a long, long time. After all, a few of the contributions to culture, to civilization, were made by people who possessed African genes—if that means a damn thing, which I doubt . . ." (Reed, Troupe, and Cannon 350, original ellipsis). As Gates notes throughout his discussion of *Mumbo Jumbo*, Reed's novel engages in an elaborate parody of several African American forerunners, including *Invisible Man*. Furthermore, Gates observes, "the themes of the relationship between words and texts echo a key passage from Ellison's short story 'And Hickman Arrives': 'Good. Don't talk like I talk; talk like I *say* talk. Words are your business, boy. Not just *the* Word. Words are everything. The key to the Rock, the answer to the Question'" (*Signifying* 220). Reed's novel is interestingly in conversation here with both the past and the future of (African) American fiction, as Ellison's short story becomes part of *Juneteenth*, almost forty years after its initial publication in 1960.

9. The archival evidence suggests that Reed wrote this jacket copy, as a copy of it is included with his correspondence to Freedgood and her assistants.

10. In addition, the letter as reproduced in the novel renders invisible the other physical elements of the original document, such as paper, ink, etc. As Genette notes with reference to a Picasso text, a perception of "'the thing itself'" depends on an individual inspection of an original document (*Work* 133).

11. See Peter J. de Voogd, "Laurence Sterne, the marbled page, and 'the use of accidents,'" *Word & Image* 1 (1985): 279–87.

12. Von Vampton also functions as a caricature of Van Vechten. As McGee notes, "Reed suggests that the support of literary authorities like Van Vechten can be dangerous insofar as they identify African American writing with a homogenous concept of ethnicity" (100).

13. The comma between "Oakland" and "California" is probably an error, as Reed's style sheet insists that "commas NEVER appear between names of city and state" (Ishmael Reed Papers).

14. As Heidegger notes, "even the much-vaunted aesthetic experience cannot get around the thingly aspect of the art work" (81). Yet for Heidegger this "thingly aspect" is ultimately unknowable except through the work of art. The same might be said for Jes Grew as a (HooDoo) art work: a physical book seems necessary for Jes Grew to spread to future generations, yet it is Jes Grew itself that "seeks" this physical form, not the material text which produces Jes Grew.

15. Madhu Dubey argues that "Reed's celebration of the subversive energy of black urban popular culture seems to become increasingly unavailable to subsequent African American writers," in part because of "the shrinking credibility, in the postmodern era, of the idea that print or vernacular culture can maintain autonomy from capitalist commodity culture" (51). Dubey cites *Mumbo Jumbo*'s first edition (though mistakenly listing the publisher as Simon and Schuster [251 n120]), but she does not address the ways in which the book already questions its commodity status, not least through the black copyright page.

16. Most critics have read the repeated copyright page as part of the novel's larger cinematic structure. Robert Eliot Fox, for example, writes that "Reed 'rolls' the title and credits before plunging back into the story" (50). Similarly, Gates notes that the "prologue functions like the prologue of a film, with the title and credits appearing next, before the action continues" (*Signifying* 227). Reed's style sheet for Doubleday confirms these readings, as his first instruction reads: "Most of book is in *present tense*, like a film script. (See in this connection position of front matter)" (Ishmael Reed Papers). No doubt these allusions to a film structure are importantly present in this and other parts of the novel, but I would argue that they work alongside, not contradict, my reading of the black copyright page as Reed's partial response to the white ownership of black texts. The cinematic repetition disrupts the usual modes of reading, perhaps compelling a recognition of alienation from the artwork as film has the greatest potential to do for Walter Benjamin, but this awareness would only enhance readers' responses to the other economic and cultural issues raised by the black page.

17. I have written to Reed on this matter, but have not received a response at the time of this writing. Freedgood died in 2002. McCormick, who served as Doubleday's editor-in-chief from 1942 to 1971, donated a wealth of company materials to the Library of Congress before his death in 1997, but the Reed files there relate only to *19 Necromancers from Now* and *Yellow Back Radio Broke Down*.

CHAPTER THREE. GWENDOLYN BROOKS'S
BIBLIOGRAPHICAL BLACKNESS

1. Harper also published the collection *The World of Gwendolyn Brooks* in 1971 and retained the rights to Brooks's earlier books following her departure.

2. Brooks also offers a more qualified assessment of her decision to leave Harper in the 1974 Madhubuti interview: "I didn't leave Harper and Row because they were doing anything to me. Or I didn't know of anything that they were doing to me that was of an evil nature. But I had been telling young poets to support the Black presses. Wherever I went to colleges to visit or read my poetry, I would tell them that this was something that they should feel as a commitment. And it seemed strange for myself to continue with a white publishing company when I was giving this advice" (quoted in Gayles 76). While Brooks here figures her relationship with Harper itself in neutral terms, she also presents as inherently impossible the production of a genuinely "Black" text through an effectively white publisher.

3. J. Sullivan notes that this typographical effect "emphasizes that these are little white words in a big black space" (561).

4. *The World of Gwendolyn Brooks* also includes *Maud Martha* as the collection's middle text, a position from which it "brings to closure the poems in 'A Street in Bronzeville' and 'Annie Allen,' while it prepares the way for 'The Bean Eaters,' and, from the sixties, the stunning poetry of *In the Mecca*" (Spillers 250). *Blacks*, Brooks's self-published anthology which is now in print from Third World Press, also includes *Maud Martha*.

5. *A Street in Bronzeville* appeared on August 15, just more than two weeks before V-J Day (Kent 73).

6. I thus disagree with Kenny J. Williams's assessment of Brooks's post-1967 career. "She herself probably gave more credence to the meaning of the 1967 Second Black Writers Conference at Fisk University than it really deserved," Williams writes. "Changing one's hair style and refusing certain amenities from a white reading public, while perhaps significant political statements, are ultimately far more cosmetic than substantive" (62–63). As I have maintained throughout this chapter, changing publishers was both a "cosmetic" and "substantive" change for Brooks, as the shift in the circumstances of textual production enabled Brooks to produce new kinds of texts.

7. On "Récitatif," see Elizabeth Abel, "Black Writing, White Reading: Race and the Politics of Feminist Interpretation," *Critical Inquiry* 19 (1993): 470–98.

CHAPTER FOUR. TONI MORRISON, OPRAH WINFREY,
AND POSTMODERN POPULAR AUDIENCES

1. Bourdieu distinguishes between "bourgeois art, which has an honoured place in society, and industrial art, which is doubly suspect, being both mercantile and 'popular' "

(50). Morrison was the only author with three Oprah's Book Club selections (although Bill Cosby appeared on one show to discuss three of his children's books). Winfrey twice selected books by Kaye Gibbons, Jane Hamilton, and Wally Lamb.

2. Franzen's *New Yorker* essay on his *Oprah* experience eloquently describes the peculiarity of having his parents' St. Louis home packaged and filmed, while including a mix of high and popular cultural reactions. (A party at a friend's house evokes the closing of *Swann's Way*, for example, while the itching that breaks out on Franzen's chest while performing his celebrity tasks reminds him of *Alien*.) Franzen here attributes his "high art" comment to "a moment of exhaustion in Oregon" (75), but does not respond directly to the debate sparked by this remark. For a more extended discussion of this episode, see Kathleen Rooney, *Reading with Oprah: The Book Club That Changed America* (Fayetteville: University of Arkansas Press, 2005), chapter 2.

3. *Song* excerpts comprise twenty-four uninterrupted pages. The magazine's table of contents demonstrates fiction's special place by beginning always with the "*Redbook* novel." As an indication of the magazine's shift away from feminist articles, consider the following examples from the September 1977 issue—" 'Farrah Fawcett Majors Makes Me Want to Scream!' "; "Is His Money Your Money Too?"; "How Do You Really Feel About Having Children?"—and from a recent issue (June 2000): "4 Things You Should Never Tell Your Guy"; "5 Sexy Things He's Dying for You to Try in Bed"; "How I Quit Dieting—And Lost Weight."

4. On the important editorial roles played by women as editors and publishers during the modernist period, see Jayne E. Marek, *Women Editing Modernism: "Little" Magazines and Literary History* (Lexington: University of Kentucky Press, 1995).

5. See Ralph D. Story, "Patronage and the Harlem Renaissance: You Get What You Pay For," *College Language Association Journal* 32 (1989): 284–95; and Thomas H. Nigel, "Patronage and the Writing of Langston Hughes's *Not without Laughter*: A Paradoxical Case," *CLA Journal* 42 (1998): 48–70. On Joyce and Eliot, see Rainey, "Consuming Investments: Joyce's *Ulysses*," *James Joyce Quarterly* 33 (1996): 531–67, and "The Price of Modernism: Reconsidering *The Waste Land*," *Yale Review* 78 (1989): 279–300. Both essays have been reprinted in *Institutions of Modernism*. On Woolf, see my "Canonicity and Commercialization in Woolf's Uniform Edition," in *Proceedings of the Ninth Annual Virginia Woolf Conference: Virginia Woolf Turning the Centuries*, ed. Bonnie Kime Scott and Ann Ardis (Pace University Press, 2000).

6. But, like Morrison, Pynchon has published in mainstream magazines: his story "The Secret Integration" appeared in the *Saturday Evening Post*, and two excerpts from *The Crying of Lot 49* appeared in *Esquire* and *Cavalier*. See my "Pynchon in Popular Magazines," *Critique* 44 (2003): 389–404.

7. An earlier, similar article in the London *Sunday Times Magazine* did include a blurry photograph of Pynchon's face, prompting Pynchon's publisher, Henry Holt, to threaten a lawsuit against the newspaper. See James Traub, "Thomas Pynchon finally loses the game of hide-and-seek," *New Yorker*, July 14, 1997, 13.

8. For a useful discussion of this format's construction of gender roles, see Masciarotte, 84–99. See also Jane M. Shattuc, "The Oprahification of America: Talk Shows and the Public Sphere," in *Television, History, and American Culture: Feminist Critical Essays*, ed. Mary Beth Haralovich and Lauren Rabinowitz (Durham: Duke University Press, 1999).

9. All references to Jacoby are taken from e-mail correspondence in September 1999. Jacoby describes the *Oprah* logo's placement as having the "greatest impact" and notes that the back cover photo of Morrison was the author's choice, as the "favorite photo of herself." *Oprah* producers approved the placement of the show's logo on book covers (Max 40).

10. The Knopf hardcover jacket for *Song of Solomon* presents the title in red lettering on a yellow field, with black wings sprouting from the two capital S's. An earlier Plume paperback echoes this design somewhat, depicting a black bird on a yellow field with a blue frame, and a larger white field for the entire cover. Neither cover conveys the sense of celebrity created by the later covers.

11. Kanaga shot "School Girl" while visiting St. Croix in 1962 (Millstein and Lowe 47).

12. One of the four viewers chosen for the discussion with Morrison was a white mother of three adopted black children. The show's opening segment includes an "explanation" of the novel from Morrison, in which she says how "astonished" she has been by responses from women of multiple racial backgrounds, who have related to Pecola's feelings of physical self-alienation in ways that are not specifically racial. Similarly, Winfrey declares while introducing the segment, "The message of *The Bluest Eye* is so universal."

13. In response to an audience member's naive query, "Has Toni Morrison written anymore [sic] books," Winfrey responds, "Yes, won a Nobel Prize for literature" ("Ashley Judd" 26).

14. Kozloff's "Audio Books in a Visual Culture" is so far the only scholarly attempt to define this experience of textuality.

15. The package for *Song* on tape, for example, is one inch shorter and one inch narrower than the Plume reprint for Oprah's Book Club.

16. *Song of Solomon* and *The Bluest Eye* are priced at $18, with *Jazz* at $16, all abridged, from Random House Audiobooks; an unabridged *Sula* lists for $26. An unabridged *Bluest Eye*, read by Morrison and Ruby Dee, lists for $23. An abridged *Beloved*, read by Lynn Whitfield, lists at $18, while Morrison reading the complete version sells for $40. The abridged *Paradise* audiobook, read by Morrison, is listed at $26, and originally bore an Oprah's Book Club sticker. Inside the package is a display of Morrison's other audio titles, encouraging consumer desire for the series.

17. On the talking book, see Gates, *Signifying Monkey* chapters 4–7.

18. See Joyce Irene Middleton, who concludes that "Morrison privileges orality so that her readers can hear and feel the unique oral character of African American language use and see how the survival of cultural consciousness, or nomos, is preserved in a highly literate culture" (29). Similarly, Gay Wilentz concludes that "Morrison's role as an Afrocentric storyteller is unmistakable, and the orature of her foremothers as well as the oral traditions of the black community is evident both in the language and the structure of the novel" (112).

19. See Huyssen's description of postmodernism: "it operates in a field of tension between tradition and innovation, conservation and renewal, mass culture and high art, in which the second terms are no longer automatically privileged over the first" ("Mapping" 48).

20. "To put it simply," Veronique Lesoinne notes, "Morrison has personified the book in a most radical way" (162). Martha J. Cutter also concludes, in a brilliant reading of *Beloved* and *Jazz*, that "the narrator is not a character within the text, although at times s/he plays that role, but rather the voice of the narrative itself" (70). See also John Leonard's review in the *Nation*, reprinted in *Toni Morrison: Critical Perspectives Past and Present*, ed. Henry Louis Gates Jr. and K. A. Appiah (New York, Amistad, 1993); Phillip Page, "Traces of Derrida in Toni Morrison's *Jazz*," *African American Review* 29 (1995): 55–66; Vincent A. O'Keefe, "From 'Other' Sides of the Realist Tracks: (A)Gnostic Narratives in Toni Morrison's *Jazz*," *Centennial Review* 41 (1997): 331–49; and Nancy J. Peterson, "'Say Make Me, Remake Me': Toni Morrison and the Reconstruction of African-American History," especially pp. 210–17; and Eusebio L. Rodrigues, "Experiencing *Jazz*," both in *Toni Morrison: Critical and Theoretical Approaches*, ed. Nancy J. Peterson (Baltimore: Johns Hopkins University Press, 1997).

CHAPTER FIVE. *JUNETEENTH* AS A TEXTUAL AND RACIAL FRAGMENT

1. *Juneteenth* thus participates in the literary revisions of whiteness and blackness outlined by Shelly Fisher Fishkin in "Interrogating 'Whiteness,' Complicating 'Blackness': Remapping American Culture."

2. For two such examples, see McGann's "*Ulysses* as a Postmodern Work" and Bornstein's *Material Modernism*, chapter 6.

3. Genette groups under the heading "paratext" those "verbal and other productions" (*Paratexts* 1) generated both by publishers and authors, although he considers the paratext to be a "conveyor of a commentary that is authorial or more or less legitimated by the author" (2). This is a potentially problematic description in a case like Ellison's, where we could certainly agree that Callahan's editorial work has, on some general level, been "legitimated" by Ellison, but in specific instances it would be difficult to distinguish authorial legitimation from editorial intervention.

4. Yukins, in contrast, analyzes *Juneteenth* as a Cubist narrative while also acknowledging a "lack of textual fixity" that leads her to "avoid making cause-and-effect claims about how the dramatic action in the story unfolds" (1262 n3). Yet Yukins also lapses into rhetorical figures of Ellison as an active, authorizing presence, as, for instance, in the claim, "In the *novel, Ellison juxtaposes* different voices, time sequences, and perspectives to create collage" (1257, emphasis added). This statement follows a paragraph in which Yukins notes that Callahan's editorial strategy is itself a kind of collage, as Callahan "gathered, selected, and pasted together a varied and, in truth,

inharmonious assortment of materials" (1257). No doubt Yukins means here to argue that Ellison's manuscripts are structured as collages, and so Callahan's editorial approach is particularly appropriate in this case, yet by asserting that in the "novel" Ellison "juxtaposes" various narrative elements, Yukins implicitly assumes a teleological fixity which the state of the manuscripts cannot sustain.

5. According to Callahan, Random House editor Scott Moyers wrote the jacket copy (De Santis 613). The preface by Charles Johnson in the Vintage paperback edition also emphasizes the degree of completedness for *Juneteenth*, for instance, referring to the "dozens of fully imagined, deeply felt passages, refined and polished to the level of poetry" in "this capacious, second novel" (xvi, xvii).

6. A similar textual contingency applies to the published version of Hughes and Hurston's play *Mule Bone*, which, as Rachel A. Rosenberg demonstrates in detail, corresponds only to those versions of the unfinished play which revolved around Hughes's insertion of a romance plot, and not to other versions upon which Hurston worked alone. See Rosenberg, "Looking for Zora's *Mule Bone*: The Battle for Artistic Authority in the Hurston-Hughes Collaboration," *Modernism/Modernity* 6 (1999): 79–105; and Bornstein, *Material*, 158–61.

7. Callahan expands on this story in the De Santis interview: "I would tell her how it was going, where I was, what I was finding, and she'd tell me, 'Well, stay with it. Stay with it, John, just keep going,' because I would convey to her that much of this material was wonderful, and the issue was form and, as always with Ralph's fiction, the transitions. Once I got through it all and attempted to lay it all out, she would again come back to her question: 'Beginning, middle, and end. Does it have a beginning, middle, and end?' After finding no way out of the labyrinth of manuscripts, I realized that within this huge, sprawling, somewhat incoherent saga of multiple narratives there was an all but finished, coherent narrative that was the heart of the saga. That was *Juneteenth*, and Fanny loved it" (606). This description, I would argue, again indirectly conveys the triumph of a desire for order, from both Callahan and Fanny Ellison, over an acceptance of the reality of the "huge, sprawling, somewhat incoherent narrative." As I contend in this chapter's conclusion, the discovery of a coherent fiction within this disorder masks the text's true, unfinished nature, substituting the fantasy of order for the reality of chaos.

8. The term "best text" refers to a debate among early twentieth-century bibliographers about how to determine which of various extant manuscripts most clearly reflect authorial intention, or at least is the least corrupt. In response to the influential Lachmann Method of organizing variant manuscripts into stemmata from which they can be traced to their "genealogical" roots, Joseph Bédier proposed a best-text method which proposed to establish one text as most representative of authorial intention, and then to follow that text throughout the editing process. Bédier therefore presumes, through what Greetham calls a "perverse logic," that an editor can "judge manuscripts by their ability to fulfill authorial preferences and yet then supposes that these preferences are otherwise unknowable, as far as emending the text is concerned" (*Scholarship* 325).

Callahan's approach to editing *Juneteenth* is not a best-text method, strictly speaking, but by applying this term to his editorial principles I mean to make the same broad criticism that Greetham advances of Bédier: by focusing on a particular portion of the manuscripts as most representative of Ellison's intentions, Callahan edits *Juneteenth* so as to shape the novel according to his own presumption of what should constitute the best text and, therefore, edits out the massive portions of the manuscripts which seem, retrospectively, to fall outside the narrative theme created by Callahan's editorial decisions themselves.

9. See also Shank's distinction here between Bliss/Sunraider as a blackface, rather than a passing, character; along these lines, Shank also reads *Juneteenth* as expressing a "fundamental recognition of the structural problem of whiteness" (50).

10. S. M. Parrish terms a "Whig interpretation of literature" an editorial approach that traces a text's retrospectively determined progress toward an established end, so that those drafts, variants, and versions which do not match up with the "final" edition of a text are seen simply as false starts. "Thus the past is pretty much wiped away except as it may in one particular or another foreshadow the present," Parrish writes (345).

Robin G. Schulze qualifies Parrish's historical metaphor in an analogy between textual development and evolution, again shifting away from a teleological view. "A version of a text becomes unremittingly historical," Schulze explains, "a product of a particular time and a particular place, designed to meet the needs of that time and place. Texts do not become better or worse, they simply become different as the world around them changes; each version achieves its own kind of fitness 'in relation to its conditions'" (275).

11. Similarly, Harryette Mullen notes in a discussion of the Optic White paint episode in *Invisible Man* that Lucius Brockway "correctly points to the unacknowledged contribution of black men and women to the production (and reproduction) of white America. The ostensibly sophisticated equipment of the factory is revealed as an elaborate 'nigger rig,' just as a significant portion of American culture turns out to be 'mammy made'" (76). On the junkyard car metaphor, see also Yukins, 1257–60.

12. I agree as well with Nadel's next claim: "By the same token, pursuing this line of regret at the expense of the text we do have in its (artificial) entirety is a great mistake. In *Juneteenth*, Callahan has made available a strong and important piece of literature rich in its exploitations and techniques Ellison devoted over half a century to refining" (400). (On Ellison's revisions of Faulkner in *Juneteenth*, for instance, see Nadel, "Integrated" 166–70.) There is no doubt that *Juneteenth* deserves to take its place among the contemporary American canon, nor that it will importantly change critical accounts of American fiction. Nevertheless, Callahan's edition is premised on an editorial illusion.

13. In his discussion of the text's "blackface sentiment," Shank similarly observes that "it is tempting here to read Hickman as Ellison, and Bliss as the impossible-to-finish project of the second novel" (60).

CONCLUSION: RACE, HISTORY, AND EDITORIAL ETHICS

1. Unbeknownst to the American public, the 761st tank battalion, known as the Black Panthers, had advanced through Europe in 1944 and 1945, playing a key role in the Battle of the Bulge and helping to liberate Buchenwald and Dachau. Yet the U.S. Army sent no members of the Signal Corps to record the tankers' arrivals, and at one point cut off gasoline supplies in order to keep the 761st from being the first American soldiers to reach the Russian front (Potter 253, 250). In what Lou Potter calls "one of the war's incredible ironies," the liberating force at Dachau also included the 442nd Regimental Combat Team, consisting largely of volunteers from Japanese internment camps within the United States (239). While this unit "was the most decorated, and had the highest casualty rate, of any unit of its size in World War II," the army "ordered the Nisei soldiers never—under pain of court-martial—to reveal their role in the liberation of Dachau" (Potter 239, 240). In order to preserve a historical record of their role in the war, the Black Panthers produced their own memoir, *Come Out Fighting*, and paid collectively for two thousand copies to be produced in Salzburg in 1945 for distribution to the unit's current and former members (Potter 265).

2. The headnote also does not specify that it includes the original published version of "The 'Pet' Negro System," rather than the condensed version that appeared in *Negro Digest* later in 1943.

3. Bornstein remarks in a similar context: "Our present criticism has sought relentlessly to demystify claims of art to 'universality,' unmasking instead the social contingency of its production and reception. Yet even as it has done that important work, current critique preserves the mystique of the text by reducing it to mere linguistic code and then to studying that code primarily through current incarnations" (*Material* 165).

4. On the ethics of memory and forgetting, see Paul Riceour, "Memory and Forgetting."

5. While "the past in *Tar Baby* is never brought to metaphoric juxtaposition with the present" (Willis 269), this absent relationship would itself be meaningful to any reading of the novel's multicultural setting.

6. On theoretical connections between postcoloniality and material textuality, see Henry Schwarz, "From Work to Text: Postcolonial Textuality," in *Reimagining Textuality: Textual Studies in the Late Age of Print*, ed. Elizabeth Bergmann Loizeaux and Neil Fraistat (Madison: University of Wisconsin Press, 2002).

7. See *The Manuscripts of* A Passage to India, ed. Oliver Stallybrass (New York: Holmes & Meier, 1979). For discussions of the draft versions of the cave scene, see June P. Levine, "An Analysis of the Manuscripts of *A Passage to India*," PMLA 85 (1970): 284–94; and Judith Scherer Herz, "Forster's Ghosts: *A Passage to India* and the Emptying of Narrative," in *Negation, Critical Theory, and Postmodern Textuality*, ed. Daniel Fischlin (Dordrecht: Kluwer Academy, 1994).

8. For an insightful discussion of narrative ethics as a way for "minority or marginalized groups to tell history in their own terms," see John Su's " 'Once I Would Have Gone Back' " (158).

9. I should note that Schulze describes her editorial principles as growing out of Shillingsburg's, and she figures her project as "an approach to text that leaves a bit more room for some form of authorial intention in the midst of the inexorable pressures of literary production" (304). In distinguishing between them here, then, I am to some extent glossing over Schulze's own expressed intention, though in ways which I would see as in keeping with her evolutionary model, for a given theory's application and usefulness should also adapt themselves to various contexts.

John Bryant also emphasizes revision as the process that generates versions more so than the particular variants or the authors or other agents responsible for those variants, with the claim that "critical and cultural meanings can be derived from the distance and direction charted by the end points of the intended revision" (96).

REFERENCES

Alfred A. Knopf. Advertisement. *New York Times*, June 6, 2002, E2.

Allen, James, Hilton Als, Congressman John Lewis, and Leon F. Litwack. *Without Sanctuary: Lynching Photography in America*. Santa Fe: Twin Palms Publishers, 2000.

Andrews, William L. "Editing 'Minority' Texts." In *The Margins of the Text*. Ed. D. C. Greetham. Ann Arbor: University of Michigan Press, 1997.

Antoni, Robert. *Divina Trace*. New York: Overlook Press, 1992.

Appiah, Kwame Anthony. "Is the Post- in Postmodernism the Post- in Postcolonial?" 1991. In *Theory of the Novel: A Historical Approach*. Ed. Michael McKeon. Baltimore: Johns Hopkins University Press, 2000.

———. "The Uncompleted Argument: Du Bois and the Illusion of Race." In *The Idea of Race*, ed. Robert Bernasconi and Tommy L. Lott. Indianapolis: Hackett, 2000.

"Ashley Judd/Oprah's Book Club." *Oprah Winfrey Show*. April 27, 2000. Transcript by Burrelle's Information Services.

"August Futures." *Esquire* August 1972: 109.

Awkward, Michael. *Negotiating Difference: Race, Gender, and the Politics of Positionality*. Chicago: University of Chicago Press, 1995.

Baker, Houston A., Jr. *Blues, Ideology, and Afro-American Literature: A Vernacular Theory*. Chicago: University of Chicago Press, 1984.

———. *Modernism and the Harlem Renaissance*. Chicago: University of Chicago Press, 1987.

Baudrillard, Jean. *Simulations*. Trans. Paul Foss, Paul Patton, and Philip Beitchman. New York: Semiotext[e], 1983.

"Behind the Scenes at Oprah's Dinner Party." *The Oprah Winfrey Show*. December 3, 1996. Transcript by Burrelle's Information Services.

Benjamin, Walter. "The Work of Art in the Age of Mechanical Reproduction." In *Illuminations*, ed. Hannah Arendt. New York: Schocken Books, 1968.

Berlant, Lauren. "National Brands/National Body: *Imitation of Life*." In *Comparative American Identities: Race, Sex, and Nationality in the Modern Text*, ed. Hortense J. Spillers. New York: Routledge, 1991.

Bernard, Emily, ed. *Remember Me to Harlem: The Letters of Langston Hughes and Carl Van Vechten, 1925–1964*. New York: Knopf, 2001.

———. "What He Did for the Race: Carl Van Vechten and the Harlem Renaissance." *Soundings* 80 (1997): 531–42.

Berry, Faith. "A Question of Publishers and a Question of Audience." *Black Scholar* 17 (1986): 41–49.

Bhabha, Homi K. *The Location of Culture*. New York: Routledge, 1994.

———. "Postcolonial Criticism." In *Redrawing the Boundaries: The Transformation of English and American Literary Studies*, ed. Stephen Greenblatt and Giles Gunn. New York: Modern Language Association, 1992.

Bigsby, C. W. E. *The Second Black Renaissance: Essays in Black Literature*. Westport, Conn.: Greenwood Press, 1980.

Bornstein, George. "Beyond Words." *Text* 8 (1995): 387–96.

———. Introduction to *Representing Modernist Texts: Editing as Interpretation*, ed. Bornstein. Ann Arbor: University of Michigan Press, 1991.

———. *Material Modernism: The Politics of the Page*. Cambridge: Cambridge University Press, 2001.

———. "What Is the Text of a Poem by Yeats?" In *Palimpsest: Editorial Theory in the Humanities*, ed. Bornstein and Ralph G. Williams. Ann Arbor: University of Michigan Press, 1993.

———. "Yeats and Textual Reincarnation: 'When You Are Old' and 'September 1913.'" In *The Iconic Page in Manuscript, Print, and Digital Culture*, ed. Bornstein and Theresa Tinkle. Ann Arbor: University of Michigan Press, 1998.

Bornstein, George, and Theresa Tinkle. Introduction to *The Iconic Page in Manuscript, Print, and Digital Culture*, ed. Bornstein and Tinkle. Ann Arbor: University of Michigan Press, 1998.

Bourdieu, Pierre. *The Field of Cultural Production: Essays on Art and Literature*. Ed. Randal Johnson. New York: Columbia University Press, 1993.

Boyd, Melba Joyce. *Wrestling with the Muse: Dudley Randall and the Broadside Press*. New York: Columbia University Press, 2003.

Boyd, Valerie. *Wrapped in Rainbows: The Life of Zora Neale Hurston*. New York: Scribner, 2003.

Brenkman, John. "Politics and Form in *Song of Solomon*." *Social Text* 39 (1994): 57–82.

Brooks, Gwendolyn. *Aloneness*. Detroit: Broadside Press, 1971.

———. *Blacks*. Chicago: Third World Press, 1987.

———. *Children Coming Home*. Chicago: David Company, 1991.

———. *Report from Part One*. Detroit: Broadside Press, 1972.

———. *Selected Poems*. 1963. New York: HarperCollins, 1999.

Browning, Barbara. "Babaluaiyé: Searching for the Text of a Pandemic." In *AIDS: The Literary Response*, ed. Emmanuel S. Nelson. New York: Twayne, 1992.

Bryant, John. *The Fluid Text: A Theory of Revision and Editing for Book and Screen*. Ann Arbor: University of Michigan Press, 2002.

Burns, Alan, and Charles Sugnet, eds. *The Imagination on Trial: British and American Writers Discuss Their Working Methods*. London: Allison & Busby, 1981.

Burr, Zofia. *Of Women, Poetry, and Power: Strategies of Address in Dickinson, Miles, Brooks, Lorde, and Angelou*. Urbana: University of Illinois Press, 2002.

Burroughs, William S. *Naked Lunch*. 1959. New York: Grove Press, 1966.

Butler, Judith. *Bodies That Matter: On the Discursive Limits of "Sex."* New York: Routledge, 1993.

Butler, Robert J. "The Structure of Ralph Ellison's *Juneteenth*." *CLA Journal* 46 (2003): 291–311.

Callahan, John F., ed. *Ralph Ellison's* Invisible Man: *A Casebook*. Oxford: Oxford University Press, 2004.

Carr, Brian. "Paranoid Interpretation, Desire's Nonobject, and Nella Larsen's *Passing*." *PMLA* 119 (2004): 282–95.

Carson, Clayborne. "Editing Martin Luther King, Jr.: Political and Scholarly Issues." In *Palimpsest: Editorial Theory in the Humanities*. Eds. George Bornstein and Ralph G. Williams. Ann Arbor: University of Michigan Press, 1993.

Caughie, Pamela L. *Passing and Pedagogy: The Dynamics of Responsibility*. Urbana: University of Illinois Press, 1999.

Chametzky, Jules. Introduction to *The Rise of David Levinsky*, by Abraham Cahan. 1917. New York: Penguin, 1993.

Chan, Jeffery Paul, Frank Chin, Lawson Fusao Inada, and Shawn Wong, eds. *The Big Aiiieeeeee! An Anthology of Chinese American and Japanese American Literature*. New York: Meridian Books, 1991.

Chaney, Michael A. "Slave Cyborgs and the Black Infovirus: Ishmael Reed's Cybernetic Aesthetics." *Modern Fiction Studies* 49 (2003): 261–83.

Chinn, Sarah E. *Technology and the Logic of American Racism: A Cultural History of the Body as Evidence*. London: Continuum, 2000.

Cohen, Philip. "Textual Scholarship in the Classroom." *Text* 9 (1996): 135–43.

Crick, Bernard R. *George Orwell: A Life*. Boston: Little, Brown, 1980.

Cunard, Nancy. *Negro: An Anthology*. 1934. Ed. Hugh Ford. New York: Continuum, 1996.

Cutter, Martha J. "The Story Must Go On and On: The Fantastic, Narration, and Intertextuality in Toni Morrison's *Song of Solomon* and *Jazz*." *African American Review* 34 (2000): 61–75.

Davis, Christina. "An Interview with Toni Morrison." In *Conversations with Toni Morrison*, ed. Danille Taylor-Guthrie. Jackson: University Press of Mississippi, 1994.

Davis, Thadious M. *Nella Larsen: Novelist of the Harlem Renaissance: A Woman's Life Unveiled*. Baton Rouge: Louisiana State University Press, 1994.

Deleuze, Gilles. "Minor Literature: Kafka." In *The Deleuze Reader*, ed. Constantin V. Boundas. New York: Columbia University Press, 1993.

Derrida, Jacques. "Aphorism Countertime." In *Acts of Literature*, ed. Derek Attridge. New York: Routledge, 1992.

————. *Archive Fever: A Freudian Impression*. Trans. Eric Prenowitz. Chicago: University of Chicago Press, 1995.

De Santis, Christopher. "'Some cord of kinship stronger and deeper than blood': An Interview with John F. Callahan, Editor of Ralph Ellison's *Juneteenth*." *African American Review* 34 (2000): 601–20.

Dick, Bruce, and Amritjit Singh, eds. *Conversations with Ishmael Reed*. Jackson: University Press of Mississippi, 1995.

Dreifus, Claudia. "Chloe Wofford Talks About Toni Morrison." *New York Times Magazine.* September 9, 1994, 72–75.

Dubey, Madhu. *Signs and Cities: Black Literary Postmodernism*. Chicago: University of Chicago Press, 2003.

Du Bois, W. E. B. "The Browsing Reader." *Crisis* 36 (1929): 234, 248–49.

————. *The Souls of Black Folk*. 1903. Ed. Henry Louis Gates Jr. and Terri Hume Oliver. New York: Norton, 1999.

Ellison, Ralph. *The Collected Essays of Ralph Ellison*. Ed. John F. Callahan. New York: Modern Library, 1995.

————. *Juneteenth*. Ed. John F. Callahan. New York: Random House, 1999.

————. "Night-Talk." *Quarterly Review of Literature* 16 (1969): 317–29.

Feldman, Gayle. "Making Book on Oprah." *New York Times Book Review* February 2, 1997, 31.

Finneran, Richard J. "Text and Interpretation in the Poems of W. B. Yeats." In *Representing Modernist Texts: Editing as Interpretation*, ed. George Bornstein. Ann Arbor: University of Michigan Press, 1991.

Fishkin, Shelley Fisher. "Interrogating 'Whiteness,' Complicating 'Blackness': Remapping American Culture." In *Criticism and the Color Line: Desegregating American Literary Studies*, ed. Henry B. Wonham. New Brunswick: Rutgers University Press, 1996.

————. *Was Huck Black? Mark Twain and African-American Voices*. New York: Oxford University Press, 1993.

Flora, Peter. "Carl Van Vechten, Blance Knopf, and the Harlem Renaissance." *Library Chronicle of the University of Texas* 22 (1992): 65–83.

Flynn, Richard. "'The Kindergarten of New Consciousness': Gwendolyn Brooks and the Social Construction of Childhood." *African American Review* 34 (2000): 483–99.

Foertsch, Jacqueline. "The Right, the Wrong, and the Ugly: Teaching Shelley's Several *Frankenstein*s." *College English* 63 (2001): 697–711.

Fox, Robert Eliot. *Conscientious Sorcerers: The Black Postmodernist Fiction of Leroi Jones/Amiri Baraka, Ishmael Reed, and Samuel R. Delany*. New York: Greenwood Press, 1987.

Franzen, Jonathan. "Meet Me in St. Louis." *New Yorker* December 24–31, 2001, 70–75.

Friedman, Alan. "Mumbo Jumbo." *New York Times Book Review* August 6, 1972, 1, 22.

Froula, Christine. "Corpse, Monument, *Hypocrite Lecteur*: Text and Transference in the Reception of *The Waste Land*." *Text* 9 (1996): 297–314.

Fusco, Coco, and Brian Wallis. *Only Skin Deep: Changing Visions of the American Self*. New York: International Center of Photography, 2003.

Gabbin, Joanne V. "Blooming in the Whirlwind: The Early Poetry of Gwendolyn Brooks." In *The Furious Flowering of African American Poetry*, ed. Gabbin. Charlottesville: University Press of Virginia, 1999.

Gates, Henry Louis, Jr. "African American Criticism." In *Redrawing the Boundaries: The Transformation of English and American Literary Studies*. Eds. Stephen Greenblatt and Giles Gunn. New York: Modern Language Association of America, 1992.

———. "Harlem on Our Minds." *Critical Inquiry* 24 (1997): 1–12.

———. *Loose Canons: Notes on the Culture Wars*. New York: Oxford University Press, 1992.

———. *The Signifying Monkey: A Theory of African-American Literary Criticism*. New York: Oxford University Press, 1988.

Gayles, Gloria Wade, ed. *Conversations with Gwendolyn Brooks*. Jackson: University Press of Mississippi, 2003.

Genette, Gérard. *Paratexts: Thresholds of Interpretation*. Trans. Jane E. Lewin. Cambridge: Cambridge University Press, 1997.

———. *The Work of Art: Immanence and Transcendence*. Trans. G. M. Goshgarian. Ithaca: Cornell University Press, 1997.

Gikandi, Simon. "Race and the Idea of the Aesthetic." *Michigan Quarterly Review* 40 (2001): 318–50.

Gilman, Sander L. *The Jew's Body*. New York: Routledge, 1991.

Gould, Stephen Jay. *Triumph and Tragedy in Mudville: A Lifelong Passion for Baseball*. New York: W. W. Norton, 2003.

Graff, Gerald. "Narrative and the Unofficial Interpretive Culture." In *Reading Narrative: Form, Ethics, Ideology*, ed. James Phelan. Columbus: Ohio State University Press, 1989.

Gray, Paul. "Paradise Found." *Time* January 19, 1998: 63–68.

———. "Winfrey's Winners." *Time* December 2, 1996, 84.

Greetham, D. C. Introduction to *The Margins of the Text*, ed. Greetham. Ann Arbor: University of Michigan Press, 1997.

———. *Textual Scholarship: An Introduction*. New York: Garland, 1994.

———. *Textual Transgressions: Essays towards the Construction of a Biobibliography*. New York: Garland, 1998.

———. *Theories of the Text*. Oxford: Oxford University Press, 1999.

Grigely, Joseph. "The Textual Event." In *Devils and Angels: Textual Editing and Literary Theory*, ed. Philip Cohen. Charlottesville: University Press of Virginia, 1991.

Gubar, Susan. *Racechanges: White Skin, Black Face in American Culture*. New York: Oxford University Press, 1997.

Harper and Brothers. Advertisement. *New York Times Book Review*. March 3, 1940, 18.

Harris, Middleton, et al. *The Black Book*. New York: Random House, 1974.

Harris-Lopez, Trudier. *South of Tradition: Essays on African American Literature*. Athens: University of Georgia Press, 2002.

Harrison-Kahan, Lori. "Her 'Nig': Returning the Gaze of Nella Larsen's *Passing*." *Modern Language Studies* 32 (2002): 109–38.

Haviland, Beverly. "Passing from Paranoia to Plagiarism: The Abject Authorship of Nella Larsen." *Modern Fiction Studies* 43 (1997): 295–318.

Hawkins, Denise B. "Conversation." In *The Furious Flowering of African American Poetry.* Ed. Joanne V. Gabbin. Charlottesville: University Press of Virginia, 1999.

Heidegger, Martin. "The Origin of the Work of Art." In *The Continental Aesthetics Reader,* ed. Clive Cazeaux. New York: Routledge, 2000.

Hemenway, Robert E. *Zora Neale Hurston: A Literary Biography.* Urbana: University of Illinois Press, 1977.

Henderson, Mae. Critical Foreword and Notes to *Passing,* by Nella Larsen. New York: Modern Library, 2002.

hooks, bell. *Black Looks: Race and Representation.* Boston: South End Press, 1992.

Hurston, Zora Neale. *I Love Myself When I Am Laughing . . . And Then Again When I Am Looking Mean and Impressive: A Zora Neale Hurston Reader.* Ed. Alice Walker. New York: Feminist Press, 1979.

———. "What White Publishers Won't Print." *Negro Digest* 8 (1950): 85–89.

Hutchinson, George. *The Harlem Renaissance in Black and White.* Cambridge: Belknap Press, 1995.

———. "Nella Larsen and the Veil of Race." *American Literary History* 9 (1997): 329–49.

Huyssen, Andreas. "Mapping the Postmodern." *New German Critique* 33 (1984): 5–52.

———. "Mass Culture as Woman: Modernism's Other." In *Studies in Entertainment: Critical Approaches to Mass Culture,* ed. Tania Modleski. Bloomington: Indiana University Press, 1986.

Ikonné, Chidi. *From DuBois to Van Vechten: The Early New Negro Literature, 1903–1926.* Westport: Greenwood Press, 1981.

Ishmael Reed Papers. Special Collections Department. University of Delaware Library.

Jackson, Lawrence. *Ralph Ellison: Emergence of Genius.* New York: John Wiley & Sons, 2002.

Jaffe, Dan. "Gwendolyn Brooks: An Appreciation from the White Suburbs." In *On Gwendolyn Brooks: Reliant Contemplation,* ed. Stephen Caldwell Wright. Ann Arbor: University of Michigan Press, 2001.

Jameson, Fredric. *The Cultural Turn: Selected Writings on the Postmodern, 1983–1998.* London: Verso, 1998.

———. *Postmodernism, or, The Cultural Logic of Late Capitalism.* Durham: Duke University Press, 1991.

Johnson, Barbara. *The Feminist Difference: Literature, Psychoanalysis, Race, and Gender.* Cambridge: Harvard University Press, 1998.

———. "Thresholds of Difference: Structures of Address in Zora Neale Hurston." *Critical Inquiry* 12 (1985): 278–89.

Johnson, Charles. Preface to *Juneteenth,* by Ralph Ellison. Ed. John F. Callahan. 1999. New York: Vintage, 2000.

Johnson, James Weldon. *The Autobiography of an Ex-Coloured Man.* 1912. New York: Alfred A. Knopf, 1927.

————, ed. *The Book of American Negro Poetry*. New York: Harcourt Brace, 1922.

————. "The Dilemma of the Negro Author." In *The Politics and Aesthetics of the "New Negro" Literature*, ed. Cary D. Wintz. New York: Garland, 1996.

Jones, Leroi, and Larry Neal, eds. *Black Fire: An Anthology of Afro-American Writing*. 2nd ed. New York: William Morrow, 1969.

Joyce, Donald Franklin. *Black Book Publishers in the United States: A Historical Dictionary of the Presses, 1817–1990*. New York: Greenwood Press, 1991.

Just, Ward. "How the Other Half Lives." *New York Times Book Review* June 9, 2002, 11.

Kawash, Samira. *Dislocating the Color Line: Identity, Hybridity, and Singularity in African-American Literature*. Stanford: Stanford University Press, 1997.

Kent, George E. *A Life of Gwendolyn Brooks*. Lexington: University Press of Kentucky, 1990.

Kinnamon, Keneth. "How *Native Son* Was Born." In *Richard Wright: Critical Perspectives Past and Present*, eds. Henry Louis Gates Jr. and K. A. Appiah. New York: Amistad, 1993.

Kinsella, Brudget. "The Oprah Effect: How TV's premier talk show host puts books over the top." *Publishers Weekly*, January 20, 1997, 276–79.

Knadler, Stephen P. *The Fugitive Race: Minority Writers Resisting Whiteness*. Jackson: University Press of Mississippi, 2002.

Kozloff, Sara. "Audio Books in a Visual Culture." *Journal of American Culture* 18 (1995): 83–95.

Lacan, Jacques. "The Subversion of the Subject and the Dialectic of Desire in the Freudian Unconscious." In *Écrits: A Selection*, trans. Alan Sheridan. New York: W. W. Norton, 1977.

Larsen, Nella. *The Complete Fiction of Nella Larsen: Passing, Quicksand, and the Stories*. Ed. Charles R. Larson. New York: Anchor Books, 2001.

————. *Passing*. 1929. Ed. Thadious M. Davis. New York: Penguin, 1997.

————. *Quicksand* and *Passing*. 1928, 1929. Ed. Deborah McDowell. New Brunswick: Rutgers University Press, 1986.

Larson, Charles R. *Invisible Darkness: Jean Toomer and Nella Larsen*. Iowa City: University of Iowa Press, 1993.

Lawson, Benjamin Sherwood. "Odysseus's Revenge: The Names on the Title Page of *The Autobiography of an Ex-Coloured Man*." *Southern Literary Journal* 21 (1989): 92–99.

Leininger-Miller, Theresa. *New Negro Artists in Paris: African American Painters and Sculptors in the City of Light, 1922–1934*. New Brunswick: Rutgers University Press, 2001.

Lesoinne, Veronique. "Answer Jazz's Call: Experiencing Toni Morrison's *Jazz*." *MELUS* 22 (1997): 151–66.

Leuders, Edward. *Carl Van Vechten and the Twenties*. Albuquerque: University of New Mexico Press, 1955.

Levy, Eugene. *James Weldon Johnson: Black Voice, Black Leader*. Chicago: University of Chicago Press, 1973.

Lewis, Randolph Robert. "'Publishing and Prejudice': Alfred A. Knopf and American Publishing, 1915–1935." MA thesis, University of Texas, 1990.

Locke, Alain. *The Critical Temper of Alain Locke: A Selection of His Essays on Art and Culture.* Ed. Jeffrey C. Stewart. New York: Garland, 1983.

———. *The New Negro: An Anthology.* 1925. Ed. Arnold Rampersad. New York: Atheneum, 1992.

Lott, Tommy. "Du Bois and Locke on the Scientific Study of the Negro." *Boundary 2* 27 (2000): 135–52.

Madhubuti, Haki R. "Gwendolyn Brooks: Beyond the Wordmaker—the Making of an African Poet." In *On Gwendolyn Brooks: Reliant Contemplation*, ed. Stephen Caldwell Wright. Ann Arbor: University of Michigan Press, 2001.

Madigan, Mark J. "'Then Everything Was Dark'?: The Two Endings of Nella Larsen's *Passing.*" *PBSA* 83 (1989): 521–23.

Madison, Charles A. *Book Publishing in America.* New York: McGraw-Hill, 1966.

Mailloux, Steven. "Reading Typos, Reading Archives." *College English* 61 (1999): 584–90.

Marcus, Jane. "Bonding and Bondage: Nancy Cunard and the Making of the *Negro* Anthology." In *Borders, Boundaries, and Frames: Essays in Cultural Criticism and Cultural Studies*, ed. Mae G. Henderson. New York: Routledge, 1995.

Marshik, Celia. "Publication and 'Public Women': Prostitution and Censorship in Three Novels by Virginia Woolf." *Modern Fiction Studies* 45 (1999): 853–86.

Marx, Steven. "Beyond Hibernation: Ralph Ellison's 1982 Version of *Invisible Man.*" *Black American Literature Forum* 23 (1989): 701–21.

Maryles, Daisy. "Behind the Bestsellers." *Publishers Weekly* October 28, 1996, 22.

Masciarotte, Gloria-Jean. "C'mon, Girl: Oprah Winfrey and the Discourse of Feminine Talk." *Genders* 11 (1991): 81–110.

Max, D. T. "The Oprah Effect." *New York Times Magazine* December 26, 1999, 36–41.

McCoy, Beth. "Perpetua(l) Notion: Typography, Economy, and Losing Nella Larsen." In *Illuminating Letters: Typography and Literary Interpretation*, ed. Paul C. Gutjahr and Megan L. Benton. Amherst: University of Massachusetts Press, 2001.

McGann, Jerome J. *Black Riders: The Visible Language of Modernism.* Princeton: Princeton University Press, 1993.

———. *A Critique of Modern Textual Criticism.* Chicago: University of Chicago Press, 1983.

———. *The Textual Condition.* Princeton: Princeton University Press, 1991.

———. "*Ulysses* as a Postmodern Work." In *Social Values and Poetic Acts: The Historical Judgment of Literary Work*, by McGann. Cambridge: Harvard University Press, 1988.

———. "What Difference Do the Circumstances of Publication Make in the Interpretation of a Literary Work?" In *Literary Pragmatics*, ed. Roger D. Sell. London: Routledge, 1991.

McGee, Patrick. *Ishmael Reed and the Ends of Race.* New York: St. Martin's, 1997.

McHenry, Elizabeth. *Forgotten Readers: Recovering the Lost History of African American Literary Societies.* Durham: Duke University Press, 2002.

McKay, Claude. *Banana Bottom.* 1933. San Diego: Harcourt Brace, 1974.

Menand, Louis. "Unfinished Business." *New York Times,* June 20, 1999, 3, 6.

Michaels, Walter Benn. *Our America: Nativism, Modernism, and Pluralism.* Durham: Duke University Press, 1995.

Middleton, Joyce Irene. "From Orality to Literacy: Oral Memory in Toni Morrison's *Song of Solomon.*" In *New Essays on* Song of Solomon, ed. Valerie Smith. Cambridge: Cambridge University Press, 1995.

Mignolo, Walter D. "Coloniality of Power and Subalternity." In *The Latin American Studies Reader,* ed. Ileana Rodríguez. Durham: Duke University Press, 2001.

Miller, Nancy K. *Subject to Change: Reading Feminist Writing.* New York: Columbia University Press, 1988.

Mills, Charles W. *Blackness Visible: Essays on Philosophy and Race.* Ithaca, N.Y.: Cornell University Press, 1998.

———. *The Racial Contract.* Ithaca, N.Y.: Cornell University Press, 1997.

Millstein, Barbara Head, and Sarah M. Lowe. *Consuelo Kanaga: An American Photographer.* New York: Brooklyn Museum, 1992.

Morrison, Toni. "Afterword." In her *The Bluest Eye.* 1970. New York: Alfred A. Knopf, 2000.

———. "Behind the Making of *The Black Book.*" *Black World* 23 (1974): 86–90.

———. *The Bluest Eye.* New York: Holt, Rinehart and Winston, 1970.

———. Foreword to her *Beloved.* 1987. New York: Vintage, 2004.

———. Foreword to her *Jazz.* 1992. New York: Vintage, 2004.

———. "Home." In *The House That Race Built,* ed. Wahneema Lubiano. New York: Vintage, 1998.

———. *Jazz.* 1992. New York: Plume, 1993.

———. *Paradise.* New York: Alfred A. Knopf, 1998.

———. *Playing in the Dark: Whiteness and the Literary Imagination.* New York: Vintage Books, 1993.

———. "Rediscovering Black History." *New York Times Magazine,* August 11, 1974, 14–24.

———. *Song of Solomon.* 1977. New York: Plume, 1987.

———. *Song of Solomon.* New York: Random House Audiobooks, 1990.

———. "Unspeakable Things Unspoken: The Afro-American Presence in American Literature." *Michigan Quarterly Review* 28 (1989): 1–34.

Mullen, Bill V. "Breaking the Signifying Chain: A New Blueprint for African-American Studies." *Modern Fiction Studies* 47 (2001): 145–63.

Mullen, Harryette. "Optic White: Blackness and the Production of Whiteness." *Diacritics* 24 (1994): 71–89.

Mulrine, Alice. "*Paradise* Follows *Beloved* and *Jazz*: Toni Morrison Talks about Her Latest Novel." *Princeton Alumni Weekly,* March 11, 1998: 22.

Nadel, Alan. "The Integrated Literary Tradition." In *A Historical Guide to Ralph Ellison,* ed. Steven C. Tracy. New York: Oxford University Press, 2004.

———. "Ralph Ellison and the American Canon." *American Literary History* 13 (2001): 393–404.

Nehamas, Alexander. "Serious Watching." *South Atlantic Quarterly* 89 (1990): 157–80.

Nelson, Cary. *Repression and Recovery: Modern American Poetry and the Politics of Cultural Memory, 1910–1945*. Madison: University of Wisconsin Press, 1989.

"Newborn Quintuplets Come Home." *The Oprah Winfrey Show*. October 18, 1996. Transcript by Burrelle's Information Services.

North, Michael. *The Dialect of Modernism: Race, Language, and Twentieth-Century Literature*. New York: Oxford University Press, 1994.

Northouse, Cameron. *Ishmael Reed: An Interview*. Dallas: Contemporary Research Press, 1993.

"A Novelist, A Talk-Show Host, and Literature High and Low." *Chronicle of Higher Education*, November 30, 2001, B4.

Ong, Walter J. *Interfaces of the Word: Studies in the Evolution of Consciousness and Culture*. Ithaca, N.Y.: Cornell University Press, 1977.

———. *Orality and Literacy: The Technologizing of the Word*. New York: Routledge, 1982.

"Oprah Helps Steinbeck Outsell Hillary." *USA Today*, July 3, 2003, D6.

"Oprah's Book Club." *Oprah Winfrey Show*. May 26, 2000.

Parks, John G. "Mining and Undermining the Old Plots: Ishmael Reed's *Mumbo Jumbo*." *Centennial Review* 39 (1995): 163–70.

Parrish, S. M. "The Whig Interpretation of Literature." *Text* 4 (1988): 343–50.

Perkins, George, and Barbara Perkins, eds. *The American Tradition in Literature*. Vol. 2. 10th ed. New York: McGraw-Hill, 2002.

Potter, Lou, with William Miles and Nina Rosenblum. *Liberators: Fighting on Two Fronts in World War II*. New York: Harcourt, 1992.

Powell, Timothy. "Toni Morrison: The Struggle to Depict the Black Figure on the White Page." *Black American Literature Forum* 24 (1990): 747–60.

Rabinowitz, Peter J. *Before Reading: Narrative Conventions and the Politics of Interpretation*. Columbus: Ohio State University Press, 1987.

———. " 'Betraying the Sender': The Rhetoric and Ethics of Fragile Texts." *Narrative* 2 (1994): 201–13.

Rainey, Lawrence. *Institutions of Modernism: Literary Elites and Public Culture*. New Haven: Yale University Press, 1998.

Rampersad, Arnold. Introduction to *Native Son*, by Richard Wright. 1940. New York: HarperCollins, 1993.

Randall, Dudley. "Black Publisher, Black Writer: An Answer." *Black World* (March 1975): 32–37.

Reed, Ishmael. *Flight to Canada*. 1976. New York: Atheneum, 1989.

———. *The Last Days of Louisiana Red*. 1974. Normal: Dalkey Archive Press, 2000.

———. *Mumbo Jumbo*. New York: Doubleday, 1972. Reprint, New York: Avon, 1978. Reprint, New York: Atheneum, 1989.

———. *Shrovetide in Old New Orleans*. 1978. New York: Atheneum, 1989.

———. *Yellow Back Radio Broke-Down*. 1969. Normal: Dalkey Archive Press, 2000.

Reed, Ishmael, Quincy Troupe, and Steve Cannon. "The Essential Ellison." In *Conversations with Ralph Ellison*, ed. Maryemma Graham and Amritjit Singh. Jackson: University Press of Mississippi, 1995.

Riceour, Paul. "Imagination, Testimony, and Trust: A Dialogue with Paul Riceour." In *Questioning Ethics: Contemporary Debates in Philosophy*, ed. Richard Kearney and Mark Dooley. London: Routledge, 1999.

———. "Memory and Forgetting." In *Questioning Ethics: Contemporary Debates in Philosophy*. Eds. Richard Kearney and Mark Dooley. London: Routledge, 1999.

Rowley, Hazel. *Richard Wright: The Life and Times*. New York: Henry Holt, 2001.

Sales, Nancy Jo. "Meet Your Neighbor, Thomas Pynchon." *New York*, November 11, 1996, 60–64.

Schappell, Elissa. "Toni Morrison: The Art of Fiction CXXXIV." *Paris Review* 128 (1993): 83–125.

Schulze, Robin G. "Textual Darwinism: Marianne Moore, the Text of Evolution, and the Evolving Text." *Text* 11 (1998): 270–305.

Scruggs, Charles, and Lee Vandemarr. *Jean Toomer and the Terrors of American History*. Philadelphia: University of Pennsylvania Press, 1998.

Shank, Barry. "Bliss, or Blackface Sentiment." *Boundary 2* 30 (2003): 47–64.

Shillingsburg, Peter. *Resisting Texts: Authority and Submission in Constructions of Meaning*. Ann Arbor: University of Michigan Press, 1997.

Silliman, Ron. *The New Sentence*. New York: Roof Books, 1978.

Silverman, Kaja. *The Acoustic Mirror: The Female Voice in Psychoanalysis and Cinema*. Bloomington: Indiana University Press, 1988.

Sollors, Werner. *Beyond Ethnicity: Consent and Descent in American Culture*. New York: Oxford University Press, 1986.

Spillers, Hortense J. "'An Order of Constancy': Notes on Brooks and the Feminine." In *Reading Black, Reading Feminist: A Critical Anthology*, ed. Henry Louis Gates Jr. New York: Meridian, 1990.

Su, John J. "'Once I Would Have Gone Back . . . But Not Any Longer': Nostalgia and Narrative Ethics in *Wide Sargasso Sea*." *Critique* 44 (2003): 157–74.

Sullivan, James D. "Killing John Cabot and Publishing Black: Gwendolyn Brooks's *Riot*." *African American Review* 36 (2002): 557–69.

Sullivan, Neil. "Nella Larsen's *Passing* and the Fading Subject." *African American Review* 32 (1998): 373–86.

Sundquist, Eric J. *To Wake the Nations: Race in the Making of American Literature*. Cambridge: Belknap Press, 1993.

Tanselle, G. Thomas. "The Editorial Problem of Final Authorial Intention." In *Textual Criticism and Scholarly Editing*. Charlottesville: University Press of Virginia, 1990.

———. *A Rationale of Textual Criticism*. Philadelphia: University of Pennsylvania Press, 1989.

Tate, Claudia, ed. *Black Women Writers at Work*. New York: Continuum, 1989.

———. "Nella Larsen's *Passing*: A Problem of Interpretation." *Black American Literature Forum* 14 (1980): 142–46.

Taylor, Henry. "Gwendolyn Brooks: An Essential Sanity." In *On Gwendolyn Brooks: Reliant Contemplation*, ed. Stephen Caldwell Wright. Ann Arbor: University of Michigan Press, 2001.

Taylor-Guthrie, Danielle, ed. *Conversations with Toni Morrison*. Jackson: University Press of Mississippi, 1994.

Thorpe, James. *Principles of Textual Criticism*. San Marino: Huntington Library, 1972.

Toomer, Jean. *Cane*. Ed. Darwin T. Turner. 1923. New York: Norton, 1988.

Van Vechten, Carl. *Nigger Heaven*. New York: Alfred A. Knopf, 1926.

Voss, Paul J., and Marta Werner. "Toward a Poetics of the Archive: Introduction." *Studies in the Literary Imagination* 32 (1999): i–vii.

Wall, Cheryl A. *Women of the Harlem Renaissance*. Bloomington: Indiana University Press, 1995.

Wallace, Michele. *Invisibility Blues: From Pop to Theory*. London: Verso, 1990.

Warren, Kenneth W. "Ralph Ellison and the Problem of Cultural Authority." *Boundary 2* 30 (2003): 157–74.

Ween, Lori. "This Is Your Book: Marketing America to Itself." *PMLA* 118 (2003): 90–102.

White, G. Edward. *Creating the National Pastime: Baseball Transforms Itself, 1903–1953*. Princeton: Princeton University Press, 1996.

Whitehead, Colson. *The Intuitionist*. 1999. New York: Anchor Books, 2000.

Whittier-Ferguson, John. "The Burden of Drafts: Woolf's Revisions of *Between the Acts*." *Text* 10 (1997): 297–319.

Wilentz, Gay. "Civilizations Underneath: African Heritage as Cultural Discourse in Toni Morrison's *Song of Solomon*." In *Toni Morrison's Fiction: Contemporary Criticism*, ed. David Middleton. New York: Garland, 2000.

Williams, Kenny J. "The World of Satin-Legs, Mrs. Sallie, and the Blackstone Rangers: The Restricted Chicago of Gwendolyn Brooks." In *A Life Distilled: Gwendolyn Brooks, Her Poetry and Fiction*, ed. Maria K. Mootry and Gary Smith. Urbana: University of Illinois Press, 1987.

Willis, Susan. "Eruptions of Funk: Historicizing Toni Morrison." In *Black Literature and Literary Theory*, ed. Henry Louis Gates Jr. New York: Routledge, 1984.

Woolf, Virginia. *The Diary of Virginia Woolf*. Vol. 3. New York: HBJ, 1980.

———. *The Essays of Virginia Woolf*. Vol. 4. Ed. Andrew McNeillie. London: Hogarth Press, 1986.

———. *The Letters of Virginia Woolf*. Vol. 3. Eds. Nigel Nicolson and Joanne Trautman. New York: HBJ, 1977.

Wright, Richard. *Native Son*. 1940. New York: Perennial Classics, 1998.

———. *Works*. Vol. 1. New York: Library of America, 1991.

Wright, Stephen Caldwell, ed. *On Gwendolyn Brooks: Reliant Contemplation*. Ann Arbor: University of Michigan Press, 2001.

Yukins, Elizabeth. "An 'Artful Juxtaposition on the Page': Memory, Perception, and Cubist Technique in Ralph Ellison's *Juneteenth*." *PMLA* 119 (2004): 1247–63.

Zeller, Hans. "A New Approach to the Critical Constitution of Literary Texts." *Studies in Bibliography* 28 (1975): 231–64.

Žižek, Slavoj. *The Sublime Object of Ideology*. London: Verso, 1989.

INDEX

References in *italics* refer to illustrations.